DEVELOPMENTAL TRANSFORMATION OF URBAN INDIA

DEVELOPMENTAL TRANSFORMATION OF URBAN INDIA
JNNURM Showcase in the South

DEEPA CHANDRAN

KALPAZ

Developmental Transformation of Urban India : JNNURM
Showcase in the South

ISBN: 978-81-7835-965-6

Published in 2013 in India by
Kalpaz Publications
C-30, Satyawati Nagar,
Delhi-110052
E-mail: kalpaz@hotmail.com
Phone : 9212142040

Laser Type Setting by: Rudra Computer Graphics, Delhi
Printed at : Chawla Offset Press, Delhi

Dedicated To

My Grandmothers, Parents, In-laws,
Husband and Brother

Contents

List of Tables

List of Figures

List of Maps

Preface

Urban areas in the country have undergone massive transformation in the recent decades. This became evident in the period after the economic reforms of 1991. Being an integral part of the dynamic global economy wherein urban centres function as the focal points or nerves, Government of India lately realised the potential of the urban centres to attain sustainable economic growth in the newly emerged circumstances and to enable the country's rise as a major global power. The fast growing importance of the urban centres in the national-regional economies in the country can be clearly read from the strategies that the policy makers followed towards urban development in the country. As Indian economy was always considered as an agrarian one (which is clear from the sayings like 'The soul of India lives in its villages), the priority of the initial five year plans had been overwhelmingly on rural development and basic industries. Investment in the urban areas was highly restricted to the creation of city development plans of few large cities and housing schemes for the economically weaker sections which usually covered very limited population.

As in any developing country, the unplanned and haphazard growth of the urban areas in the country has created numerous challenges in their functioning as a system. Acute shortage of the funds available for investing in the urban infrastructure had always been a major challenge in urban development in India. The already existing shortages of the urban basic services were aggravated by the fast growth of the urban population and by the rural to urban migration predominantly of semi-skilled and unskilled workers. Thus, the interplay of various negative factors along with an outdated urban governance system, led to the growth of urban centres in the country which were characterized by features such as large slum and squatter population, poor infrastructure facilities, poor industrial and revenue bases, unattractive environment for private and foreign investment, etc. The introduction of the economic reforms to overcome the then prevailed circumstances of an economic crisis in 1991, necessitated the Government of India to restructure the urban development strategies as well as to reshape the urban space in the country to suit the newer demands of global capitalistic market.

First major response from the policy makers to mould the urban centres in the country to suit the opportunities and demands in the global economy can be traced to the Mega city scheme initiated in 1993 covering the five large cities of the country. But, the realization about the necessity of a large scale initiative in urban development covering major urban centres spread across the country in order to find its own place in the world economy, led to the introduction of Jawaharlal Nehru National Urban Renewal Mission (JNNURM) in December 2005. It is the most ambitious program introduced by the Government of India in the history of urban development. The ultimate goal of the Mission is to transform the selected 63 cities (to which 2 more i.e. Tirupati and Porbander were added in 2009) into economic centres of global, national and regional importance. Perhaps the best aspect about the Mission in my perception is that an urban development program of such a vast scale covered the urban centres spread across the country including those areas which could never find a place in any major urban development scheme in the past.

The present study was done when the Mission was half way. Thus, it enables one to examine if the Mission could bring in real positive changes in the urban areas of the country in general. In the country as a whole, the very less number of projects completed as compared to the expectations that everybody had at the times of its launch, points out the very slow pace of the progress of the Mission projects. In majority of the cases it is either because of the inability of the urban local body to attract private investment which in fact is crucial in the success of the cities under JNNURM. Yet another important reason for the slow progress of the Mission projects especially in the cities falling in the second and third category is that of severe capacity constraints of the urban local bodies to match with the various demands to handle such a large scale program. It is also clear that, the cities are more enthusiastic in implementing the pro-market reforms rather than implementing the reforms for increasing community participation or decentralization. The direct link between the level of privatization and the success of cities/states under the Mission is evident from the fact that the cities/ states which have performed well under JNNURM are the same ones which could implement all/majority of pro-market reforms.

The detailed study of the Mission cities in Kerala, i.e. Kochi and Thiruvananthapuram enables the reader to understand the ground realities about the progress made under the Mission and to examine the challenges on the way ahead. It was observed that the failure of the state (Kerala) in attracting the private sector investment because of its legacies of 'public action', 'labour militancy' and the 'unfriendly investment atmosphere' proved to be costly under JNNURM. Nonetheless, it was clear that in spite of the poor private sector participation, the sectors which enabled the active participation of the people in various stages of project formulation, implementation and service delivery could yield appreciable outcomes. Thus, it is suggested that rather than merely focusing on the private sector investment, JNNURM should restructure itself in such a way that it will give ample scope for community participation not only in papers but also in reality.

I am sure that this book will be useful for those who are interested in urban development and planning in the country.

December 2012 **Deepa Chandran**

Acknowledgements

First of all, I would like to express gratitude to my supervisor Prof. Atiya Habeeb Kidwai for her patient guidance throughout the period of this study. She has been the source of inspiration to me for this research work as well as during the difficult times in my personal life. I could learn quite a lot of valuable lessons from her guidance and I firmly believe that they will remain as the base for my future research. Besides her, I am very grateful to Prof. B.S. Butola for enabling me to learn the essential qualities of good research where shortcuts do not have a place. Words fail to convey my gratitude when it comes to my dear parents. I believe that I could not have completed this work without the moral support they had given. The support that my husband Mr. Renjith Kumar, gave me in the course of my research works often watered my eyes in happiness. I am very indebted to him for the overwhelming encouragement that he had given me to fulfil my dream of getting this research work published in the form of a book.

I express my gratitude to my brother Deepu and my friend Chrisatbel from Kerala University, for accompanying me during the slum surveys in Kochi and Thiruvananthapuram. In their absence, I would have failed to complete the field work in the limited time available. I thank my friends in JNU for giving me the moral support during the course of this work. After long hours of work and tensions, the sweetness of the friendship that I enjoyed through them could refresh my tired brain and bring in new ideas for this study. Some of them could also give me valuable suggestions and healthy criticisms which further strengthened my arguments. But the fact which hurts me most at this juncture is the absence of my grandmother who could not have a look at the piece of research I have done.

I am very thankful to the system analyst-CSRD, Mr.Varghese, the staffs in JNNURM wing of both the cities, Kudumbasree Offices in both cities, TCPO office of Kerala, and the KSUDP/JNNURM office in Thiruvananthapuram. The help given by Mr. Ashok Kumar, Mr. Hari Kumar (both from Kudumbasree office), Mr. Shyam (from Thiruvananthapuram Corporation), Mr. Rajeev (KSUDP/JNNURM Office) and Mrs. Sathy (TCPO, Kerala) during the data collection needs special mention. Above all, I express my sincere gratitude to Council for Scientific and Industrial Research (CSIR) for funding the study.

December 2012 **Deepa Chandran**

List of Abbreviations

ADB	-	Asian Development Bank
ADS	-	Area Development Society
BSUP	-	Basic Services for the Urban Poor
CAA	-	Constitutional Amendment Act
CDP	-	City Development Plan
CDS	-	Community Development Society
DPR	-	Detailed Project Report
DFID	-	Department for International Development
EWS	-	Economically Weaker Sections
GDP	-	Gross Domestic Product
GoI	-	Government of India
HUDCO	-	Housing and Urban Development Corporation
H.P	-	Himachal Pradesh
IHSDP	-	Integrated Housing and Slum Development Program
JNNURM	-	Jawaharlal Nehru National Urban Renewal Mission
KSUDP	-	Kerala Sustainable Urban Development Program
LIG	-	Low Income Group
MoA	-	Memorandum of Agreement
MoHUPA	-	Ministry of Housing and Urban Poverty Alleviation
MoU	-	Memorandum of Understanding
MoUD	-	Ministry of Urban Development
M.P	-	Madhya Pradesh
MPCI	-	Monthly Per Capita Income

NABARD	-	National Bank for Agricultural and Rural Development
NGO	-	Non-Governmental Organization
NHG	-	Neighbourhood Groups
NIUA	-	National Institute of urban Affairs
NSDP	-	National Slum Development Programme
NSG	-	National Steering Group
NTPRC	-	National Transportation Planning and Research Centre
OBC	-	Other Backward Caste
PEARL	-	Peer Experience and Reflective Learning Initiative
PEM	-	Poverty Eradication Mission
PPP	-	Public Private Partnership
RDF	-	Refused Derived Fuel
SC	-	Scheduled Caste
SJSRY	-	Swarna Jayanthy Shahariy Rozgar Yojana
SLNA	-	State Level Nodal Agency
SLSC	-	State Level Steering Committee
ST	-	Scheduled Tribe
TCMC	-	Thiruvananthapuram City Municipal Corporation
UAs	-	Urban Agglomerations
UIDSMT	-	Urban Infrastructural Development of Small and Medium Towns
UIG	-	Urban Infrastructure and Governance
ULB	-	Urban Local Body
ULCRA	-	Urban Land Ceiling Regulation Act
UNICEF	-	United Nations International Children's Emergency Fund
U.P	-	Uttar Pradesh
VAMBAY	-	Valmiki Ambedkar Awaz Yojana
VRS	-	Voluntary Retirement Scheme
WAPCOS	-	Water and Power Consultancy Services India Limited

1

Introduction

Urban Development in India

India, with an urban population of 286 million in 2001, has the second largest urban system in the world. At present, growing at a rate of nearly 3 percent per annum, the urban population of the country constitutes nearly 28 percent of the total population. As a result of the liberalization policies adopted by the government of India, the share of the urban population is expected to reach 40 percent of the total population by 2021.[1] It is estimated that by 2012, urban economic activities will be contributing 65 percent to the total GDP of the country which again is totally dependent on the quality and the availability of the urban infrastructure.[2] In the post reform period, cities which are considered as the 'engines of economic development' are not only linked with the regional or national economy, but are also highly intertwined with the international economy. Thus it is accepted that in today's world 'urbanization' has to be considered as a spatially grounded social process in which a wide range of different actors with quite different objectives and agendas interact through a particular configuration of interlocking spatial practices'.[3]

The share of urban population living in a country is considered as one of the indicators of the level of economic

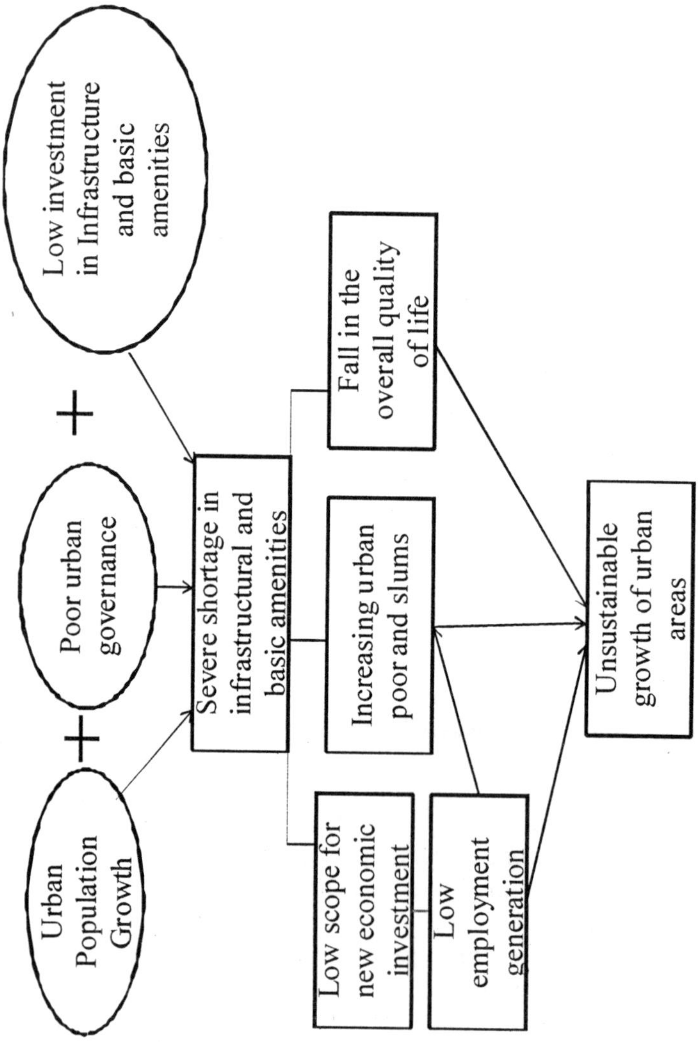

Fig. 1.1 Conceptual Framework-Urbanization in India

development that it has achieved. Constituting close to 28 percent of the total population of the country, nearly 57 percent of the GDP of the Indian economy is generated from urban areas.[4] India's economic growth since the 1970s is largely based on the growth of the service sector which is predominantly based in the urban areas.[5] According to a UN projection[6], urban India is expected to race ahead of rural India in terms of the total population by 2025. Almost very close to this, some other studies project that the urban population will take over the rural population by 2030.[7] Owing to the increasing importance of urban areas in the new global settings, formulation of a strong urbanization strategy has become unavoidable in national planning.

The unplanned and haphazard growth of the urban areas has created numerous challenges in their functioning as a system. As any other developing economy, the funds available for investing in the urban infrastructure fall short of the actual need in India. The already existing shortages of the urban basic services are aggravated by the fast growth of the urban population and by the rural to urban migration predominantly of semi-skilled and unskilled workers. When the total population of the country annually grew at the rate of 2 percent during 1991-2001, the respective urban annual growth was 3 percent, while that of the mega cities and slum population were of 4 percent and 5 percent.[8] Apart from these challenges, lack of capability of the urban governance mechanisms and outdated institutions has left the urban areas in the country unsustainable and almost unmanageable. The very poor level of the urban infrastructural facilities available in the country are clear from the fact that the share of the households with access to tap water, closed latrines and closed drainage facilities are 68.7 percent, 46.1 percent and 34.5 percent respectively.[9] Considering all these factors, the Eleventh Five Year Plan has summarized the following facts about the urban areas of the country.

- Urban sector contributed 63 percent of the GDP of the country in 2007, while the respective shares were merely 29 percent and 47 percent in 1950-51 and 1980-81.

- There is continued concentration of urban population in the large cities. The pattern of the spatial variation in the population concentration reflects the spatial polarization of employment opportunities.

- The poor and the outdated mechanisms of urban governance neutralize the benefits of the agglomeration economies making the cities non credit worthy and expensive but with poorly functioning urban services. The severe inadequacy in the urban infrastructure services in addition to the low quality of the services provided has become the biggest constraint in the country against achieving rapid economic growth in the future.

- The number of the urban poor is continuously rising in the country from 1973-74 but the share of the urban poor has fallen down. A total of 640 towns spread across the country report the existence of slums and they accommodate 42.6 million people and 8.2 million households. This also points out the acute shortage of housing in the urban areas especially among the poorer sections of urban population.

- Very low level of private sector participation in the provision of urban infrastructural amenities. Considering the severe paucity of government funds to invest in these areas and the huge gap between the demand and supply of the essential urban services at present, private sector investment in urban areas should be promoted through various mechanisms.

Statement of the Problem

The urban areas of the country have undergone massive transformation in various degrees in the post economic reform period. In the milieu of liberalization, globalization and privatization, economic growth began to be fully centered on the large cities across the globe which necessitated every country to evolve various mechanisms to attract private and foreign investments. (C,Vaidya, 2006). It was with this background that the urban development program named Jawaharlal Nehru National Urban Renewal Mission (JNNURM) was initiated by the Central Government of India. The Mission was initiated by the Ministries of Urban Development and Housing and Urban Poverty Alleviation on 3rd December 2005. The broad aspects which are covered under the Mission are : (i) urban infrastructure and governance; and (ii) alleviation of urban poverty and ensuring the basic minimum amenities to all the sections of urban society.

In general, studies available about the Mission can be broadly classified into two categories. The first group of studies supports the Mission as it is the crucial step taken by the Government of India (GoI) for the development of urban areas of the country and to raise India as a global power. They support the set of reforms proposed under the Mission stressing that outdated governance mechanisms are one of the major lacunae of the urban areas in the country and these institutions have to be replaced by the newer and more efficient ones to make the cities sustainable in every aspect. In contradiction to this, the other group of studies explains the Mission as the agenda propagated by the external funding agencies and the bilateral agencies but with the face of a Central Government initiative. They observe that the set of reforms as the new method to implement the neo liberal strategies of economic development by expanding the role of private sector and through delimiting the role of the Government as mere facilitator.

The present study attempts to examine if JNNURM could yield results in comparison to the expectations that the Government of India had at the time of its launching. As it is the largest ongoing urban development program in the country, it is very important to find out the challenges that the Mission is facing if any and to suggest solutions to tackle them. Though the Mission covers urban areas of very wide range in terms of size, it has to be also examined that if all the categories of urban areas are equitably benefitting from the Mission. In addition to this, through the case studies of Kochi and Thiruvananthapuram, the two cities covered under JNNURM from Kerala, the implementation of various projects under the Mission is studied in depth.

Objectives of the study

In the backdrop of ever increasing role of the urban areas in the national economy, JNNURM was initiated as an effective tool to tap the economic potential of the urban areas in India. Considering the importance of this urban development scheme the present study has the following objectives :

(1) To analyze the disparity in the funds allocated as well as the performance of the cities and states under the Mission and Sub-Missions of JNNURM.

(2) To examine the importance of reforms in urban governance under JNNRUM in determining the progress of city or state under JNNURM.

(3) To study JNNURM in the context of current level of infrastructural facilities attained by the state of Kerala.

(4) To scrutinize the Sub-Mission of Basic Services for the Urban Poor (BSUP) in tackling the problem of urban poverty in Kochi and Thiruvananthapuram in the contexts of community participation, structural mechanisms involved, population covered and urban governance reforms. The basic characteristics of the slums in both the cities will also be studied through field surveys as a part of this objective.

(5) To suggest policy suggestions to improve the progress of the various schemes under JNNURM in the Mission cities in Kerala and at the national level.

Research questions

The above objectives of the study lead us to ask the following research questions :

(1) Are there spatial disparities across states and cities in the benefits derived from JNNURM and if there are any, what are the causes for these disparities?

(2) To what degree JNNURM will benefit the state in the backdrop of the current infrastructural facilities attained by Kerala?

(3) How efficient is the Sub Mission of Basic services for the Urban Poor in tackling the problem of urban poverty in the Mission cities of Kochi and Thiruvananthapuram?

Literature review

This part of the chapter tries to build up theoretical framework of the study. The literature review is broadly divided into six sections as follows :

(1) Urban Development strategies; A global view

(2) Urbanization processes and pattern in India

(3) Urban areas in India in the Post economic reform period

(4) Urban Infrastructure and governance in India

(5) Jawaharlal Nehru National Urban Renewal Mission (JNNURM)

(6) An introduction to economy and urban processes in Kerala

Urban Development Strategies - A global view

In the western world, urbanization was always a process associated with industrialization wherein the labor force engaged in primary activities (particularly agricultural activities) gradually migrated to the centers of industrial activities which in course of time became the hub of population concentration. The immense importance attached with the urban areas in the national development is evident from the Keynesian argument that rising industrial productivity and close ties to the federal government are keys for sustained growth. During the initial stages of urbanization in the Western countries, the unplanned growth of cities created blighted areas and their demolition was believed to be necessary for the entire city as they were found to be the centers of crime and diseases. (Quinones, 1994 as cited in R Weber 2002). Thus, urban development in these countries including USA focused mainly on the demolition of these unattractive areas which were noticed in large numbers in non white localities. (Chicago Planning Commission,1942, quoted in Swatzberg, 2001, as cited in R Weber 2002). This bulldozer approach in urban development continued in the middle of the century which made the government authorities to take up the role of an insurance company, absorbing the cost of demolition and land preparation. Through these steps, it was generally believed that economic regeneration of cities will lead to improved social welfare for local residents in general. (DoE circular quoted in Higgens, 1983). The shifting of strategy from slum clearance and the broadening of the concept of blight resulted in the flow of white population to the Suburbs. (Von Hoffman, 2000).

It was in the 1950s that Growth pole strategy gained currency in the area of regional and urban development. It was accepted to be very useful if harmonized with the local economic and social conditions. (N. M. Hansen, 1967), (H.W. Richardson (1978). Quite contradictory to this some studies proved that it further favored concentrated accumulations in selected locations and could not give the promised results due to the loopholes in implementation. (J, Friedman (1972) as sited in H Benjamin, 1983). The post 1977 period, before the advent of full scale Thatcherism, can be considered as a brief 'golden' age for urban policy in which social and economic factors were overtly linked together in the development strategy. (Wilks- Heeg, 1996). By the end of 1970s, the redistributive spatial policies by extending urban industrial growth into underdeveloped peripheral regions underwent massive changes because of the challenges from urban industrial decline, welfare state retrenchment and economic globalization. (Martin and Sunley, 1997).

The early 1980s witnessed the shift in responsibility of the state in providing public services to the neoliberal perspective of private sector oriented development of infrastructure and provision of public services, where the state remained as a monitor of these activities. (Cheema,1983, as cited in F. Miraftab, 2004). It was widely proposed that the privatization or outsourcing of an activity will reduce the government control over it and in turn will reduce the possibilities of corruption and are more accountable to the recipients of services. (Sheifar, 1998 as cited in B.H. Nordtveit (2005). The beginning of 1980s also witnessed the emergence of the property led solutions for the urban problems. This marked an important stage in the transformation of urban development strategy from the Public sector initiatives to market based or private solutions. (M. Richerson, 1989), (Turok, 1992), (Headly, 1992). The growth of urban centers such as Hong Kong which solely illustrates the role of private players by means of monopoly in property renting, have full control in determining the local investment pattern in physical and social infrastructures. (D. Harvey, 2002). But most of these initiatives left out the urban poor and the peripheral areas of the city from making any substantial gains; one such example is the Urban Development Corporations (which was expected to attract private investment in urban infrastructure through property markets) introduced in the 1980s in Britain. (R. Imrie., H. Thomas, 1999).

A Marxian perspective to the studies about urban development was added through the works of David Harvey. It was believed that in the framework of uneven capitalistic geographical development, the priority was and will be given to the rules of capital accumulation rather than to the goals of meeting local needs and maximizing local welfare. Besides, it was also assumed that the rise of entrepreneurialism will deepen the uneven geographical development and will have prominent role from the geopolitical sense. (D. Harvey, 1989). In the contemporary world economy, the basis of the post modern city's economy is the 'production of fictitious capital to lend to the real estate agents who cut deals for the highly paid professionals who manufacture fictitious capital'. (D. Harvey, 1989). In addition to these, the concentration of political and economic power in the hands of few people have resulted in the growth of urban giants. Quite ironically, the social policy formulated under these circumstances, contributed very little in the provision of welfare services. (A.F. Ades, E.L. Glaeser, 1995).

In spite of the limitations in the market based urban development, taking account of their economic importance it was accepted that the priorities in national development should be given to policies which promote economic growth through cities. (P.E. Peterson, 1981). Under this regime, it was believed that any deviations from the urban based economic growth strategy will lead to failure of the market ending up in huge losses in private investments, jobs and tax revenue. Thus, the cities were considered as the business corporations or as efficiency maximizing organizations, which take various steps to enhance economic productivity. (K. R. Conner, 1991). To establish themselves in the highly competitive and rapidly changing local, regional and global milieu, the Metropolitan city local authorities mostly with silent approval of the private sector began to heavily depend on large scale urban development projects. (Erik-Swyngedouw, Frank-Moulaert and Arantxa Rodriguez, 2002).

These mammoth projects which are part of the neo-liberal policy, its selective middle and upper class democracy, and new forms of urban governance interventions, are characterized by less democratic and more elite oriented participation. Nonetheless, though very few grass root movements could manage to change the course of these lopsided development policies. (E. Swyngedouw., F. Moulaert & A. Rodriguez, 2002). The highly disproportionate focus that the elites receive in urban development strategies is evident from the fact that the present urban regeneration strategies primarily dominated by combination of aesthetic, economic and marketing considerations are oriented to appease the urban elite class. (F. Bianchini and M. Parkinson, 1994). However, the role of political forces operating in the country is another major factor in shaping the urban development strategies and thus to determine the development priorities. (J.R. Logan and H.L. Molotch, 2007).

There is wide consensus on the fact that globalization processes since 1970s have transformed urban areas as important geographical targets for numerous institutional changes and policies aiming at fast economic growth creating new spaces through contemporary capitalism. (N. Brenner, 2004). The 'new localism' or the recent stress for the decentralized governance is often misused as a forceful tool through which local, political and economic elites are aggressively attempting to promote economic rejuvenation to suit their interests. (N. Brenner and N. Theodore, 2002). As a result of these the neoliberal policies resulted in economic polarization and social exclusion rather than trickle down. Its failure in many instances is evident through the unexpected social costs, financial and industrial crisis that threatened to spread through the highly connected global market. (B. Jessop, 2002). Apart from this, the blurring of the conceptual distinction between private and public sectors in the aftermath of PPP (Public Private Partnership) initiatives in urban development restructured the local governments to treat the residents merely as customers with stratified entitlements to basic services rather as citizens leading to deepening of social segmentation. (F. Mirftab, 2004).

The dynamics of neo-liberalization has loosened various constraints related to marketization, commodification, and hyper exploitation of workers, and the discretionary power of private capital. Thus, the voice raised in demand for urban life based on grass root democratic participation and the satisfaction of social needs rather than the greediness for private profit, can be heard in many large cities. (N. Brenner, and N Theodore, 2002). Rejecting the serious long and short term negative implications of the neoliberal strategy on urban socio-economic space, it is argued by many scholars that the new circumstances have opened the gateway for numerous development opportunities to many countries around the globe. They argue that the rise of China as a global power in the economic map of the world is the proof for the triumph of neo-liberalism and the unsustainability of capitalism, M Li, (2005), (2008)

Urbanization Processes and Patterns in India

The policy makers have always had a half-hearted attitude towards the development of urban areas in the country. This can be mainly because of the low share of the urban population in the country just after independence. (R. Ramachandran, 1991). At present, the urban areas in the country have a two hierarchy structure in which the high consistent growth rate of the large cities shows the stability of their economy, while the falling growth rate of the small cities as the proof for the instability of their economies. (A. Kundu, 1983). It has to be noticed that the investments in urban areas were mainly centered on the less developed areas with proximity to the core cities without any ecological and sustainability considerations and this resulted in the growth of the metropolitan area without any link with the regional development. (S.B. Guha, 1999). Besides, there is huge imbalance in the fund allocation across the various size classes of urban areas in the country. Lion's share of the total subsidized infrastructure and urban amenities funds provided through the governmental programs from 1960s-1980s went to few large cities of the country and benefitted mostly the higher and the middle income neighborhoods. It was argued that this kind of an urban development strategy in the post reform period, aimed to promote the growth of selected cities to raise them to the level of 'global cities' will prove to be disastrous sooner or later. (A. Kundu, 2002).

The fast growth of the population in the large cities has deteriorated the quality of urban life and has become a major challenge in attracting the investment for funding in economic activities. (S. Banerjee). These fast growing urban centers have very poor capacity to generate employment opportunities for their increasing population. (Mukharji, 1995). Within the category of first class towns itself, it is the million plus cities which have noticed the larger growth rates than rest of the first class cities and this is another implication of the top heavy structure of the urban areas in the country. (A. Kundu, Saranagi, 2007). The most important challenges in front of the small towns at present are the lack of growth of the employment opportunities and the poor basic urban amenities available. (B. Chattopadhayay, 2006).

The disparity between the small and large towns in various aspects can be attributed, firstly to the capacity of the large cities to attract both the national and global investments and to the decline in the public investments in infrastructure and other basic amenities of the small towns. (A. Kundu, 2006). This has resulted in the wide variation in the financial performance of the cities in the country and across the cities within the same state. (S. Thakur, 2007). The constitutionally built in imbalances in the functions and the functions assigned to various levels of government is evident from their poor performance and the high dependency of the lower levels of urban governing bodies on the state and center (P.K. Mohanty, B.M. Misra, R. Goyal and P.D. Jermi, 2007). In the midst of all these challenges, keeping an eye on the urgency to meet the capitalistic demand for liquidity, some of the states have developed mechanisms to make the built environment more flexible and responsive to investment criteria of real estate capital (R. Webber, 2002).

Urban India in the Post Economic Reform Period

Globalization is important for economic growth as it affects the spatial allocation of resources and creates spatial impacts (Lim, 2007). It has added further focus to the importance of city level efficiency, and rapid economic gains in economic efficiency at the national level are achievable through its leading cities (Mohan, 2007). Thus, it is generally agreed that the changes that are taking place in cities and the city related policies in the country can be well understood in relation to the emergence of globalization. (Mathur, 2005). The increasing importance of urban areas in the national, regional and global economy has made planned development of urban areas a necessity in the post economic reform period. (K.N. Singh, 2000). Unluckily, the lack of planning for the urban areas has resulted in the poor capacity of our urban areas to generate employment opportunities for the ever increasing population especially in case of the larger cities. Mukharji (1996). Though the programs of liberalization have accelerated the process of economic growth and reduction in disparity at the global level, the regional disparity within the country has gone up. (A. Kundu, S. Gupta, 1996, and UN 2009).

In the globalised milieu, there had been clear cut transformations in the functions and nature of urban areas in the country. These centers act as the windows of global economy whose most evident manifestations are traced in the presence of large human agglomerations or large cities (N. Sharma, 2000). In other words, the cities of today are growing as the gatekeepers of globalization in terms of international investment and national entry points for global, economic socio-cultural and financial forces (A. Kundu, 2003). The new patterns of investment which were established as the responses to these changes, have led to the concentration of economic activities in a few large cities and the corridor joining them that attract most of the rural migrants (A. Kundu, 2002). Besides, the increasing privatization of land and civic amenities has led to the shooting up of the land values and this became the main reason for the slowing down of migration of the poor to the urban areas since the 1990s (A. Kundu, B. Pradhan, and A. Subrahmaniyam, 2003). Today, the older forms of urban governance are not fitting with the dynamic urban environment in the post globalization world, which calls for the need to establish newer and dynamic urban governing institutions to suit the present needs (I.Baud, 2003). These newly emerged urban governing institutions try their level best to provide land at preferred sites to the newly arising economic activities through the capitalistic market and this tendency is almost the same across all the states. (A. Kundu, B. Pradhan and A. Subrahmaniyam, 2003).

In the post economic reform period it was also widely appreciated that the huge gap in the demand and supply of urban amenities in the country can be filled up through private and foreign investment. (S. Narayanan, 2002). The promotion of the ULBs to borrow from the capital market for financing in urban infrastructure and the promotion of the private sector under the recent urban development initiatives like JNNURM and UIDSSMT are appropriate examples for globalization needs moulding the urban development strategy in our country (M.R. Narayana, 2008). There is no doubt in the fact that the involvement of the international funding agencies in the management of urban centers in the country during the post economic reform period has increased immensely in comparison to the pre-economic reform period (NIUA, 2009). As a setback to this trend, the payment of huge sum of municipal revenue in the form of interest for the loans availed from the external funding and bilateral agencies have made our large cities very vulnerable to economic shocks at the global arena. But the degree of vulnerability can be reduced through careful planning of the municipal expenditure. (A. Kundu, 2002).

Urban Infrastructure and Governance in India

In the initial years of planning itself, it was observed that there is acute shortage of urban infrastructure in the country. As in any other country it was the urban poor who were worst affected by the inadequacy of these services. (Zakaria Committee Report, 1963). Various multilateral agencies, bilateral agencies, and external commercial borrowings have played vital role in restructuring the urban development strategies in the country at present, especially in the post reform period (S. Narayanan, 2002). Though ADB investments in urban infrastructure had clearly helped the country in removing the infrastructure bottlenecks and contributed to economic growth, the sustainability of these projects were affected by prevailing policy and institutional constraints (ADB, 2007). At present, the potential improvements in the provision and maintenance of urban infrastructure and services are constrained by poor urban governance, management and finance. (World Bank, 2003). In order to keep the urban areas in the country vibrant to the changes taking place across the global economy, it is necessary to keep the urban institutions and various management mechanisms also dynamic (Isa. Baud, 2004).

The external funding agencies have always been a major critique of the urban governance institutions in India. It is believed that the current changes taking place in the area of urban governance in the country is largely due to the pressure exerted by the external funding agencies in various ways (V. Baindur, L. Kamath, 2009). Though the 74th CAA (Constitutional Amendment Act) was a milestone in the area of urban governance in the country, as its implementation and provisions remained only in papers it failed to ensure people's participation to a satisfactory level and the functioning of the ULBs as independent governing bodies (Mathur, 2005). The outdated urban governing institutions in addition to the poor revenue base of urban areas in India made it necessary for the local bodies to evolve strategies to tap private investment through capital markets and Public Private Partnerships. (S. Bagchi, 2001). At the same time, the role of the government as the supplier, buyer and seller of these services remains very important, especially in developing countries. (A. Pethe and M. Gorkhe, 2002).

On the negative side, the fall in the public investment in basic amenities and increasing role of the private sector in urban management has increased the regional disparity and across the different sizes of urban areas in the levels of the basic amenities available. (A. Kundu, D. Kundu and S. Bagchi, 1999). Beyond this, loosening of government control over the local bodies has increasingly made the ULBs under the control of Corporate and financial institutions and this in turn has deepened the segmentation within the cities of the country (A. Kundu, 2002). It was noted that there is a huge disparity between urban-rural and the poor-rich sections in the provisions of urban basic services. The privatization of basic services is expected to further widen the gap between the various sections of urban society to avail these services (V.R. Reddy, 2007). Contrary to this, some studies have proved that the privatization of the services will not affect the urban poor as usually expected, because they are the ones who are more willing to pay user charges than the better off people if they are ensured a more adequate and efficient supply. (D. Ghosh, S. Ghosh and L. Bounsley, 2006).

In spite of having taken several initiatives to boost up the urban infrastructure in the country, it is very hard to accept the fact that even though there was improvement in the level of basic urban services available, there had been clear cut decline in both the quality as well as the quantity of these services. (NIUA, 2007). Thus, in order to improve the efficiency in the provision of urban amenities and urban revenue base in the country, it is inevitable to implement innovative resource mobilization methods and governance reforms like restructuring of the property tax, market based financing systems, and management innovations in ULBs. These are necessary in order to survive the competition among the cities across the globe to attract the private and foreign investments. (C. Vaidya and H. Vaidya, 2008). Along with implementing the governance reforms, necessary manpower and technical expertise are also very important to improve the governance of the ULBs. Where ever it was not done, extra pressure exerted on the ULBs was observed to have added further stress on the inefficient service delivery at present. (NIUA, 2007). In the market oriented development of the urban areas, it is evident that the incapability of the ULBs to generate the matching share of revenue has become one of the most important obstacles to utilize many of the governmental schemes. Thus, it is suggested that the funding for urban infrastructure and basic amenities by the agencies like HUDCO should not be solely guided by the mechanisms of the capital market, but also by the considerations for social equity (UN, 2008).

Jawaharlal Nehru National Urban Renewal Mission (JNNURM)

JNNURM is widely appreciated as a comprehensive urban renewal program which will enable the 63 selected urban centers to place themselves as important centers of economic activities at the global level. (NIUA, 2007). It is also viewed as the most recent and the positive response given by the Government of India (GoI) to meet the increasing demands of globalization in urban development strategy (M.R. Narayana, 2008). The Mission came as the response arising out of the rapid and unplanned urban growth and economic disparities that have created the 'dual cities'. (K. Renu, 2008). It has became very crucial in the economic growth of the country as it is the most recent and comprehensive urban structure strategic framework through which the GoI intends to direct future investments, institutional, fiscal and management reforms in urban areas. And it is widely agreed that the degree of institutionalisation of various sets of reform initiatives taken under the Mission will determine the degree of its success. (ADB, 2008). In order to sustain the competition at the regional, national and global levels, and also to mobilize the resources needed for investment, it is agreed that new strategies of urban management in the country, especially, PPPs (Public Private Partnership) have to be promoted in a large way under JNNURM. (C. Vaidya, 2009).

Withstanding the shower of appreciation that JNNURM received from different corners, it is also criticized by some scholars as the strong symbol of the current urban development strategy adopted by GoI keeping focus on the development of the large cities of the country (B. Chattopadhayay, 2007). It is also believed that the current reforms under JNNURM are the ultimate results of the influence on country's urban development strategies by the international financial institutions and bilateral donors. (V. Baindur and L. Kamath, 2008). The second basis for the criticism of the Mission is the half hearted inclusion of BSUP (Basic Services for the Urban Poor) under JNNURM as the second Sub Mission to ensure the access of basic amenities to all sections of urban society. (V.Baindur and L.Kamath, 2008). It is clear from the fact that even in cities like Delhi with huge chunk of urban poor population, the funds for the poverty alleviation through JNNURM remain unutilized, while other remunerative construction projects are completed on or before time with Public Private Partnership (PPP). (S. Mitra, 2008). In disagreement to the pro-market oriented urban development strategy of the Mission, it is widely criticized that the private sector investment under JNNURM will not benefit the poor and the middle class as they are not interested in investing in basic services but only in the huge projects which will give them huge sum of profit. (V. Baindur and L. Kamath, 2007).

Economy and Urbanization Processes in Kerala

Kerala, a small state located in the south western part of the country, had often been in the centre of academic discussion owing to its peculiar model of development. Except in the area of political economy, there is very close resemblance between the development experience of Kerala and that of Sri Lanka (R. Casinader, 1995). The backwardness and the unemployment of the state can be neglected in the glory of achieving high social development at the peril of the state itself. (K.P. Kannan, 1990). It was observed by some scholars that investing in the manufacturing industry of the modern variety is the most vital factor for the sustenance of the state economy and the government should be able to convince the profitable working of the modern industries by improving the efficiency of public enterprises. (K.K. Subrahmanyam and P.M. Pillai, 1986). But in the later years, it was widely accepted that the main solution to overcome the stagnation of the state economy is to encourage private investment with emphasis on the setting up of technology based skill intensive industries. (K.K. Subrahmanyam, 1990). Along with promoting private sector in the state, it is argued that the revival of the industrial sector, labor reforms, adequate power supply and good infrastructure are very important to tackle this challenge. (N. Padmabhan, 1990; B.A. Prakash, 1998 and (Jeromi, 2003).

The Urban processes experienced in the state can be well correlated with its commercial factors and geographical location. It is interesting to note that the urban population growth in the state is not due to the concentration of the population in the large cities but due to the increase in the number of urban areas and also due to the urbanization of the peripheral areas of the existing major centers. (T.T. Sreekumar, 1990). In addition to this, the role of colonial and ecological factors is also equally important in the evolution of the present urbanization pattern. (B. Dasgupta, 2000). The urbanization pattern can also be studied through analyzing the rural urban linkages in the state and vice versa. (K.P Aniyan, 1991). Urban areas in the state had played the role of catalysts in speeding up the urbanization process in the state largely by propelling the diversification of densely populated rural settlements resulting in the emergence of new towns. (T.T. Sreekumar, 1993 and M. Eppen, 1999).

The large size and density of villages in the state, the dispersed urban settlement pattern and the historically well developed transport system making every village accessible by the road, etc make the distinction between the rural and urban areas very arbitrary in the state. (M. Eppen,1999). Similarly, uniqueness in the urbanization processes is also evident in the characteristics of the urban population of the state, especially in case of the slum population. (NIUA, 1993). Residential flat construction and the flat culture in the urban areas are on an increase in the state due to the increasing over all density. (Town Planning Department, Government of Kerala, 2002). The study by the Ministry of Local Self Governance proposes that through the recent urban development schemes of KSUDP and JNNURM, emphasis should be given to adopt various urban governance mechanisms which were successfully implemented in many other cities of the country. (Kerala Institute for Local Administration, 2008). In contradiction to this, it is widely condemned that the strict guidelines and the conditions to avail the funds under these projects have undermined democratic participation of the common people in development process and aims to privatize the urban sectors. (B. Kuruvilla, 2006).

Role of the state in urban development

The activities in the urban areas cannot be left to themselves. It needs careful planning and it is in this field the government policies play a major role. Government intervention in urban activities and planning is important due to the following reasons :

- The government intervention becomes very necessary as there is always conflict between the interests of the various sections of urban population. This is very clear in case of urban land policy, slum policy, etc.
- Through various policies, the government can direct the spatial pattern and nature of urbanization in the country as a whole and can determine the priority in the development of various classes of urban areas.
- The government through various provisions can ensure the accessibility of urban amenities to the entire urban population. Thus, the government policies have direct implications on improving the quality of life in the urban areas.
- 'Through various steps, public policies and programs can reduce the gap in standard of living between the various social groups living in urban areas. These policies can also play a major role in reducing the regional disparity within the country.
- The government policies can determine the extent of sustainability in the growth and development of the urban areas. They also take account of the environmental sustainability which can be ensured through regulating the various economic activities and framing policies for shaping urban areas.

In general, the state interventions in development are planned tools in service of 'rationalization' which will eliminate the smallest government units, orient investments to places with greatest development potential, and to improve the technical level of planning.[10] At present, Government is not the only player in regulating the direction and momentum of urban growth. The importance of the private investments, public private partnership and that of the NGOs has increased immensely during the post economic reform period. The shortage of government funds for investments in urban infrastructure has necessitated the government to open numerous areas of urban development for private investors. This is supported by the argument that private sector is more efficient and faster in increasing the coverage of various services than the public sector counterpart.[11] The examining of the Five Year Plans will enable us to understand the shifting focus of urban development strategy adopted in the country.

Mainly owing to the agrarian nature of Indian economy, urban areas have not got the adequate attention from the beginning of the Five Year Planning in the country.[12] The initial plans mainly addressed the areas of rural development, industrialization, poverty, agriculture, etc, while problems of urban areas were not given attention except in case of urban housing shortage. In spite of this, several non prominent initiatives were taken by the Central as well as by the State Governments for solving the problems of urban areas but mainly restricted to urban housing. The half-hearted attitude of the policy makers towards urban development had continued till the Eighth Five Year Plan, the plan in which a massive urban development scheme, Mega City Project was introduced.

The later plans well addressed the acute shortage of the basic amenities in our urban areas and stressed on the critical need to increase investments in urban infrastructure in the background of changed global milieu. Opening of the economy also had its own replications on the urban policy in our country. Some of the noticeable changes which can be seen from this point of view in urban policies are increasing stress on the concept

Table 1.1 Schemes for Urban Development in the Five Year Plans

Serial No.	*Five Year Plan*	*Priority areas / Schemes in Urban Development*
1.	1st Five Year Plan (1951-56)	1. Urban housing
2.	2nd Five Year Plan (1956-61)	2. Urban housing
3.	3rd Five Year Plan (1961-66)	1. Low income housing
		2. Slum clearance and improvement
4.	4th Five Year Plan (1969-74)	1. Housing
		2. Water supply and sanitation
5.	5th Five Year Plan (1974-79)	1. Housing
		2. Water supply and sanitation
		3. Environmental Improvement of Urban Slums
6.	6th Five Year Plan (1980-85)	1. Housing
		2. Environmental Improvement of Urban Slums
		3. Integrated development of Small and Medium Towns
7.	7th Five Year Plan (1985-90)	1. Housing
		2. Environmental Improvement of Urban Slums
		Integrated Development of Small and Medium Towns
		3. Urban Basic Services for the Poor
		4. National Capital Region Development
		5. Sanitation and water supply

(Contd.)

(Contd. Table 1.1)

Serial No.	*Five Year Plan*		*Priority areas/Schemes in Urban Development*
8.	8th Five Year Plan (1992-97)	1.	Nehru Rozgar Yojana
		2.	Environmental Improvement of Urban Slums
		3.	Urban Basic Services for the Poor
		4.	Integrated Development of Small and Medium Towns
		5.	Prime Ministers Integrated Urban Poverty Eradication Program
		6.	Indira Awaas Yojana
		7.	Accelerated Urban Water Supply Programme
		8.	Mega city scheme
		9.	Transport
		10.	National Slum Development Programme
9.	9th Five Year Plan (1997-02)	1.	Accelerated Urban Water Supply Programme
		2.	Integrated Development of Small and Medium Towns
		3.	Urban Basic Services for the Poor
		4.	Mega city scheme
		5.	Swarna Jayanti Shahari Rozgar Yojana
		6.	National Slum Development Programme
		7.	Valmiki Ambedkar Awas Yojana

(Contd.)

(Contd. Table 1.1)

Serial No.	*Five Year Plan*	*Priority areas / Schemes in Urban Development*
10.	10th Five Year Plan (2002-07)	1. Mega city project 2. Accelerated Urban Water Supply Program 3. Integrated Development of Small and Medium Towns (all were later Subsumed under Jawaharlal Nehru National Urban Renewal Mission (JNNURM) and Urban Infrastructure Development Scheme for Small and Medium Towns (UIDSSMT) 4. National Slum Development Programme 5. Valmiki Ambedkar Awas Yojana (Both Subsumed under Basic Services for the Urban Poor (BSUP) and Integrated Housing and Slum Development Program (IHSDP) 6. Swarna Jayanti Shahari Rozgar Yojana
11.	11th Five Year Plan (2007-12)	1. Jawaharlal Nehru National Urban Renewal Mission 2. Urban Infrastructure Development Scheme for Small and Medium Towns 3. Swarna Jayanti Shahari Rozgar Yojana

Source- Five Year Plans, Planning Commission of India.

of user charges for the sustainability of services, opening up of the urban infrastructure to private investors, increase in the use of urban local body assets to finance themselves through capitalistic market. The reflections of the urban development strategies advocated by the international agencies can be seen in our five year plans, especially from the eighth five year plan.

Mega City Project which was initiated in 1993 was the first urban development initiative entirely based on the above mentioned principles in the creation of urban infrastructure in the cities of Bombay, Calcutta, Chennai, Bangalore and Hyderabad. The base of the neoliberal urban governance institutions were laid in the large cities of the country through this scheme. But the realization that the investment in urban development should not be restricted only to very few large urban centers of the country, but to a larger number of cities spread across the country, made it necessary for the Government of India to design a large scale urban development programme.

The increasing complexity of urban activities and urban governance made the integrated urban planning necessary in the recent decades. JNNURM or Jawaharlal Nehru National Urban Renewal Mission was introduced in the country in December 2005 as the single powerful solution to tackle the numerous challenges of our urban areas. A close assessment of the Mission guidelines throws light on the fact that this program has taken a 'u' turn in urban development strategy in the country from that of the past. It can be also considered as the replication of Mega City Project on a larger scale. It is expected through the Mission through urban governance reforms and the investment in urban infrastructure, the major urban challenges can be solved to a large extent. In total, the major aspect that we can observe is the gradual shift from the welfare oriented approach to market oriented approach in urban development and management.

Data base

In the present study both primary and secondary data were used. The state level analysis is based entirely on the secondary data while for the detailed study of the Mission cities from Kerala, both primary and secondary data were used. In total, for the present study, data from the following sources were used.

(1) Census of India, Primary Census Abstract, 2001.

(2) Town directory, Census of India, 1991, 2001.

(3) JNNURM website, Ministries of Urban Development and Housing and Poverty Alleviation.

(4) City Development Plans (CDPs) of the 63 Mission cities.

(5) Corporation websites of Kochi and Thiruvananthapuram.

(6) Slum primary census abstract, 2001.

(7) District Census Handbooks of Kochi and Ernakulam, 1991, 2001.

(8) Data directly collected from the corporation offices of Kochi and Thiruvananthapuram.

(9) Primary household level survey of slum population in the cities of Kochi and Thiruvananthapuram.

(10) Detailed Project Reports (DPRs) of the various Mission projects under the corporations of Kochi and Thiruvananthapuram.

Methodology

Various statistical and analytical techniques are used in the study. These are as follows :

(1) To analyze the performance of various states and cities under the Mission, simple statistical tools are used. The percentage values of the share of various state and cities out of the total released fund under the Mission is calculated to get the overall picture of the Mission.

(2) Fund- Population Ratio (FPR) - The share of the funds released cannot be taken as the criteria for understanding the performance as it is not scale free due to the population factor. In order to neutralize the factor of population, ratio between the shares of the fund released under the Mission and the share of the population covered under the Mission is calculated. This is done both in case of the Mission cities and in case of states. The formula can be written as-

$$FPR = \frac{\text{percentage of share of the city or state in the released fund under JNNURM}}{\text{percentage of share of City or state in the total population covered under JNNURM}}$$

(3) Concentration index of urban poor (CIUP) - The variation in the concentration of urban poor in various categories of cities under the Mission is calculated. The formula used is;

$$CIUP = \frac{\text{Share of the urban poor population under each category of cities}}{\text{Share of the category in the total population covered under Mission}}$$

(4) Distribution of funds across the various categories of Mission cities (DOF) – In order to find the variation in the allocation of the funds for the various categories of Mission cities, share of the funds allocated under each category per 1000 population is calculated. This will neutralize the factor of population variation across the various categories of Mission cities. The formula is;

$$DOF = \frac{\text{Funds to be allocated under a given category of cities}}{\text{Share of the given category in the total population covered under Mission}} \times 1000$$

(5) Funds.Population Ratio of the 3 Categories of Mission cities- This is calculated to understand the pattern of distribution of the Mission funds across the three categories of cities. The formula is;

$$FPR = \frac{\text{Percentage share of a given category in the released fund under JNNURM}}{\text{Share of the given category in the total population covered under Mission}}$$

(6) Cross tabulation. Cross tabulation of respective shares of the cities falling under the various categories of urban poor population with that of the share of BSUP under Mission investments plans is done to examine if the cities give adequate importance to the second Sub Mission for urban poor.

(7) Correlation. Correlation between various aspects of slum population with the income level of the surveyed households is done to assess if the income level of the families have impact on the various aspects of their life in slum.

(8) Ranking. Ranking of the cities is done to analyze the implementation of the Mission reforms. All the selected reforms at the ULB level are given equal weight. The ranks are added up to get the final ranking of the cities in implementing the reforms.

(9) Percentages. Simple percentages are calculated to analyze various socio-economic data collected from the field survey. The share of the households in the total surveyed households in various aspects like land ownership, length of stay in slum, payment of user charges, etc. are calculated for both the cities separately.

(10) Graphical methods. In order to illustrate statistics related to the projects, various graphical methods like bar diagram, pie diagrams, line graphs, radar diagram etc are drawn.

Study area

In the first part of the study, the performance of the states and cities across the country under JNNURM is assessed. Though Tirupati and Porbandar were added to the list of the Mission cities in the beginning of 2009, these two cities are not included in this study. Among the 63 Mission cities which were covered from the commencement of JNNURM, Delhi is excluded from the study as major portion of the investments in the urban infrastructure and in other areas are made in this city under the tag of 'Common Wealth Games'. The inclusion of Delhi may give a wrong impression that the city is performing best in the country which may not be the reality. Thus, 62 Mission cities are covered under the first part of the study. The second part of the study focuses on the Mission cities in Kerala, i.e. Kochi and Thiruvananthapuram. The detailed study on the progress of the JNNURM projects in these cities is done through field work and data collected from the Corporation Websites and the CDPs and DPRs. The maps of the study areas are given in the next page.

Chapter scheme of the study

The study is divided into five chapters. The major contents of the chapters are as follows.

Introduction

The chapter tries to build up a strong theoretical framework on urbanization, processes involved, management mechanisms and other aspects related to the urban development in the country. Since the area of study is JNNURM with special reference to the Mission cities in Kerala, a part of the literature review covers these two aspects too.

Progress of Jawaharlal Nehru National Urban Renewal Mission (JNNURM) in India

The first part of Chapter 1 gives a broad introduction to the urban development Mission. It covers Mission guidelines, funding structure and fund allocation under the CDPs and other linked facets of the Mission. The second part of the chapter analyzes the performance on the states and cities under the

Map 1.1 JNNURM Cities Covered under the Study

Source : Government of India.

JNNURM - Jawaharlal Nehru National Urban Renewal Mission

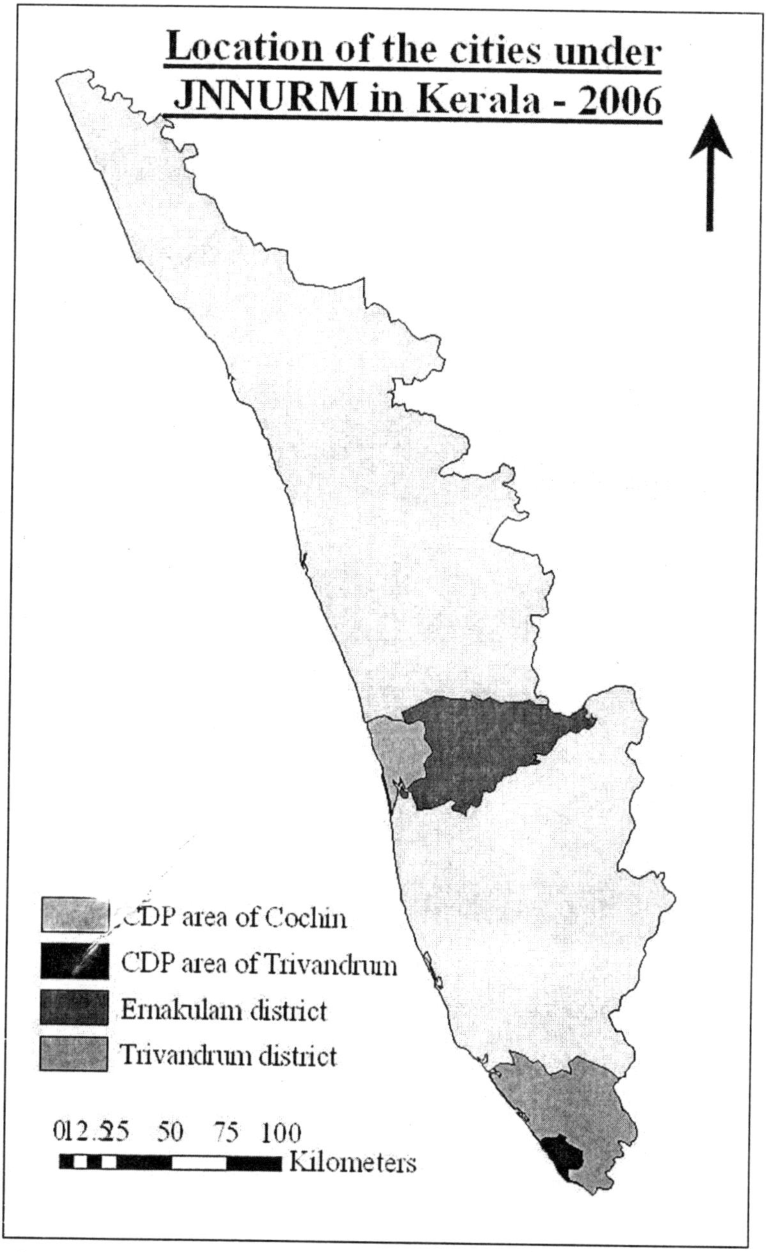

Map 1.2 Area of Case Study- JNNURM Cities in Kerala

Mission. This is entirely based on the statistics on the Mission available from the official website of the Mission managed by the Ministries of Urban Development and Housing and Urban Poverty Alleviation.

Urbanization, Urban Infrastructure and Urban Governance in Kerala

A brief study on the basic characteristics of urbanization processes and patterns in the state is done in the first part of Chapter 2. It is done to understand the background in which JNNURM was introduced in the state. In the backdrop of the current urban amenities available in the state, the second part of the chapter analyzes the progress of the first Sub Mission, UIG (Urban Infrastructure and Governance). The analysis is based on the statistics available from the official websites of Kochi and Thiruvananthapuram Corporations and from the JNNURM official website by the Government of India.

Basic Services and the Urban Poor in Kerala

A brief study of Kudumbasree, the poverty alleviation nodal agency in the state, is done in the first part of Chapter 3. In order to understand the nature of urban poverty in the state is done a slum survey in the two cities . This is covered in the second part of the chapter. The third part of the chapter deals exclusively with the analysis of the progress of the BSUP projects in the two cities. The analysis is based on the statistics available from the official websites of Kochi and Thiruvananthapuram Corporations and from the JNNURM official website by the Government of India. In addition to this, field survey data is also analyzed in this chapter.

Conclusion

This chapter can be broadly divided into two parts. With special focus on Mission cities from Kerala, the first part summarizes the progress of JNNURM projects in the country in a comprehensive manner. The policy suggestions evolved from the study for the better implementation of JNNURM both at the country level and also specific to the two Mission cities in Kerala is dealt in the second part of the chapter.

References

1. Government of India, (2002), "Eleventh Five Year Plan, (2007-12)", Planning Commission of India, p. 394.
2. Ibid, p. 396.
3. Harvey, D. (1989), "From Managerialism to Entrepreneurialism: The Transformation in Urban Governance in the Late Capitalism", *Geographiska Annaler*, Vol. 71, No 1, (1-16), p. 4
4. Government of India, (2002), "Eleventh Five Year Plan, (2007-12)", Planning Commission of India, p. 395.
5. "India, infrastructural report", 2003, Published by Oxford University Press, New Delhi, p. 12.
6. "Mckinsey Report on Urban India 2030 ; Projections and Statistics", (2010), Mckinsey Global Institute, p. 2.
7. Barnhardt, M., Supriti S., Ramanathan, R. (2002) *"Urban Poverty Reduction Initiatives in India; A General Assessment and a Particular Perspective"*, Published by Ramanathan Foundation, p. 2.
8. "Urban Poverty Reduction Strategies in Select Cities of India", (2008), NIUA, p. 6.
9. Census of India, 2001, as cited in *Urban Poverty Reduction Strategies in Select Cities of India*, (2008), NIUA", p. 6.
10. Evers, (1976), as cited in J. R. Logan, H. L. Molotch, (2007), *"Urban fortunes; The Political Economy of Place"*, Published by California University Press, p. 149.
11. Clarke, G.G., Kosec, K., Wallasten, S. (2008), "Has Private Participation in Water and Sewerage Improved the Coverage? Empirical Evidence From Latin America", *Journal of International Development*, Vol. 21, No. 3, p. 327.
12. Ramachandran, R. (1990), *"Urbanization and Urban Systems in India"*, Published by Oxford University Press, p. 282.

2

Progress of Jawaharlal Nehru National Urban Renewal Mission (JNNURM) in India

Jawaharlal Nehru National Urban Renewal Mission (JNNURM)- An Introduction

Jawaharlal Nehru National Urban Renewal Mission (JNNURM) is the most recent and the largest urban development initiative undertaken by the Government of India. It is larger than any previous urban development scheme not only in terms of investment, but also in terms of the number of cities covered, sectoral coverage and in terms of the integration of the peripheral areas also in the planning process. The first part of this chapter deals with the basic aspects about the Mission Jawaharlal Nehru National Urban Renewal Mission (JNNURM) which is mainly based on the government documents on the Mission. The second part of the chapter tries to analyze the progress of the JNNURM projects at the state and city levels in the first four years of the Mission period. The entire analysis is based on the data available on the Mission projects from the JNNURM website managed by Ministry of Urban Development and Ministry of Housing and Urban Poverty Alleviation.

The Urban Development Mission, which was inaugurated on 3rd December 2005 aims at the overall and sustainable development of the selected cities throughout the country within a period of seven years. The statement on the Mission clearly points out that JNNURM solely aims at the reform driven, fast track planned development of cities with focus on efficiency in urban infrastructure, service delivery mechanisms, community participation and accountability of urban local bodies and parastatal agencies. In other words, the Mission which covers 63 cities under three population size categories aims at the transformation of these cities into efficient, growing, equitable and sustainable centers for future economic growth. In 2009 two more urban centers; Porbandar and Tirupathy were added to this list making the total number of Mission cities to 65. But these two cities are not included in this study as they are at the initial stages of Mission formalities. Similarly Delhi, the capital city is also not included as there are so many infrastructural and other projects taking place in the city as it is the host of the Common Wealth Games 2010. The Mission which was launched under the Ministries of Urban Development and Housing and Poverty Alleviation and functions under the overall guidance and supervision of the National Steering Group (NSG) which is further coordinated by the State Level Steering Committees (SLSC). The broad objectives of the Mission are :

- Integrated development of the infrastructure services.
- Securing linkages between asset creation and maintenance for long run project sustainability.
- Accelerating the flow of the investment into the urban infrastructure services.
- Planned development of the cities including the peri-urban areas[1], outgrowths[2], and urban corridors.[3]
- Renewal and the redevelopment of the inner city areas.
- Universalization of the urban basic services to ensure their availability to the urban poor.

The Mission can be considered as the milestone in the history of urban planning in the country in many respects. It is the result of the late realization of our planners about the increasing importance of the urban areas in the globalised world. 'The new urban policy developed in parallel with the neoliberal economic policy revolves around the city. The old forms and functions, traditional political and organizational configuration, had to give way to a new urbanity that would stand the tests imposed by the global and liberal world order.'[4] The achievement of the high economic growth will be beyond our reach unless we change the poor image of our urban areas in the global economy. Though it is not for the first time, the importance of the urban areas was given emphasis by the planners, however, it is for the first time such a large scale and integrated approach for the sustainable growth of the urban areas is taken in the country. Experiences in the past show that urban development investments will not be meaningful and the benefits from them will not be sustainable without the implementation of the urban governance reforms and decentralization of urban governance. Thus, the two major thrusts given in the Mission are firstly on the implementation of a set of mandatory and optional reforms to ensure the sustainable and efficient functioning of the Urban Local Bodies (ULBs) and secondly on the fuller implementation of the 74th Constitutional Amendment Act (CAA) which will ensure the peoples participation in developmental activities.

As in any other developing economy, India also faces severe shortage in the urban infrastructural facilities. The ever increasing population in the urban areas and the increasing importance of the urban areas in terms of the economic activities exert further pressure on the already stressed urban amenities. In addition to this, the inefficient and outdated urban governance mechanism and the governance institutions is another major challenge that our cities are facing at present. JNNURM has taken a sudden leap in the areas of transforming urban governance institutions and the governing mechanisms. In order to avail the central government share of funds under the JNNURM projects, implementation of minimum level of reforms in each year is the pre-requisite condition. The fuller participation of the common man in urban planning and developmental activities is aimed to be achieved during the Mission period through the inclusion of the 74th CAA[5] in the mandatory reforms.

The poor management of the urban areas and the poor infrastructural facilities in the country had always been a point to be criticized by the external funding agencies. A closer observation at the urban development programs in the past funded by the external agencies, throw light on the fact that these agencies in the country have always stressed on the reforms of urban governance and institutions. Thus, introduction of JNNURM in the country was widely appreciated by these agencies, and also are very closely associated with the Urban Development Mission through various means like monitoring, training and capacity building. The Mission is supported by the external funding agencies like ADB and had approved $ 2 million in Feb 2006 in its support. Other than this, it has also deployed a team of consultants (in the areas of city planning, project development, financial planning, capacity building, legal regulatory reforms and monitoring and evaluation systems) which is an integral part of the Mission.

JNNURM and Sub-Missions

JNNURM, the urban development Mission, has adopted an integrated approach towards developing the urban areas. The Mission not only aims at the creation of urban infrastructure, but also at the efficient and sustainable service delivery, reforms in the urban governance, to ensure the basic civic amenities to the entire urban population, and thus to trigger the overall development of the urban areas in the selected cities of the country. It has two Sub-Missions namely Urban Infrastructure and Governance (UIG), and Basic Services for the Urban Poor (BSUP).

Sub-Mission for Urban Infrastructure and Governance : This Sub Mission is administered by the Ministry of Urban Development. The admissible components under this Sub Mission are as follows :

- Water supply including setting up of desalination plants
- Sewerage and sanitation
- Solid waste management including hospital waste management
- Construction and improvement of the drains and the storm water drainage system
- Urban transport
- Renewal and redevelopment of the inner city areas
- Development of the heritage areas
- Preservation of water bodies
- Street lighting
- Prevention and rehabilitation of soil erosion and landslides only in cases of special category States where such problems are common.
- Parking lots and spaces on PPP basis.

Sub-Mission for Basic Services to the Urban Poor : This Sub Mission is administered by the Ministry of Urban Employment and Poverty Alleviation through the Sub-Mission Directorate for Basic Services to the Urban Poor. The main components under BSUP are as follows :

- Integrated development of slums, housing and development of infrastructure projects in slums in the identified cities.
- Projects involving development, improvement, and maintenance of basic services to the urban poor.
- Slum improvement and rehabilitation projects.

- Projects to provide houses at affordable cost for slum dwellers, urban poor, Economically Weaker Sections (EWS) and Lower Income Group (LIG) categories.

- Civic amenities like community halls, child care centres etc.

- Convergence of health, education and social security schemes for the urban poor.

In spite of covering very wide range of sectors under the Mission, projects pertaining to power, telecom, health, education, employment creation are not considered as eligible for JNNURM assistance. Unfortunately, most of those sectors which are not covered under the Mission have strong and direct link with the level of social development. Non- coverage of these sectors in spite of their immense importance in improving the living condition of the population is one of the major criticisms faced by JNNURM.

Strategy of the Mission

Various steps are involved in the implementation of the Mission. These are :

- Preparation of city development plan indicating policies, programs and financial plans following which the memorandum of understanding will be signed between the Ministry of Urban Development of GoI, State Urban Development Ministry and the respective Urban Local Body (ULB).

- Preparation of Detailed Project Reports (DPRs) by the Urban Local Bodies/Parastatal agencies to undertake the projects in the identified areas. The projects which involve PPPs or private investments are given priority while approval is given.

- Flow of the funds from the state and the center directly to the nodal agency designated by the state. The funds for identified projects across cities would be disbursed to the ULB/ Parastatal agency through the designated State Level Nodal Agency (SLNA) as soft loan[6] or grant-cum-loan or grant.

- Incorporating the private sector efficiencies in management, implementation, and financing of the projects through public private partnership arrangements. The quarterly reports are to be submitted to the centre on the progress of the Mission at the state level, at the city level and at the project level.

Expected Outcomes of JNNURM

On completion of the Mission period, it is expected that ULBs will have achieved the following:

- Adoption of modern and transparent budgeting, accounting, financial management systems for all urban service and governance functions.

- Establishing and operation of city-wide framework for planning and governance.

- Accessibility of all urban basic services to all sections of urban population.

- Establishment of financially self-sustaining agencies for urban governance and service delivery, through reforms to tap the revenue potentials.

- Conducting of local services and governance in transparent and accountable manner.

- Introduction of E-governance[7] applications in core functions of ULBs/ Parastatal[8] resulting in reduced cost and time of service delivery processes.

Urban Governance Reforms under JNNURM

The thrust of JNNURM is to ensure improvement in urban governance and service delivery, so that ULBs will become financially sound and sustainable for undertaking new programs. The institutionalization of these fiscal, financial management and governance reforms initiatives taken by the GoI is considered to be the basis for success of the Mission.'[9]. The reforms under the Mission can be divided into the following ways :

Mandatory Reforms (Compulsory Reforms)

The compulsory reforms under the Mission are at the state level, local body level and at the parastatal agencies level. The area of coverage under the first set of reforms is quite different from that of the second and the third sets of reforms.

(i) *Mandatory Reforms at the Level of ULBs, and Parastatal Agencies*

- Adoption of modern accrual-based double entry system of accounting in ULBs and parastatal agencies.
- Introduction of a system of e-governance using IT applications, such as Geographical Information System (GIS) for various services provided by ULBs and parastatal agencies.
- Reform of property tax with GIS. It becomes a major source of revenue for ULBs and arrangements for its effective implementation so that collection efficiency reaches at least 85 per cent within next seven years.
- Levy of reasonable user charges[10] by ULBs and Parastatals with the objective that the full cost of operation and monitoring or recurring cost is collected within the next seven years. However, cities and towns in the North East and other special category States will have to recover only 50 percent of operation and monitoring charges initially. Should graduate later to full O&M (Operation and Monitoring) cost recovery in a phased manner.
- Internal earmarking, within local bodies, budgets for basic services to the urban poor.
- Provision of basic services to the urban poor including security of tenure at affordable prices, improved housing,

water supply and sanitation. Delivery of other existing universal services of the government for education, health and social security is ensured.

(ii) *Mandatory Reforms at the Level of States*-These reforms are as follows :

- Implementation of decentralization measures as envisaged in 74th Constitutional Amendment Act. The State should ensure meaningful association and engagement of ULBs in planning the function of parastatal agencies as well as the delivery of services to the citizens.
- Repeal of ULCRA[11] (Urban Land Ceiling Regulation Act).
- Reform of Rent Control Laws balancing the interests of landlords and tenants.
- Rationalization of Stamp Duty[12] to bring it down to no more than 5 per cent within next seven years.
- Enactment of the Public Disclosure Law[13] to ensure preparation of medium-term fiscal plan of ULBs and parastatal agencies and release of quarterly performance information to all stakeholders.
- Enactment of the Community Participation Law.[14]
- Assigning or associating elected ULBs with "city planning function". Over a period of seven years, transferring all special agencies that deliver civic services in urban areas to ULBs and creating accountability platforms for all urban civic service providers in transition.

Optional Reforms

Under the Mission, the following optional reforms will have to be undertaken by ULBs (urban local bodies), parastatal agencies and State governments. All the reforms have to be implemented during the Mission period.

- Revision of bye-laws to streamline the approval process for construction of buildings, development of site, etc.

- Simplification of legal and procedural frameworks for conversion of land from agricultural to non-agricultural purposes.

- Introduction of Property Title Certification System[15] in ULBs.

- Earmarking at least 20-25 per cent of developed land in all housing projects (both public and private agencies) for EWS (Economically Weaker Section) and LIG (Low Income Group) category with a system of cross Subsidization.

- Introduction of computerized process of registration of land and property.

- Revision of byelaws to make rain-water harvesting mandatory in all buildings and adoption of water conservation measures.

- Bye laws for reuse of recycled water.

- Administrative reforms i.e. reduction in establishment costs by adopting the Voluntary Retirement Scheme (VRS), not filling posts falling vacant due to retirement etc., and achieving specified milestones in this regard.

- Structural reforms which mainly include the restructuring of the ULBs to align with the current needs, creation of trained groups of municipal staffs in technical areas.

- Encouraging PPP.(Public Private Partnership)[16.]

The urban governance reforms to be implemented under JNNURM aims to promote the market oriented development of the urban areas in order to better the financial performance and service delivery. At the same time, the set of reforms under the Mission appreciates the need to achieve complete decentralization of urban governance so that the active participation of common people in decision making will be ensured. JNNURM is the most recent and a firm step taken by the GoI appreciating the urgency to reform the existing outdated urban governance institutions and governance mechanisms in the country which were very much outdated. Ironically, there are many contradictions in the various sets of reforms under the Mission. For example, on the one hand, the reforms exert great pressure on the ULBs to work efficiently which in turn demands additional manpower, but on the other the reforms stress the ULBs to cut short the cost of governance, by not filling the vacant posts and promoting voluntary retirement. This will only create huge gap between the demand and supply of the men power needed to manage these fast growing cities and will further deteriorate urban governance. The reforms under the Mission will be analyzed in detail in a separate section of this chapter.

JNNURM - The Cities under the Mission

The citie of JNNURM cover 42.1 percent of the total urban population in the country. The cities covered under the Mission are categorized into three groups on the basis of the population criteria of their inclusion in the Mission. These categories are megacities, million plus cities and other identified cities of special importance.

Mega cities

This category comprises of the large urban centers of the country which have a population of above 4 million according to the 2001 Census of India. These cities are Delhi, Greater Mumbai, Kolkata, Bangalore, Chennai, Hyderabad, and Ahemadabad. Though they are only seven in number, they have a total population of 64.9 crores, i.e. roughly 54 percent of the total population covered under the Mission and close to 23 percent of the urban population of the country.

Other million plus cities

The number of cities falling under this category is 28 and covers all those cities with a population ranging between 1 to 4 million as per the Census of India records in 2001. These cities

Categories of Cities/Towns Covered under JNNURM

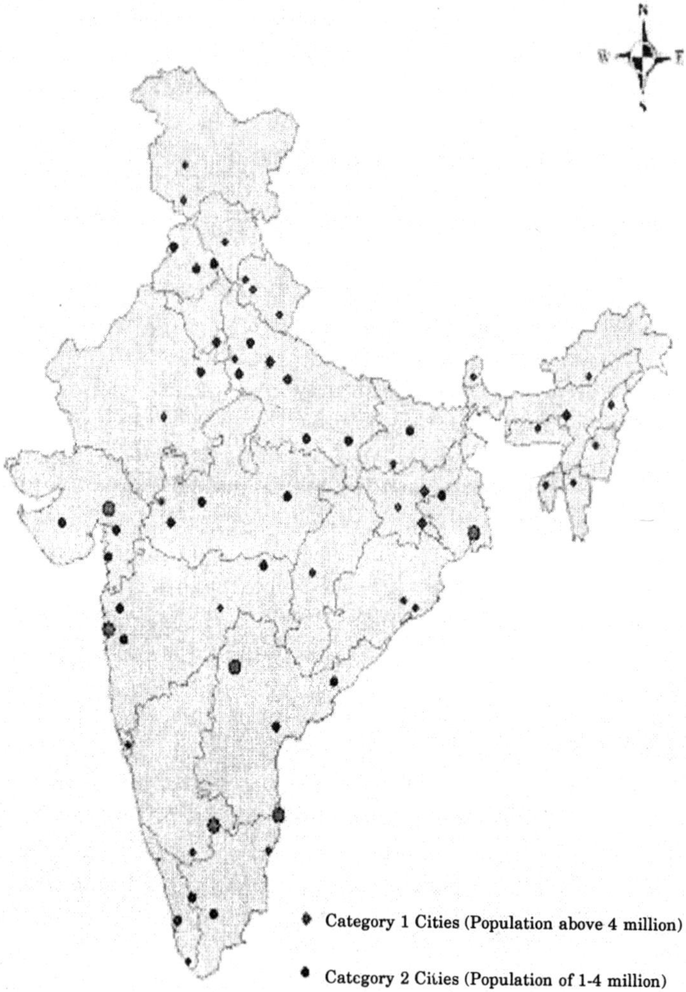

- Category 1 Cities (Population above 4 million)
- Category 2 Cities (Population of 1-4 million)
- Category 3 Cities (Population below 1 million)

Map not to scale

Source : Government of India

JNNURM-Jawaharlal Nehru National Urban Renewal Mission.

Map 2.1

with a population of 43.4 crores in total cover 36 percent of the population covered under this Mission and 15.1 percent of the total urban population of the country.

Other cites identified

The cities coming under this category are:

(i) Capital cities of the states which are not covered under category 1 and category 2 (e.g. Itanagar, Panaji, Kohima etc.).

(ii) Those cities of historical, national, tourist and religious importance in the country with a population of below 1 million according to the 2001 census. (e.g. Mysore, Bodh Gaya, Mathura, Ujjain, Nainital etc.). Thus, the total number of the cities in the third category is 28. With a total population of 12.1 crores, they have only 10.1 percent of the total population covered under the Mission. There is large scale variation in the population size across the cities of this category.

Table 2.1 Population Categories of cities under JNNURM

Categories of cities under JNNURM	*Number of cities*
Cities / UAs with 4 million plus population as per 2001 census	07
Cities/ UAs with 1 million plus but less than 4 million population as per 2001 census	28
Selected Cities/ UAs (State Capitals and other cities/ UA of religious/historic and tourist importance)	28
Total number of cities under JNNURM	63

Source- Official Website of JNNURM, http://jnnurm.nic.in/

2.1.6 Fund allocation across various categories of cities

The investment plan across various categories of Mission cities is given in Table 2.2:

Table 2.2 Investment plan across the categories of cities under JNNURM

Category	*Number of cities*	*Planned investment (for 7 years, Rs in crores)*	*Planned annual requirements (Rs in crores)*
Cities with over 4 million population	7	57143	8163.3
Cities with 1-4 million population	28	57143	8613.3
Selected cities with less than 1 million population	28	6250	892.9
Total	63	120536	17219.5

Source- Official Website of JNNURM, http://jnnurm.nic.in/

The following facts were revealed from the data on the Planned Mission investments.

1. Under the Mission the total amount of the funds allocated to be spent during the Mission period in the three categories of Mission cities are 57143, 57143, 6250 crores respectively. In the total funds for the Mission, 47.4 percent will be invested in the seven mega cities, while the same amount will be invested in other 28 million plus cities and the share of the third category cities in the funds to be invested is only 5.2 percent.

2. The average fund that a city in the first category will get during the Mission period is Rs.1166 crores in case of the mega cities, while it is Rs.72.9 crores and 30.4 crores in the case of the second and the third categories of cities under the Mission.

3. To know the intensity of investment in the various categories of cities under the Mission, the funds to be spent per thousand population in the three categories can be calculated. In the mega cities, on an average Rs.18000 will be spent during the Mission period for every 1000

population. This is only Rs.1680 and Rs.660 in the case of the other two categories.

The Figure 2.2 shows that when the major bulk of the funds will be invested in large cities, the cities coming in the third category will get very meager fund.

Figure 2.1

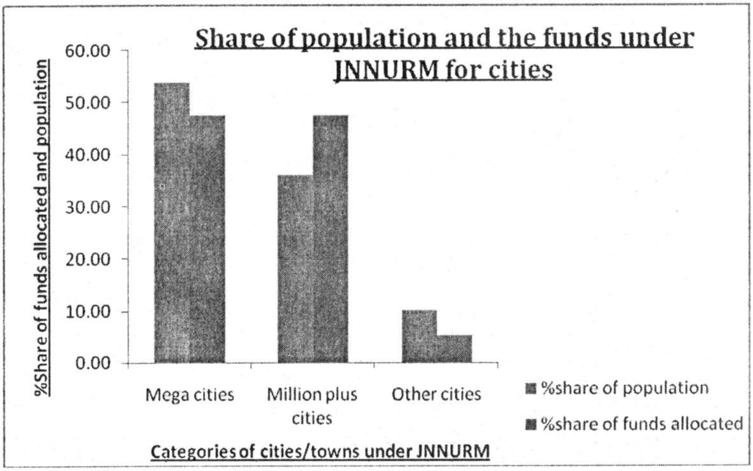

Figure 2.2

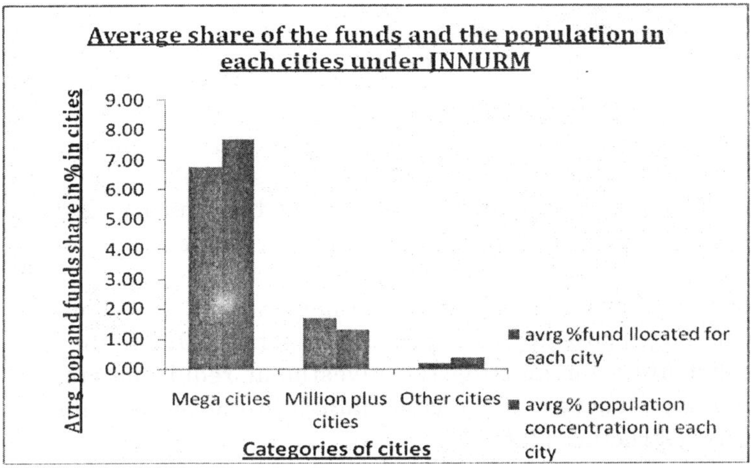

It is widely accepted that the small cities in the country falling in the third category have much poorer revenue base and urban infrastructural amenities as compared to the large cities falling in the first and second categories. This necessitates huge investment in urban infrastructure in these cities through the Mission in order to overcome the current challenges. An investment of Rs.660 for every 1000 population during the Mission period of seven years in the area of urban infrastructure will prove to be insufficient.

Funding of the Mission Projects

The funding pattern of the urban infrastructure projects under JNNURM, when it was initiated is given in Table 2.3.

Table 2.3 Funding pattern of the projects under JNNRUM

Category of cities / towns / UAs	*Centre*	*State*	*Urban Local Body*
Cities with 4 million plus population (2001)	35 percent	15 percent	50 percent
Cities with 1-4 million population	50 percent	20 percent	30 percent
Cities/towns in north east and J & K	90 percent	10 percent	-
Cities other than mentioned above	80 percent	10 percent	10 percent

Source- Official Website of JNNURM, http://jnnurm.nic.in/

It is evident from the Table 2.3 that the funding pattern for the Mission projects between the center, state and the ULB varies from one city to another depending on population size and other special considerations. The special consideration given to the cities of North East region and Jammu and Kashmir is an important step taken by the Government of India to facilitate the development of urban areas in these geographically less attractive areas for investment and to overcome the challenges posed by their poor revenue base. Due to the fund constraints for meeting the investment requirements, the funding structure of the cities falling in the second category was restructured later.

Mechanisms under JNNURM to Ensure Efficiency

There are various mechanisms employed under JNNURM to ensure efficient and better working of the Mission cities. Some of them are as follows :

PEARL (Peer Experience and Reflective Learning Initiative)

It is an initiative to support the cities to actively network among themselves for cross learning. In other words, the aim of PEARL is to create manageable network between JNNURM cities for cross learning and knowledge sharing on urban management, reforms and governance to achieve the Mission objectives.[17] The cities under the Mission are categorized into various groups on the basis of the population size, socio-economic profile and key economic indicators, urban growth pattern and urban character and complexities. Thus, the cities with similar problems are networked to share the best practices and solutions in the problem areas that they have in common. There are five categories of cities under PEARL and these are the following.

Group (A) Mega cities with global character in socio economic profile (9 cities)
Group (B) Major industrial cities (14 cities)
Group (C) Mixed economy cities (14 cities)
Group (D) Cultural and religious cities (15 cities)
Group (E) Hill and environmentally sensitive cities (11 cities)

The practice of knowledge sharing through PEARL connects the ULBs of the Mission cities and it helps the smaller cities in comparison to the larger ones to get exposure and to learn from others beyond the administrative boundaries. NIUA (National Institute of Urban Affairs) is the national coordinator of the PEARL program for coordinating the overall functioning of the network.

Investment Rating of the Urban Local Bodies

JNNURM Mission directorate has introduced rating of the Urban Local Bodies on the basis of investment and development of baseline data for various municipal services. It primarily aims to strengthen the concept of cities as enterprise capable of raising revenues for services delivered and leveraging funds from the capital market to renew or build new assets.[18]. The third annual meeting on JNNURM revealed the fact that in the 39 cities where the rating exercise has been completed, 21 Mission cities have received investment grade ratings while the other cities will have to reach the investment rating within the Mission period.

Awards for the best performing cities under various sectors

It aims to recognize the achievements of the Urban Local Bodies in undertaking various initiatives in the area of urban development through JNNURM. Assessment will be done on the basis of a set of indicators which is entirely based on the standardized services level benchmarks prepared by the Technical cell of JNNURM. Each indicator is scaled as 1 (low), 2 (medium) and 3 (high).

Establishment of City Voluntary Technical Group

These are voluntary groups of professionally qualified people, in the sectors of urban planning, governance, urban engineering, legal and financial services and urban poverty. The team advices on matters related to governance of the city, building urban poverty reduction programme etc.

Allocation of funds under JNNURM in the CDPs of the cities

City Development Plans which summarizes the developmental visions of the cities under JNNURM broadly divides the total planned investment under the Mission into two heads of Urban Infrastructure and Governance (UIG) and Basic Services for the Urban Poor (BSUP). It has to be examined if adequate attention had been given for the Sub Mission for the urban poor as compared to the Sub Mission for urban infrastructure. The share of BSUP projects in CDP investment plan, roughly in half of the cities is as low as 10 percent and below. Close to 1/3rd of the cities have BSUP share in investment of 15 percent and above. But these percentages alone do not mean that these cities are not paying adequate attention for ensuring minimum access to the civic amenities for the urban poor. To get a more meaningful picture, the planned investment under BSUP has to be compared with that of the share of the urban poor population in each city. This can show the gap between the actual needs and the allocated funds for improving the life of the urban poor as a whole.

Table 2.4 Share of BSUP in CDP investment layout and the share of urban poor population

Percentage of BSUP in CDP investment layout	*Percentage of the Mission cities*	*Percentage of share of urban poor in total population of the cities*	*Percentage of share of Mission cities*
5 and below	11.9	10 and below	22.0
5- 10	33.9	10 - 20	25.4
10 - 15	20.3	20- 30	27.1
15 - 20	15.3	30 - 40	18.6
20 and above	18.6	40 and above	6.8

Source- CDPs of the Mission Cities, http://jnnurm.nic.in/

Figure 2.3

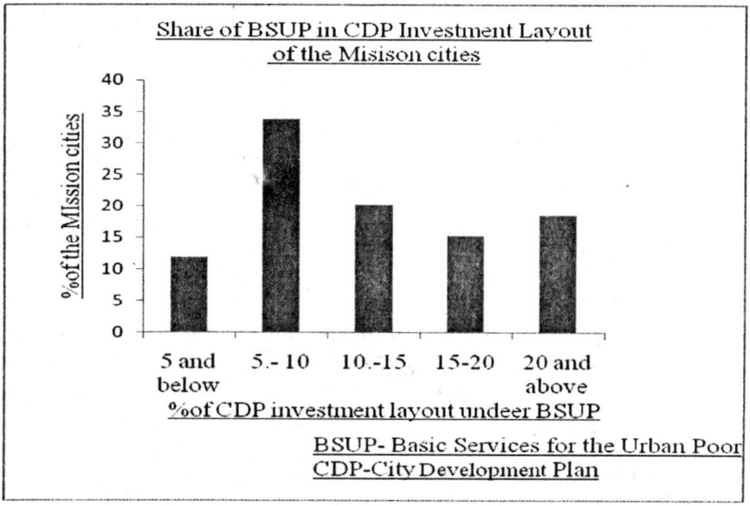

On one hand, close to 1/4th of the Mission cities have less than 10 percent of their population living in poverty, but on the other more than 1/4th of the Mission cities have their respective shares of urban poor population above 30 percent. Only 1/5th of the Mission cities have allocated a share of 20 percent and above under BSUP as per the CDP. Quite contrarily, more than half of the Mission cities have more than 1/5th of population falling in the urban poor category. This shows that there is a mismatch in the division of funds between the two Sub-Missions of JNNURM in relation to the size of the urban poor population in these cities. This will be clearer if we cross examine the proportionate share of the funds allocated under BSUP in the CDPs of the Mission cities and the proportionate share of the urban poor population in each Mission city.

Figure 2.4

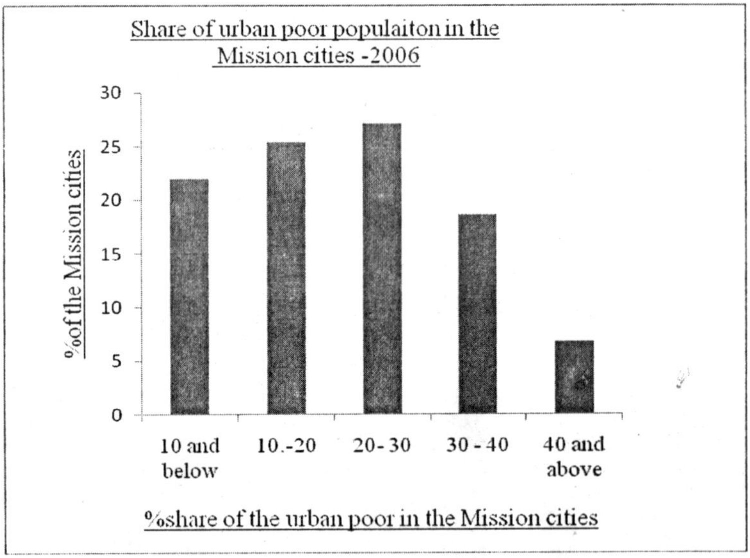

Table 2.4 shows that 75 percent of the Mission cities which have less than 5 percent of funds allocated under BSUP, have more than 20 percent of their population living in poverty. On the other hand, in case of the cities with more than 20 percent of the plan investment of JNNURM under BSUP, 3/4th of the cities have more than 20 percent population in urban poor category. The Table 2.5, given in appendix illustrates that in the cities with more than 40 percent of the population living in poverty, 1/4th cities have planned investment share of 5 percent

and below under BSUP. This shows that there is severe shortage in the investments under BSUP in the Mission investments plans under JNNURM. In the same category of cities, only 1/4th cities have investment share of 20 percent and above under BSUP. In other words, we find that 3/4th of the Mission cities with more than 40 percent population categorized as urban poor, have share as low as 10 percent and below under BSUP in the investment plan. It proves that the fund allocation in the CDPs of the Mission cities between BSUP and UIG is highly skewed. There are very few cities which have the share of funds allocated under BSUP almost equal in proportion to the share of urban poor population. Though Basic Services for the Urban Poor is one of the two Sub Missions under JNNURM, from the above analysis it is clear that it has not received the adequate priority under the city development plans prepared under the Mission.

Performance of States under JNNURM

In this part of the chapter an attempt is done to analyze the performance of the various cities and states in getting the funds from the Urban Development Mission. The first part will analyze the performance of the states under the Mission as a whole, while the second part will assess the state-wise performance separately under the two Sub Missions.

Overall Performance of states under JNNURM

The progress of the states under the Mission is assessed in various aspects like number of projects approved, share of the state in funds released etc.

Total number of the projects and the share of the states

In the country as a whole, the total number of the projects approved under the Mission is 929. In terms of the total number of the approved projects, Maharashtra stands first with 132 projects. It is followed by West Bengal (130), Tamil Nadu (102), U.P (98), and Andhra Pradesh (84), Gujarat (83) etc. In percentage terms of the projects approved, Maharashtra alone has close to 15 percent of the total Mission projects and is closely

Figure 2.5

Total Number of Projects Approved Under JNNURM Till Nov 2009

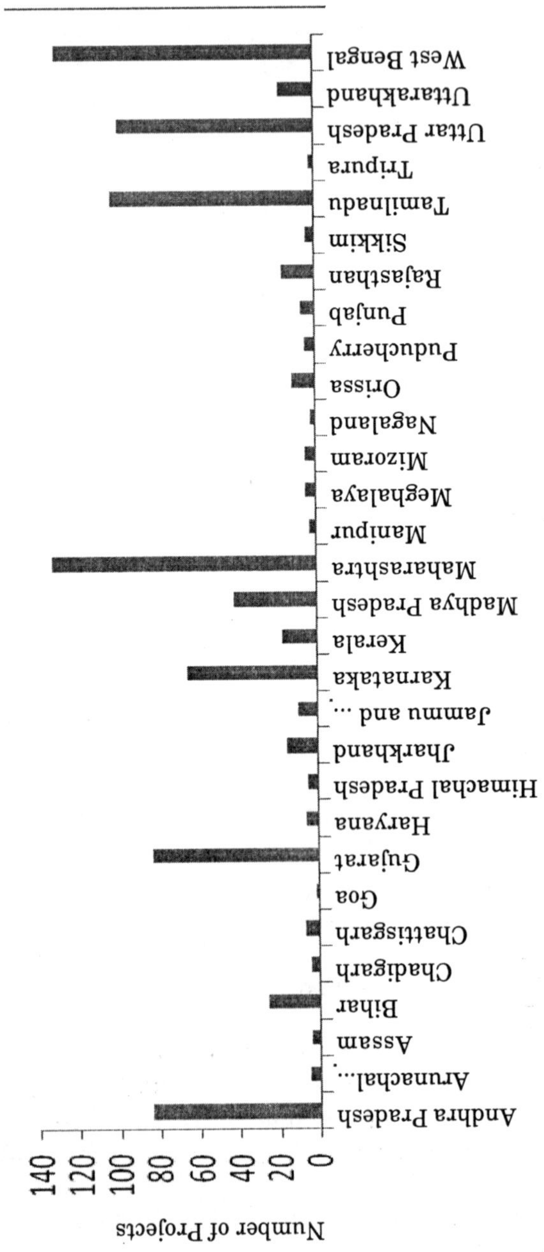

JNNURM-Jawaharlal Nehru National Urban Renewal Mission

followed by West Bengal (14 percent). These two states along with Tamil Nadu (11 percent), U.P (10.6 percent), Andhra Pradesh (9 percent) and Gujarat (9 percent) constitute roughly 68 percent of the total sanctioned Mission projects in the country.

The argument that the benefits from the Mission goes only to a few selected states can be understood to be baseless when one appreciates the fact that close to 70 percent of the population covered under the Mission resides in the Mission cities of these six states. The north eastern states of the country have 30 Mission projects in total which comprises 3.2 percent of the total share. Compared to this, the share of the population of these states to the total population covered under the Mission is only 1.76 percent.

Total funds released under the Mission

The total funds released under the Mission projects until November 2009 is Rs.18462.05 crores, in which Rs.4191.15 crores was disbursed for BSUP projects and Rs.14270.90 crores for UIG projects. Thus, the shares of BSUP and UIG to the total funds released are 22.7 percent and 77.3 percent respectively. At the state level, Maharashtra received the highest share of the released Mission funds ie 25.81 percent.

Table. 2.5. Fund allocation pattern across states under JNNURM

No. of Mission cities	*States / UTs*	*Percentage of share in funds released under JNNURM*	*Cumulative share in funds released under JNNURM*
3	Maharashtra, Gujarat, Andhra Pradesh	54	54%
4	Karnataka, West Bengal, Tamil Nadu, Uttar Pradesh	28	82%
23	Others	18	100%

Source- JNNURM mission website.

The state with the second highest share of the released fund is Gujarat (16 percent) which is followed by Andhra Pradesh (12.1 percent), Uttar Pradesh (8 percent), West Bengal (6.2 percent), etc. The three states of Maharashtra, Gujarat and Andhra Pradesh together have received close to 54 percent of the total Mission funds released.

The ratio between the share in funds released and the share in population

The simple share of the various states in getting the released funds under the Mission cannot be considered as the sole indicator to decide the level of the performance of the states and cities. It is very natural that the larger states and the larger cities will get larger share of the funds released and vice versa. In order to neutralize the factor of population in this analysis, the ratio between the share of the population of these states and cities in the total Mission population and the share of funds released under the Mission can be assessed. It means that if a state or city has the adequate share of the funds released in terms of the size of its population, the value of this ratio will be '1'.

Similarly, those states and cities which have got a higher share of the funds than their share of the population will have a ratio of above 1 while for those cities and states which have not received the adequate funds in relation to the population covered under them will have a ratio below '1'. From this point of view, Arunachal Pradesh has the highest ratio of 8.65, which shows that the share of the funds released under the Mission as a whole is 8.65 times higher than in relation to the population of the state covered under the Mission. The state is followed by Nagaland and Sikkim with the ratios of 4.2 and 3.71 respectively. The other states which have a ratio above '1' are Gujarat (1.76), Andhra Pradesh (1.62), Chhattisgarh (1.38), Haryana (1.22), Rajasthan (1.18), Maharashtra (1.18) and Orissa (1.06). Among the larger states which have received high shares of the funds released under the Mission, but whose values of the respective ratio is lower than '1' are Karnataka (.98), Uttar Pradesh (.87) and Tamil Nadu (.72).

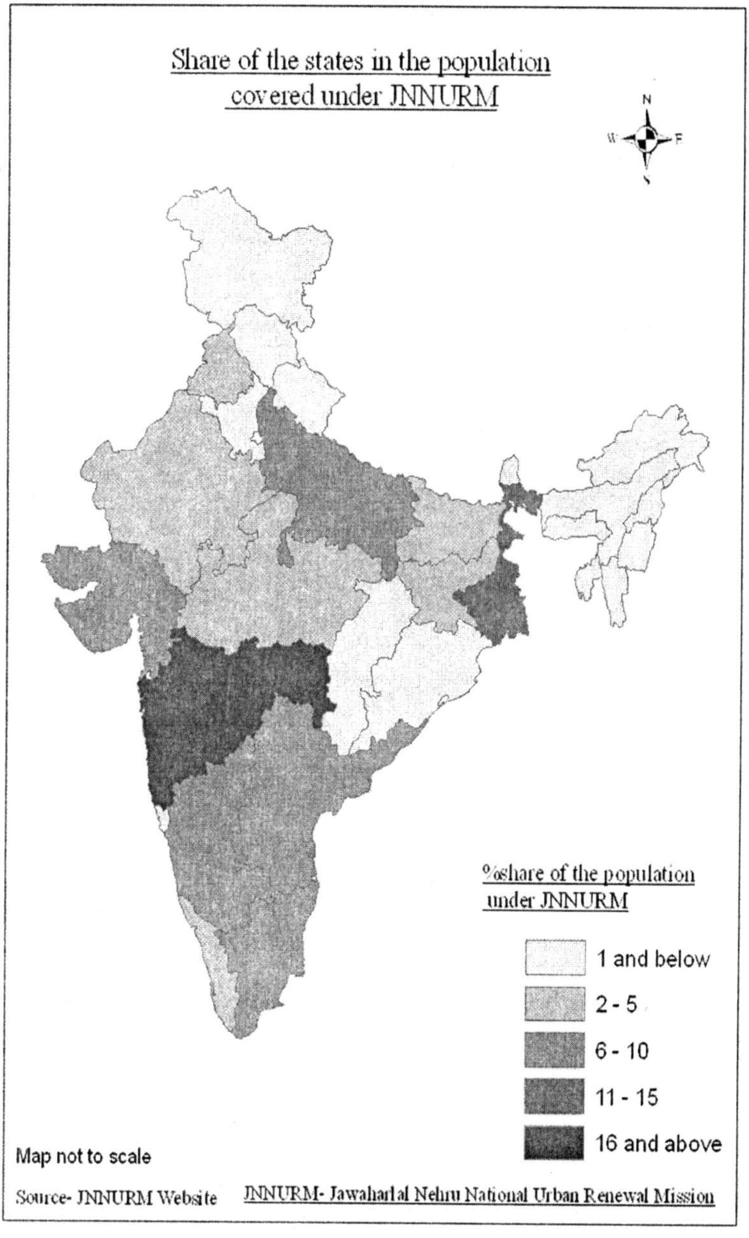
Share of the states in the population covered under JNNURM
N
W
E
S
%share of the population under JNNURM
1 and below
2 - 5
6 - 10
11 - 15
16 and above
Map not to scale
Source- JNNURM Website
JNNURM- Jawaharlal Nehru National Urban Renewal Mission

Map 2.2

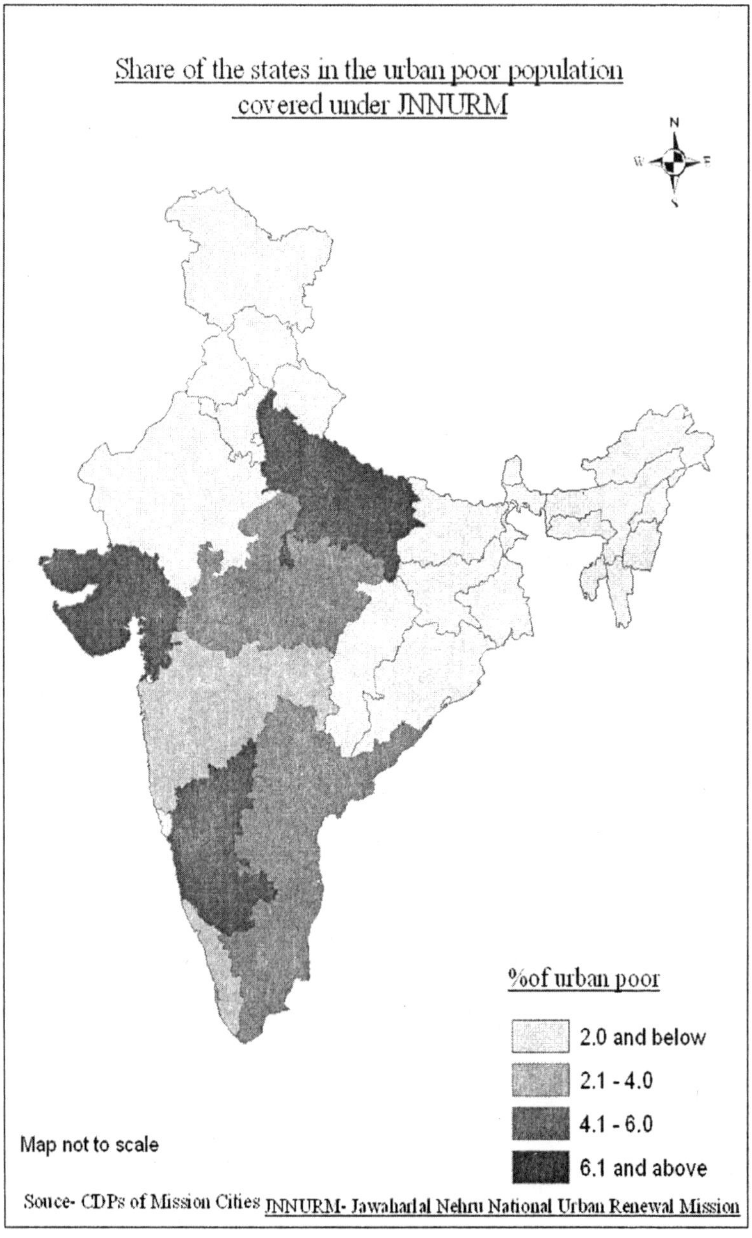
Share of the states in the urban poor population
covered under JNNURM
N
%of urban poor
2.0 and below
2.1 - 4.0
4.1 - 6.0
6.1 and above
Map not to scale
Souce- CDPs of Mission Cities JNNURM- Jawaharlal Nehru National Urban Renewal Mission

Map 2.3

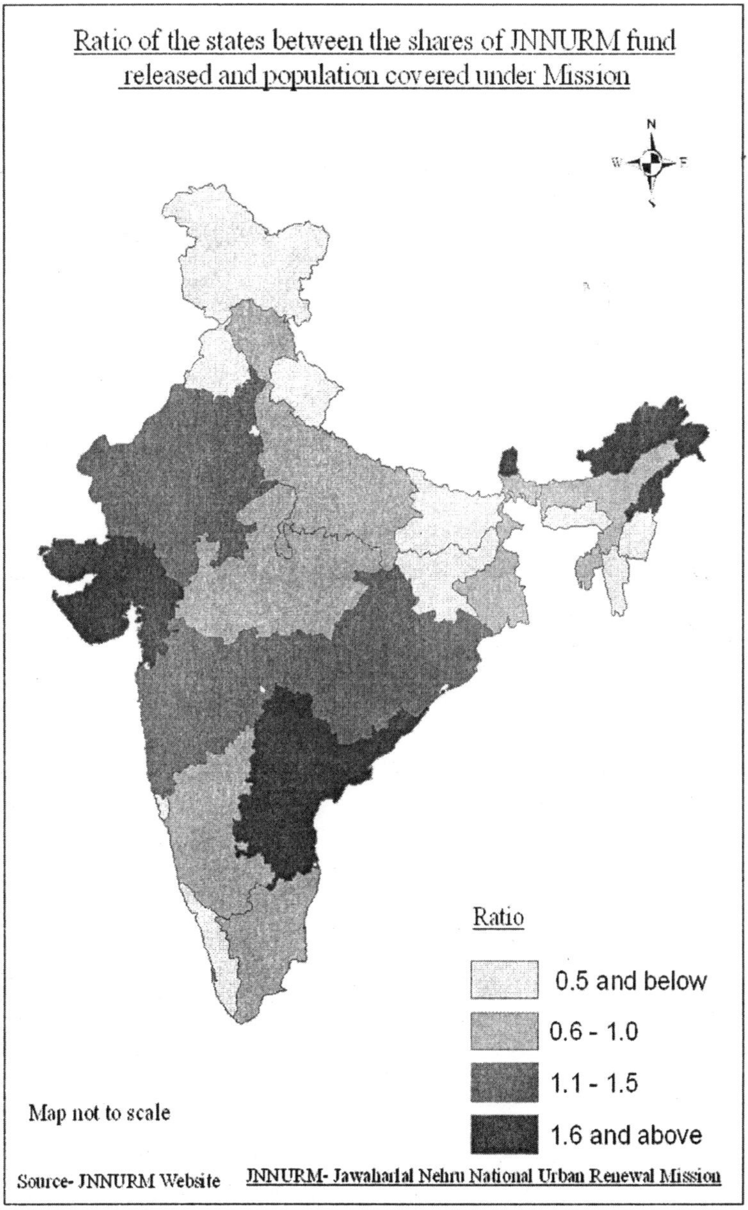
Ratio of the states between the shares of JNNURM fund released and population covered under Mission
N
Ratio
0.5 and below
0.6 - 1.0
1.1 - 1.5
1.6 and above
Map not to scale
Source- JNNURM Website
JNNURM- Jawaharlal Nehru National Urban Renewal Mission

Map 2.4

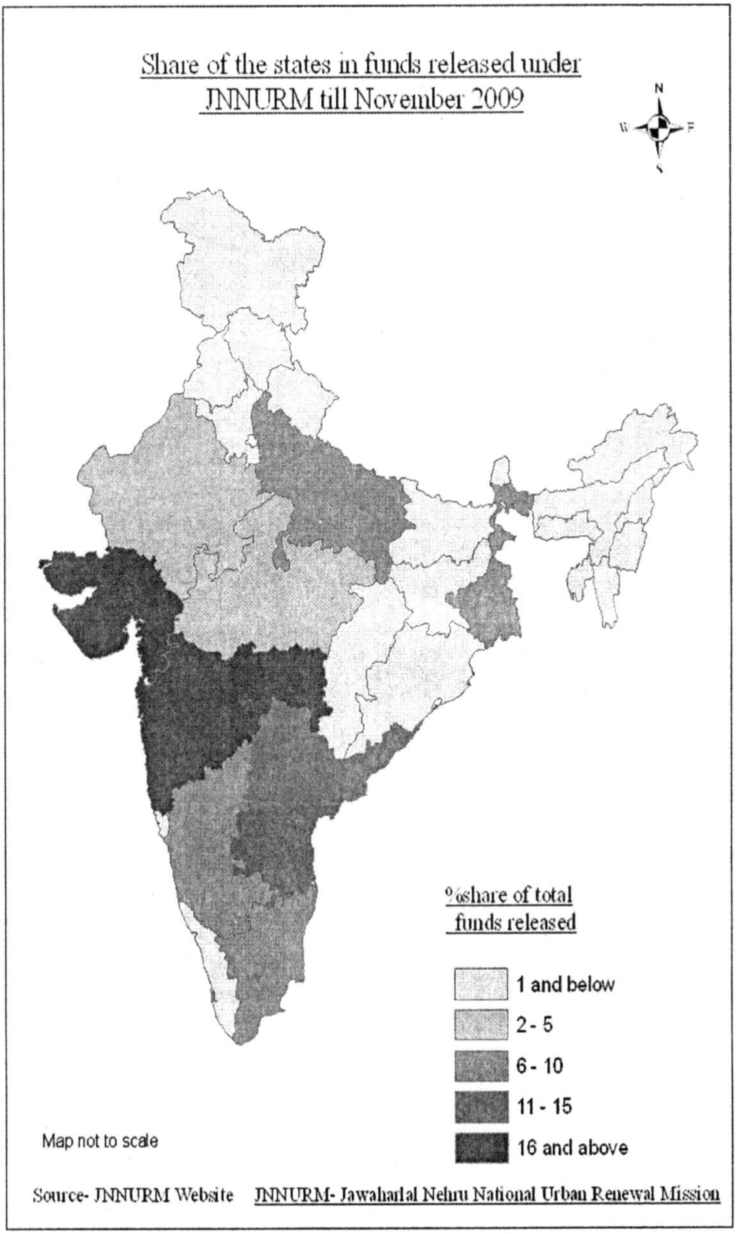
Share of the states in funds released under
JNNURM till November 2009
N
%share of total
funds released
1 and below
2 - 5
6 - 10
11 - 15
16 and above
Map not to scale
Source- JNNURM Website
JNNURM- Jawaharlal Nehru National Urban Renewal Mission

Map 2.5

Table. 2.6. Progress assessment of states under JNNURM

Percentage of funds released / Percentage population	*States*	*Private Investment*	*Exceptional cases*
1.5 and above	Andhra Pradesh, Gujarat	Very successful	Sikkim, Arunachal Pradesh, Nagaland,
1.0 – 1.5	Maharashtra, Rajasthan, Haryana,	Successful	Chhatisgarh, Orissa,
0.5 – 1.0	M.P, Assam, Kerala, H.P, Tripura, Punjab, Chandigarh, Pondichery,	Less successful	Tamil Nadu, Karnataka, U.P, West Bengal,
0.5 and below	Bihar, Jharkhand, J&K, Manipur, Meghalaya, Uttarakhand, Mizoram	Least successful	Goa

Source- Author's own assessment.

The three states of the North Eastern region, namely Arunachal Pradesh, Nagaland and Sikkim which have high ratio between the share of the funds allocated and the population covered under the Mission are characterized by very low level of infrastructural facilities. This makes it necessary to invest in the urban areas of these states much more than in case of those states where the level of infrastructural facilities have already crossed the incipient stages. At the same time, the values above '1' in case of the states like Gujarat, Andhra Pradesh and Maharashtra proves that these states are performing better than other states.

In spite of the large share of the population under the Mission in these states, these states have managed to receive larger shares of the funds released. Bihar is the only major state where the ratio of the population under the Mission and the fund released is very low compared to any other major state. This proves that the state did not perform well in getting through the Mission. Low fund-population ratios of many of the north eastern states and some other hilly states are also a major matter of concern as they may be left out from adequate benefitting through the Mission in spite of their poor infrastructural facilities in the urban areas.

On the basis of the fund population ratio, the Mission cities can be categorized as in Table 2.6. The ratio describes the level of the success that a state has achieved under JNNURM. The column 'exceptional' means that in these particular states the direct link between the level of privatization and the level of success under JNNURM is not directly linked. It is clearly understood that Andhra Pradesh, Gujarat, Mahasrashtra, etc were successful under the Mission while in Bihar and most of the states falling in the hilly tracts of the country, the Mission could not bring in noticeable change.

Performance of the states under the Sub-Missions

This part of the chapter tries to analyze the performance of the states under the two Sub-Missions of JNNURM.

Urban Governance and Infrastructure

In this Sub section, various aspects regarding the first Sub-Mission of urban Infrastructure and Governance (UIG) are analyzed.

(i) Sector wise distribution of the projects

Under the infrastructure creation in the urban areas through the Mission, there are eleven broad sectors. These sectors are given differential weights on the basis of their degree of importance in determining the quality of life in urban areas. The basic statistics regarding the allocation of the funds among the various infrastructural sectors under the Mission is given below.

From Table 2.5, it can be easily understood that water supply projects are given the highest priority under the Mission. Close to 30 percent of the total sanctioned projects under the urban infrastructural projects belong exclusively to this sector. The sector which is given the second highest priority under the Mission is sewerage which has more than $1/5^{th}$ of the total projects sanctioned under UIG. Other sectors with noticeable shares of the projects approved under UIG are Roads and flyovers (16 percent), Drainage (13 percent), Solid waste management (8.4 percent) etc. The difference is more evident in case of the funds released and the funds sanctioned under the infrastructural projects. More than 37 percent of the project funds released under UIG are solely for water supply. This is followed by the sectors of sewerage (22 percent), drainage (12 percent) etc.

The priority under the Mission is to fill the gap in demand and supply of infrastructural facilities in the essential sectors like water supply, sewerage, solid waste management. Thus, the investment in these infrastructural amenities brings a clear cut positive impact on quality of life in urban areas, as compared to the investments in other sectors of urban infrastructure. Besides the high priority given to these sectors under UIG guidelines, another reason for the huge investment under these sectors is because of their ability to attract private sector

Table 2.7 Sector-Wise Allocation of JNNURM funds under Urban Infrastructure Projects

Sector	*Percentage of share of total projects sanctioned*	*Percentage of share of funds sanctioned*	*Percentage of share of the funds released*
Drainage/Storm water drainage	12.97	15.1	12.48
Roads/Flyovers	15.9	6.74	8.27
Water supply	29.92	36.57	39.66
Sewerage	21.97	25.25	21.96
Urban Renewal	2.09	.89	.65
Mass rapid transport system	4.18	9.17	11
Other urban transport	2.93	1.55	1.37
Solid waste management	8.37	4.2	3.86
Development of the heritage areas	.42	.09	.36
Preservation of the water bodies	.84	.22	.19
Parking	.42	.2	.19

Source- Official Website of JNNURM, http://jnnurm.nic.in/

Pattern of Distribution of Funds Released Under UIG Till Nov 2009

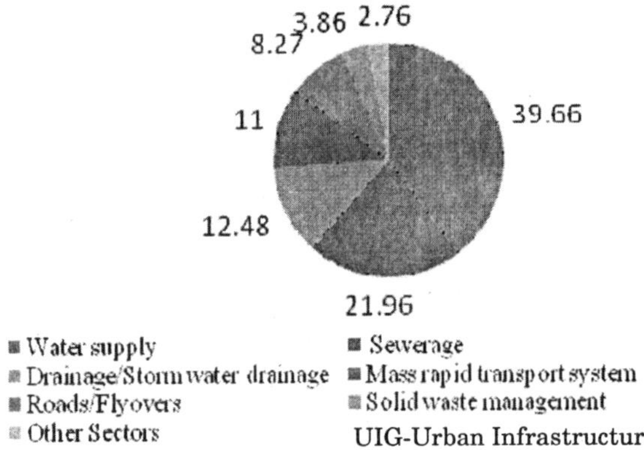

UIG-Urban Infrastructure and Governance

Figure 2.6

participation as compared to the other sectors of urban infrastructure. This assumption is based on the findings by several studies that 'irrespective of the city where it is implemented, the transition of the services like water supply, sewerage and solid waste management from the public sector into private sector management are likely to be very successful than the other sectors'.[19]

(ii) Total projects approved at the state level

In the country as a whole, the total number of the approved projects under this Sub-Mission is 467. In terms of the number of the projects approved, Maharashtra stands first with 77 projects approved, followed by Gujarat (67), Tamil Nadu (51), Andhra Pradesh (48) and Karnataka (47), etc. Goa is the only state with no project approved under the Sub Mission.

(iii) Funds released under UIG

The first Sub Mission of urban infrastructure and governance has received 77.3 percent of the total Mission funds released till November 2009.

Maharashtra has received the largest share of the released funds, i.e. 27 percent and is followed by Gujarat (17.9 percent), Andhra Pradesh (10.9 percent), U.P (8.1 percent), Karnataka

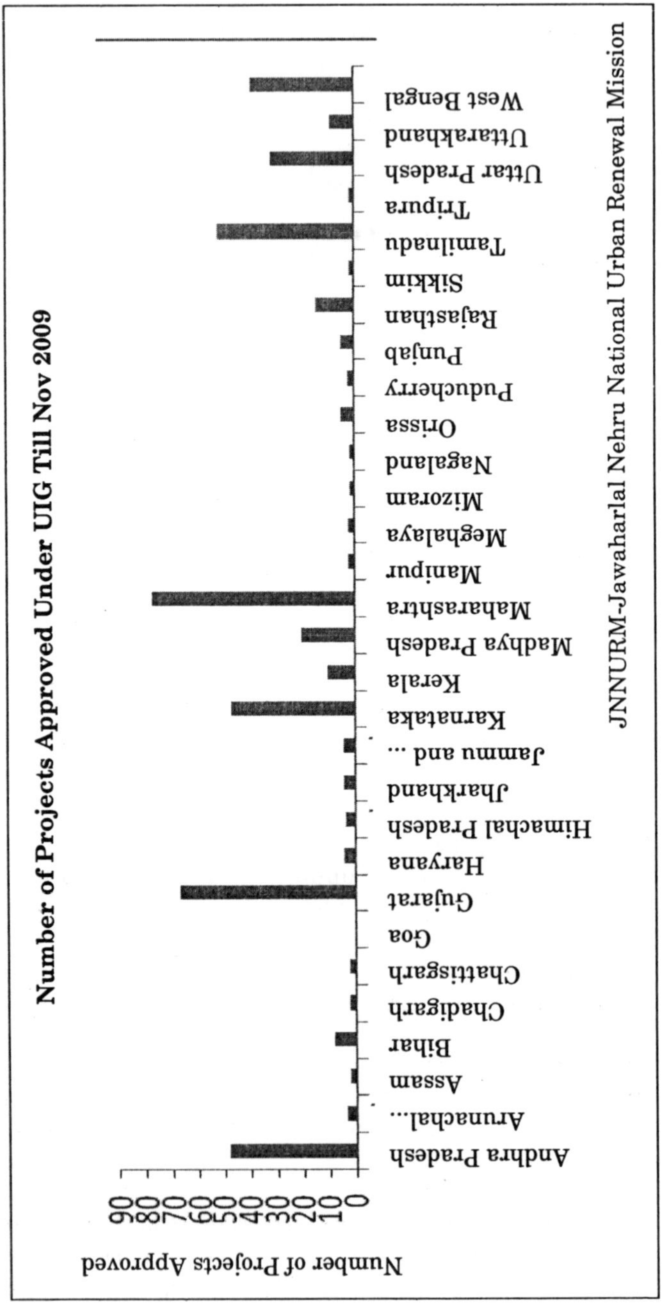
Number of Projects Approved Under UIG Till Nov 2009
Number of Projects Approved
0
10
20
30
40
50
60
70
80
90
Andhra Pradesh
Arunachal...
Assam
Bihar
Chadigarh
Chattisgarh
Goa
Gujarat
Haryana
Himachal Pradesh
Jharkhand
Jammu and ...
Karnataka
Kerala
Madhya Pradesh
Maharashtra
Manipur
Meghalaya
Mizoram
Nagaland
Orissa
Puducherry
Punjab
Rajasthan
Sikkim
Tamilnadu
Tripura
Uttar Pradesh
Uttarakhand
West Bengal
JNNURM-Jawaharlal Nehru National Urban Renewal Mission

Figure 2.7

Ratio of the states between the shares of UIG fund released and population covered under Mission

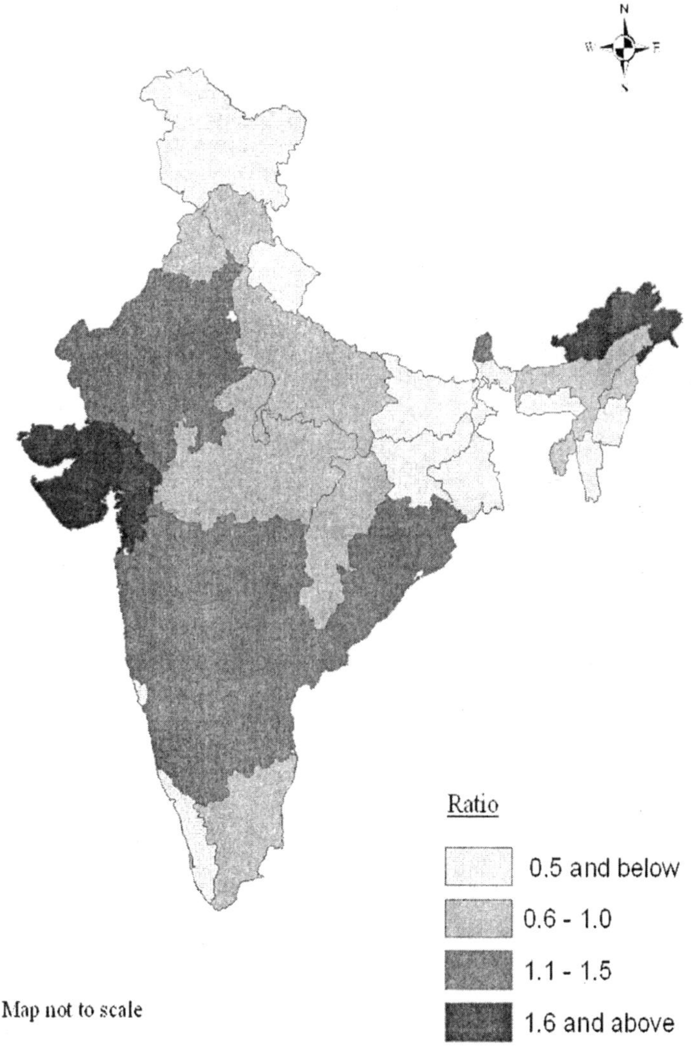

Map not to scale

Source - JNNURM Website.

UIG-Urban Infrastructure and Governance

Map 2.6

Share of the states in funds released under UIG till November 2009

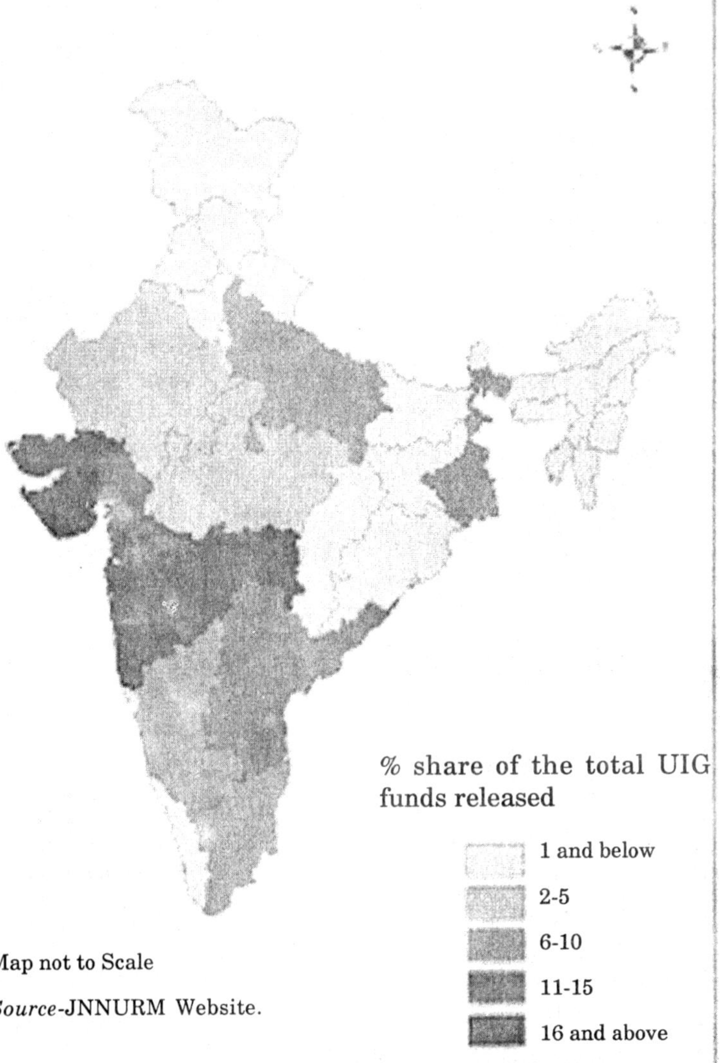

Map 2.7

(6.8 percent), West Bengal (6.3 percent), Tamilnadu (5.7 percent), etc. The share of these six states together in the total funds released is close to 83 percent. The state with no fund released under the Sub Mission is Goa. The slow progress of the Mission projects in various states is a matter of serious concern, especially considering the fact that more than half of the Mission period is already over.

iv) Completed projects under UIG

In the 467 projects approved under Urban Infrastructure and Governance, the number of the completed projects till November 2009, is 48. With 20 projects completed, roads and the flyover sector has the largest share in the completed projects. The sector is followed by water supply with 17 projects completed. The other sectors with at least one project completed are sewerage (5), drainage (2), Solid waste management (1), Urban renewal (2) and other urban transport (1). The interest of the private investors to invest in urban development varies highly from one sector to another on the basis of profitability. Sectors like water supply, roads/flyovers, sewerage, etc. were able to attract private investment more than the other sectors as these are more profitable to invest. This also can be the reason for the fact that large shares of the projects approved and projects completed, fall in those sectors where the complete cost recovery is easier than other urban infrastructure sectors. Priority is also given to the approval of the projects falling in those sectors which are considered as vital in determining the quality of urban life. At the state level, Gujarat has the highest number of the projects completed ie, 13 (27 per cent) which is followed by Andhra Pradesh (12 projects), Karnataka and Tamilnadu (seven projects each). The other states with completed projects are Maharashtra (4), Madhya Pradesh (3) and West Bengal (2). The very low number of projects completed in comparison to the number of projects approved shows the slow implementation of the projects throughout the country.

Basic Services for the Urban Poor

In this Sub section, various aspects regarding the second Sub-Mission of Basic Services for the urban Poor (BSUP) will be analyzed.

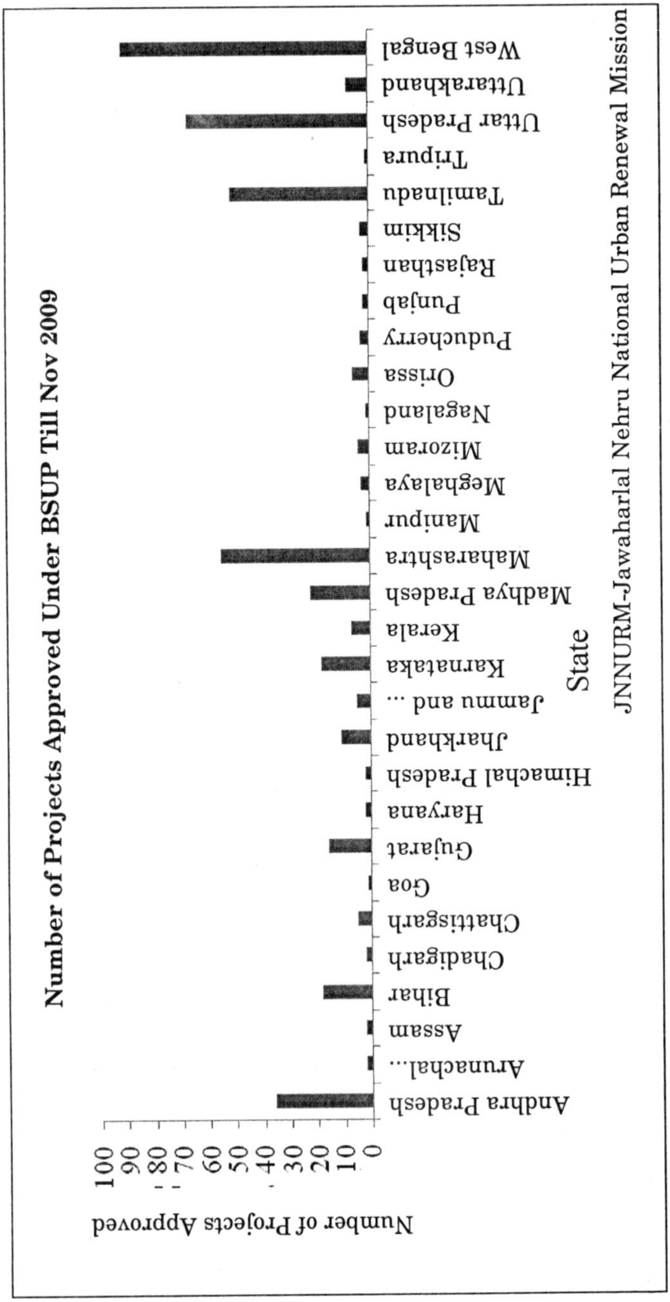
Number of Projects Approved Under BSUP Till Nov 2009
Number of Projects Approved
100
90
80
70
60
50
40
30
20
10
0
Andhra Pradesh
Arunachal...
Assam
Bihar
Chadigarh
Chattisgarh
Goa
Gujarat
Haryana
Himachal Pradesh
Jharkhand
Jammu and ...
Karnataka
Kerala
Madhya Pradesh
Maharashtra
Manipur
Meghalaya
Mizoram
Nagaland
Orissa
Puducherry
Punjab
Rajasthan
Sikkim
Tamilnadu
Tripura
Uttar Pradesh
Uttarakhand
West Bengal
State
JNNURM-Jawaharlal Nehru National Urban Renewal Mission

Figure 2.8

(i) Total projects approved under BSUP

The total number of the approved projects at the national level under this second Sub Mission of JNNURM is 462. West Bengal with 91 projects stands ahead of all other states in terms of the projects approved. It is followed by Andhra Pradesh (67), Maharashtra (55), U.P (51), Gujarat (36) etc. There are no states where no projects are approved under the Sub Mission.

(ii) Funds released under BSUP

The Sub-Mission of BSUP has received 22.7 percent of the total Mission funds approved. This is a positive sign about the Mission, as in most of the City Development Plans of the Mission cities, the share of the funds allocated under BSUP was very negligible and were much lower than the actual share of the BSUP funds released. Maharashtra alone has received 22.2 percent of the funds released under the Sub-Mission and is followed by the states of Andhra Pradesh (16.1percent), West Bengal (11.3 percent), Gujarat (9.6 percent), U.P (7.6 percent) and Tamilnadu (7.5 percent). It means these six states together, received 74 percent of the total funds released under BSUP.

(iii) Completed Projects under BSUP

In the country as a whole, the number of houses sanctioned under the program is roughly 10 lakhs in which the construction of 4.5 lakh houses is completed. But the data shows that the number of houses aimed to be constructed under the Mission is much lower than the actual shortage in housing for the economically weaker sections in these cities. Besides this, the number of houses covered under the Mission during the four years is also not very impressive. For example, in Vishakhapatnam, about 1.27 lakh households required housing of which only 67000 households were covered under the Mission, leaving roughly the same number of households out of the housing scheme.[20]

The data on the completed group housing projects is not available as most of them are passing through the implementation stage at present. Though the provision to give legal ownership of land to the slum households by the ULB at affordable cost is included under BSUP, it appears that in ground reality, slum development through group housing projects is often pushed by the ULBs for implementation especially the provision of multi- storied flats located either in a part of the same slum or in a different area. This enables the ULB to clear up large expanses of the city area which were occupied by slum population prior to this. It can be seen as a hidden agenda to root out the slum population from the important areas of the city, pushing them towards the margins and to encourage real estate business.

Performance of Mission Cities under JNNURM

As mentioned earlier in this chapter, 62 Mission cities excluding Delhi, Porbander and Tirupati, are taken for the city level analysis of the Mission. The analysis is done in case of the Mission as a whole in the first part, and separately for the two Sub Missions in the later part.

Total Mission funds released

Mumbai has received the highest share of the released funds under the Mission as a whole (11.3 percent). Mumbai is followed by Pune (8 percent), Hyderabad (7.8 percent), Ahmadabad (7.1 percent), Kolkata (6.6 percent), Surat (5.4 percent), Bangalore (4.6 percent), etc. These seven mega cities together constitute about 51 percent of the total funds released under the Mission projects.

Jamshedpur is the only city which has not received funds released under the Mission as a whole. This indicates the very slow progress of the Mission projects. Without taking adequate steps to tackle this problem, the cities will not benefit from the Mission and will be unable to raise themselves to the level of expectation. Under JNNURM, it is obvious that the ULBs have to be highly competitive to get enough funds from the center to satisfy their needs. The levels of success of the cities in getting the Mission funds depend on their efficiency to fasten up the Mission procedures involved. As this is a major factor in determining the competency of the cities in the neoliberal world economy [21], more strategies are needed to be evolved to reduce

Table 2.8 Fund allocation pattern across the Mission cities under JNNURM

No of cities	*Mission cities*	*Percentage of share in funds released under JNNURM*	*Cumulative share in funds released under JNNURM*
8	Mumbai. Pune, Hyderabad, Ahmadabad, Bangalore, Chennai, Kolkata, Surat	55%	55%
11	Ajmer, Jaipur, Kanpur, Bhopal, Vadodara, Nagpur, Nanded, Nasik, Vishakhapatnam, Vijayawada, Madurai	24%	79%
43	Other Mission cities	21%	100%

Source- JNNURM official website.

the time lag of the cities in various stages of project designing and implementation.

Ratio between the shares of funds released and population

The ratio between the shares of the city in the funds released under the Mission and in the population covered under the Mission shows that Itanagar (8.93) stands ahead of all the other cities. The very low level of the basic amenities available in the cities is a major problem of the North Eastern region. The high ratio between the funds released and the population share indicates that these cities were also able to get their own share of funds under the Mission. The other small cities with high ratio of the funds released vis-à-vis to population share are Nanded (8.03), Kohima (4.7), Ajmer (3.5), Gangtok (2.7) etc. The small base of the infrastructural facilities makes it very necessary for the ULBs and the central Government to search for solutions to add extra momentum to urban infrastructural development in these states. The special consideration given to the Mission cities in the North Eastern region and Jammu and Kashmir in the funding pattern under the Mission projects is a good example for this.

It has to be noticed that majority of the cities which have performed well in investing in urban infrastructure and basic amenities through JNNURM are from Gujarat, Andhra Pradesh and Maharashtra. Some of these cities are Pune, Surat, Ahmadabad, Hyderabad, Vadodara, Nashik etc. The studies have shown that those states, which have gone ahead of rest of the country in implementing the globalization and liberalization strategies of urban growth, were able to gain enormously in the form of foreign and private investments and Gujarat is the best example for this.[22] Thus, the numerous steps that the state government and the ULBs have taken in the field of privatization of major sectors and commercialization of basic amenities to a great extent, can be considered as the major reason for the appealing performance of the cities in Gujarat and other cities such as Pune, Hyderabad, etc under JNNURM.

Table.2.9 Progress Assessment of Cities Under JNNURM

Percentage of funds Released / Percentage Pop	*Mission Cities*	*Private Investment*	*Exceptional Cities*
1.5 and above	Ahmedabad, Pune, Vadodara, Surat, Nashik, Vishakhapatnam, Bhopal, Vijayawada	Very successful	Ajmer, Gangtok, Itanagar, Kohima, Nanded, Mysore
1.0 – 1.5	Hyderabad, Faridabad, Rajkot, Nagpur, Madurai, Asansol, Varanasi,	Successful	Raipur, Bhubaneswar,
0.5 – 1.0	Ranchi, Srinagar, Haridwar, Chandigarh, Shimla, Meerut, Thiruvananthapuram, Pondichery, Puri, Guwahati, Agartala, Aizwal, Allahabad,	Less successful	Chennai, Mumbai, Coimbatore, Jaipur, Indore, Banglore, Kolkatta
0.5 and below	Panaji, Jamshedpur, Gaya, Dehradun, Nainital, Ujjain, Shillong, Imphal, Patna, Jammu, Ludhiana	Least successful	Kochi, Jabalpur, Dhanbad,

Source- Author's own assessment.

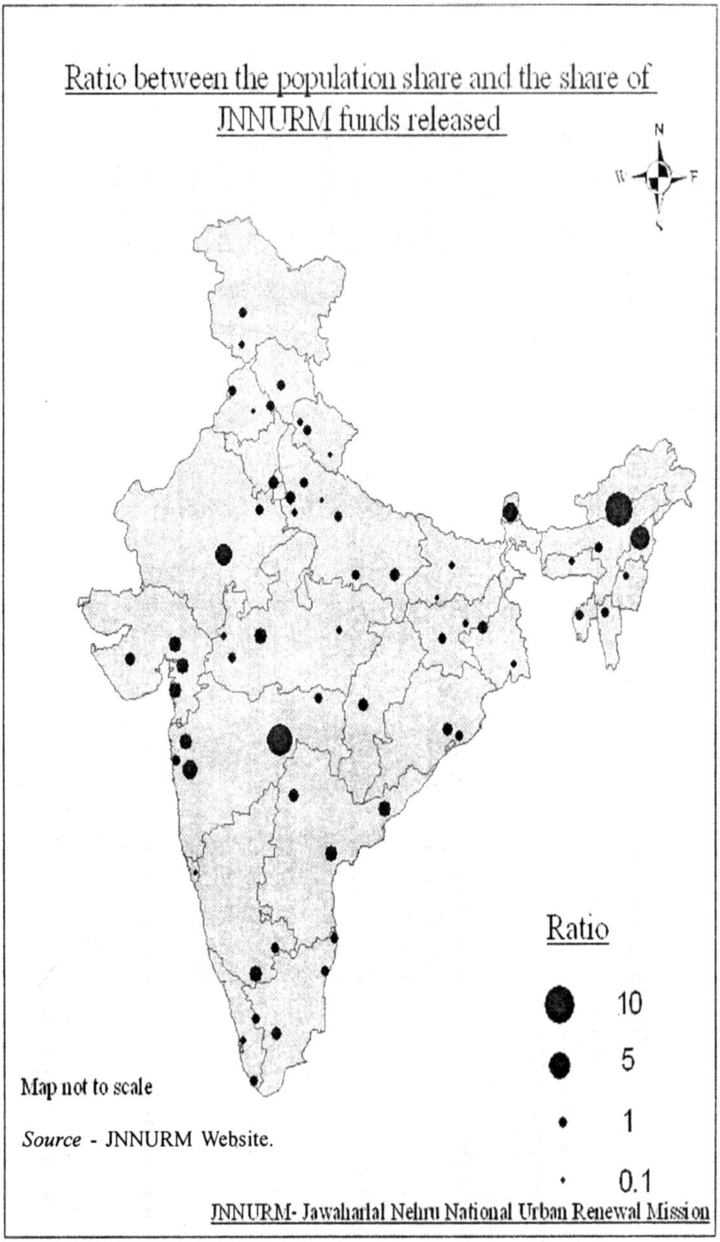
Ratio between the population share and the share of JNNURM funds released
N
W
E
S
Ratio
10
5
1
0.1
Map not to scale
Source - JNNURM Website.
JNNURM- Jawaharlal Nehru National Urban Renewal Mission

Map 2.8

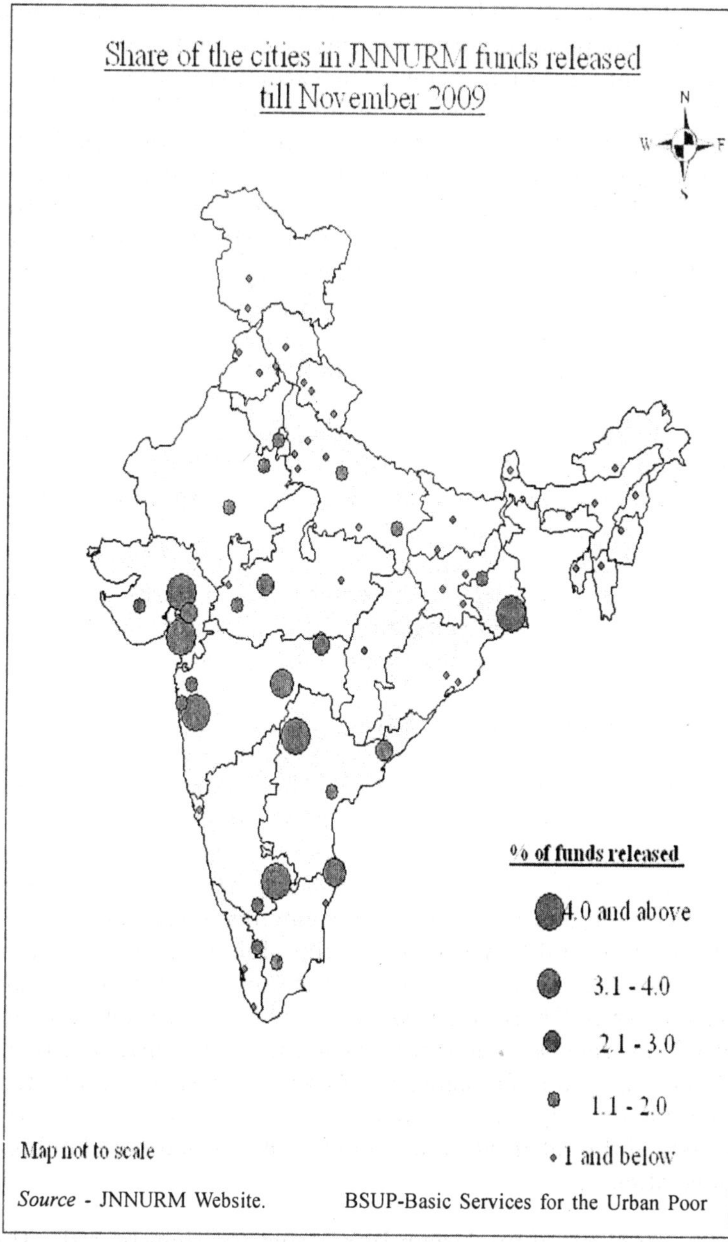
Share of the cities in JNNURM funds released
till November 2009
N
% of funds released
4.0 and above
3.1 - 4.0
2.1 - 3.0
1.1 - 2.0
1 and below
Map not to scale
Source - JNNURM Website.
BSUP-Basic Services for the Urban Poor

Map 2.9

From Table 2.9 it is evident that those cities which had a high fund population ratio were successful in attracting private investments in urban sectors. The exceptional cities are those where the level of success or the failure under JNNURM is not directly linked to privatization but other factors (especially the size of population). From the Mission guidelines itself it is evident that the success of the state or ULB in tapping the potential of Public Private Partnerships (PPPs) is very crucial in determining its capacity to make investments under JNNURM. Thus, it is natural that those cities or states which do not have investment friendly atmosphere failed to attract private sector investment in urban infrastructure.

As a setback to this trend, the growth of PPP initiatives in urban infrastructure and provision of basic amenities while meeting the needs of those sections which have the capacity to pay for the services provided, may leave negative impact on the economically weaker sections in ensuring the availability of basic services. Thus, the present trend of pushing forward the agenda of PPPs will only widen the gap in standard of living between various groups within the urban society.[23]

Release of funds under UIG

Mumbai alone received 12 percent of the total funds released under UIG-Sub Mission. It is followed by Pune (8.6 percent), Ahmadabad (8.2 percent), Hyderabad (7.5 percent), Kolkata (5.9 percent), Surat (5.7 percent) and Bangalore (5.6 percent). These seven cities together received about 54 percent of the total funds released under urban infrastructure projects. Many of the million plus cities like Jabalpur, Meerut, and Ludhiana have very low shares of the funds released under the Sub Mission. There are three cities which have not received any funds released under the projects and these cities are Bodh Gaya, Panaji and Jamshedpur. At the same time, small cities like Nanded, Ajmer, etc have received comparatively better shares of the released funds than the above mentioned million plus cities.

Analysis of the Urban Infrastructure projects under the three categories of the Mission cities gives an interesting

Table 2.10 Investment under UIG across the various categories of cities till November 2009

Population Size Category	*Percentage of Share of the Approved Funds under UIG*	*Percentage of Share of the Released Funds under UIG*	*Percentage of Share of the Total Population Covered Under the Mission*	*Ratio Between the Population and the Funds Released*
Category 1 cities	38.78	42.30	48.44	0.87
Category 2 cities	44.92	45.07	40.26	1.12
Category 3 cities	16.29	12.64	11.30	1.12

Source- Official Website of JNNURM, http://jnnurm.nic.in/

picture. The share of the various categories of cities in case of the total sanctioned and released funds under UIG, and the performance of three categories of cities in relation to the population covered, etc. are given in Table 2.6. Under the projects for urban infrastructure, category 1 cities have got close to 42 percent of the total funds released, whereas the shares of the second and third category cities which cover 28 cities each are close to 45 percent and 13 percent respectively. At the same time, the comparatively much lower shares of the third category cities have to be understood from the point of view of very low share of the population of these cities.

The ratio between the share of the funds released under the Sub-Mission and the share of the population covered, gives a different picture. The respective ratios of the first, second and the third categories of Mission cities are 0.87, 1.12 and 1.12. This shows that the category 1 Mission cities were not successful in getting the adequate funds under the Sub-Mission in relation to the huge population covered under them. On the other hand, in relation to the population covered, the 2nd and 3rd category cities were able to get more funds released under the Sub-Mission. The possible explanation for this can be the low infrastructural base in the smaller cities in the country in comparison to the mega cities, which necessitated more investment in the second and third categories for infrastructural development.

At present, there is acute shortage of the infrastructural amenities in the small and medium towns of the country and this challenge can be solved only through adequate investment in infrastructure and basic amenities.[24] From this view point, the higher ratios of the second and the third category cities than the first category can be considered as a positive hint towards the increasing investment in urban infrastructure in the smaller urban areas through the Mission. It also reveals the fact that unlike the previous urban development initiatives it is not only the few selected larger cities which have benefitted from the Mission projects, but also the smaller cities throughout the country.

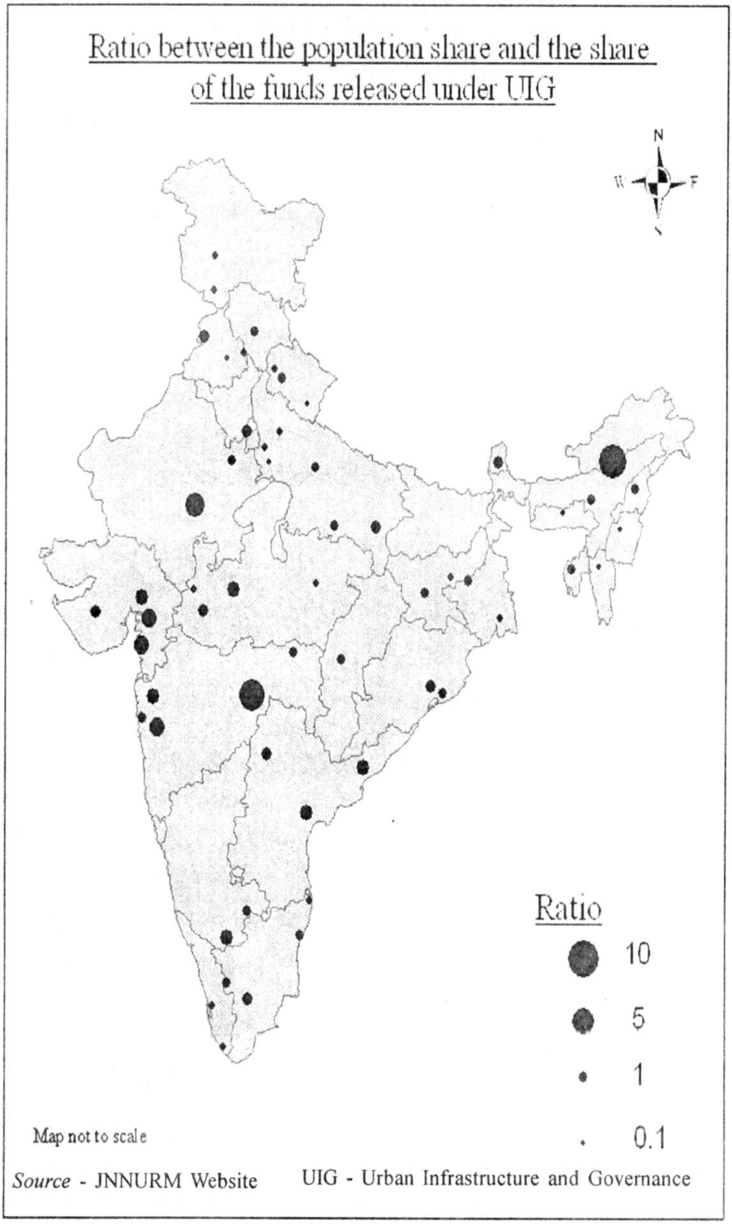
Ratio between the population share and the share of the funds released under UIG
N
Ratio
10
5
1
0.1
Map not to scale
Source - JNNURM Website
UIG - Urban Infrastructure and Governance

Map 2.10

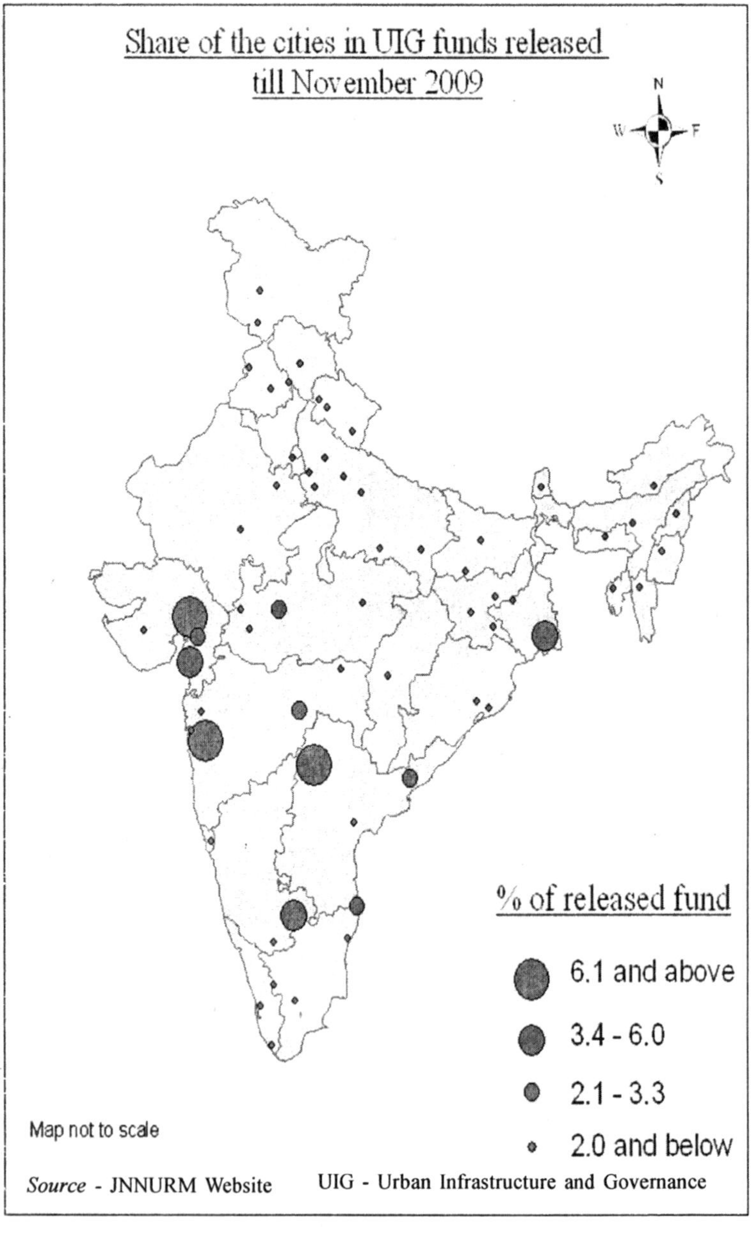
Share of the cities in UIG funds released
till November 2009
N
W
E
S
% of released fund
6.1 and above
3.4 - 6.0
2.1 - 3.3
2.0 and below
Map not to scale
Source - JNNURM Website
UIG - Urban Infrastructure and Governance

Map 2.11

Total projects completed under UIG

During the last four years of the Mission period, only 15 cities have at least one project completed under the Mission. Surat, Hyderabad and Bangalore with seven projects each completed have the largest shares of the projects completed. Ahmadabad (6), Vishakhapatnam (4), Chennai (4), Madurai (3), Bhopal (2), Mumbai (2), Asansol, Calcutta, Indore, Nagpur, Pune, Vijayawada (all one project each) are the other cities where at least one project under JNNURM is completed till date. The cities which have high share of the projects completed under the Mission are those which have succeeded in a large way in reforming the urban governance especially in encouraging private sector investment. Thus, it can be understood that the neoliberal strategy of present economic development focused on the city centered economic growth and punishes those cities which do not take policies for economic development by losses in investment, jobs and tax revenue.[25]

Release of funds under BSUP

In terms of the funds released under the sub-mission of the Basic Services for the Urban Poor, Mumbai has received the largest share (9.4 percent) of funds. The other cities which have received noticeable shares of the funds released are Hyderabad (8.9 percent), Kolkatta (8.8 percent), Pune (6.1 percent) etc. These four cities together have got close to 1/3rd of the total funds released under the BSUP projects. Jamshedpur is the only city which has not got funds released under BSUP. At the same time, it is very shocking that million plus cities like Allahabad and Ludhiana with huge urban poor population, have only negligible shares of funds released to the total.

The performance of the cities under the Mission can also be analyzed on the basis of the three population categories. The Table 2.7 illustrates that in the total urban poor population in the Mission cities, the share of the category 1 cities is 51 percent, while the share of these cities out of the total population covered under the Mission is 48.4 percent. The corresponding shares of the second and third categories of cities are 36 percent and 13 percent. But since these figures alone cannot tell

Table 2.11 Investment under BSUP-JNNURM across the various categories of cities till November 2009

Category of Cities	*Percentage of Share in Urban Poor Population Under the Mission*	*Share of Urban Poor in the Total Population*	*Concentration Index of Urban Poor Population*	*Percentage Share of the BSUP Funds Released*	*Ratio Between Share in BSUP Funds Released and Share in Urban Poor Population*
Category 1	51.19	22.31	1.06	36.05	0.70
Category 2	35.83	19.38	0.89	42.07	1.17
Category 3	12.98	25.01	1.15	17.74	1.37

Source- Official Website of JNNURM, http://jnnurm.nic.in/

anything more about the extent of concentration of the urban poor population within various categories of cities, the concentration index of the urban poor population in these cities are calculated.

The concentration index of urban poor population shows that they are primarily concentrated in the third category of the Mission cities as compared to the other two. This is due to the very poor urban infrastructural facilities in the smaller cities which result in the mushrooming of the slum and squatter settlements within the city and in its peripheral areas. The very poor physical infrastructural facilities in these urban centers (on the basis of which slums are identified), in turn results in large share of their urban population being categorized as urban poor.

The fast growth of the population in the large cities has deteriorated the quality of urban life and has become a major challenge in attracting the investment for funding in economic activities. Among the first and the second categories of cities, it is in the first category of cities where the urban poor are comparatively more concentrated.[26] The large urban areas of the country have very poor capacity to generate employment opportunities for the ever increasing population in these cities.[27] In spite of the fact that it is the service sector activities which are important in the larger cities which need skilled workers, the unskilled rural migrants are forced to get absorbed into the informal sector which most often give poverty level of returns.[28] The funds released under the Sub-Mission is the highest in case of the second category of cities (42 percent) and the respective shares of the first and the third categories are 36 percent and 18 percent.

The ratios of the shares of the funds released and the urban poor population under BSUP in each category proves that it is the third category of cities which are performing better than the other two categories. At the same time, it also has to be pointed out that the percentage share of the urban poor population to the total population under each category is the

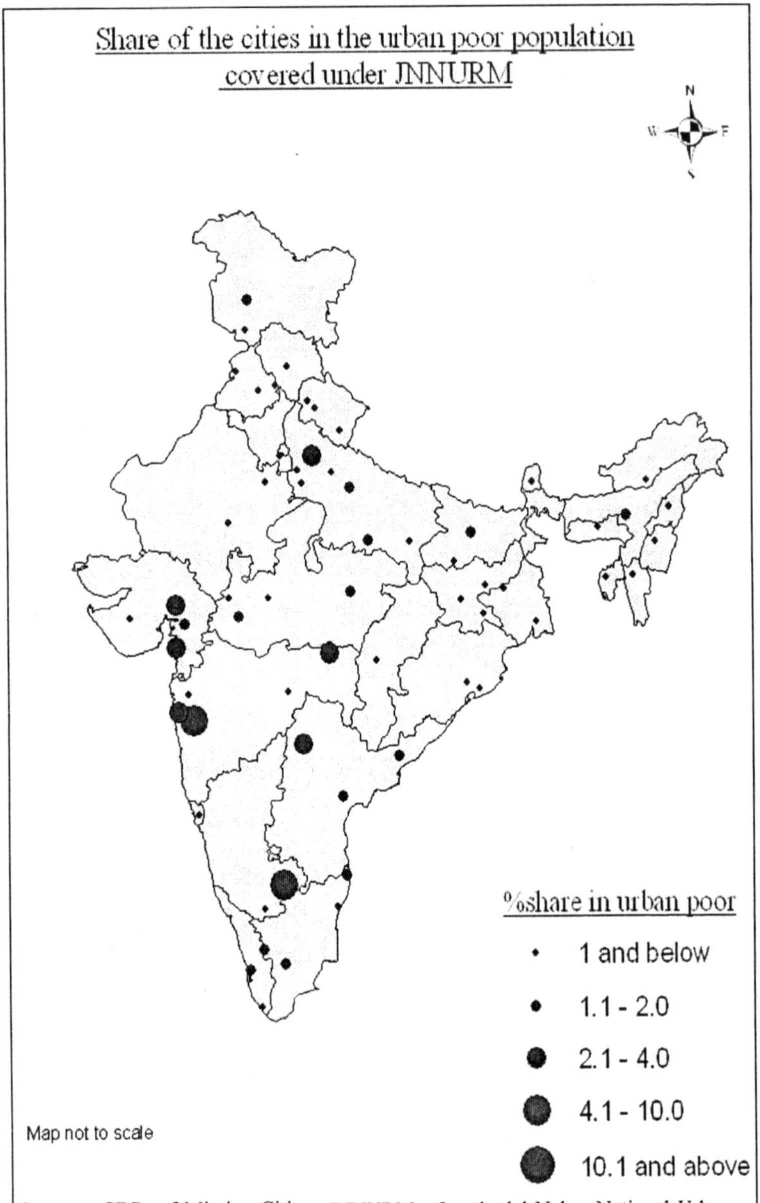

Source - CDPs of Mission Cities JNNURM - Jawaharlal Nehru National Urban Renewal Mission

Map 2.12

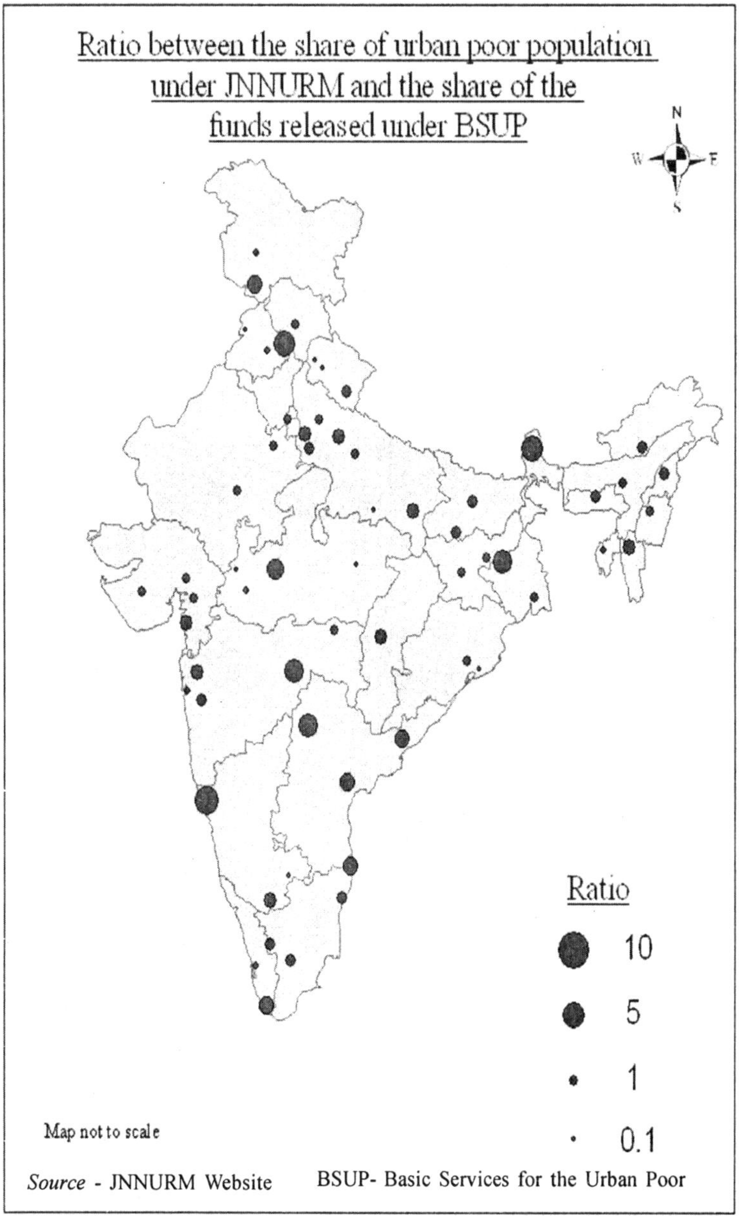
Ratio between the share of urban poor population under JNNURM and the share of the funds released under BSUP
N
W
E
S
Ratio
10
5
1
0.1
Map not to scale
Source - JNNURM Website
BSUP- Basic Services for the Urban Poor

Map 2.13

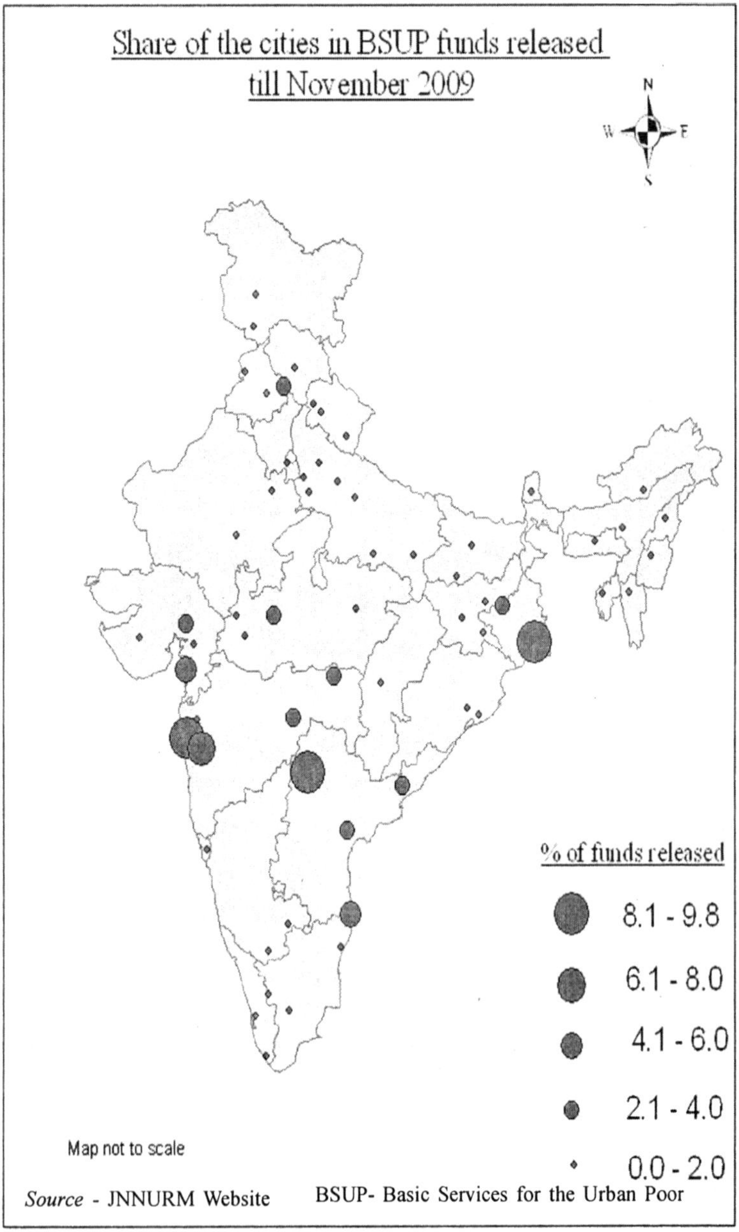
Share of the cities in BSUP funds released
till November 2009
N
W
E
S
% of funds released
8.1 - 9.8
6.1 - 8.0
4.1 - 6.0
2.1 - 4.0
0.0 - 2.0
Map not to scale
Source - JNNURM Website
BSUP- Basic Services for the Urban Poor

Map 2.14

Share of the released funds from the approved fund under BSUP till November 2009

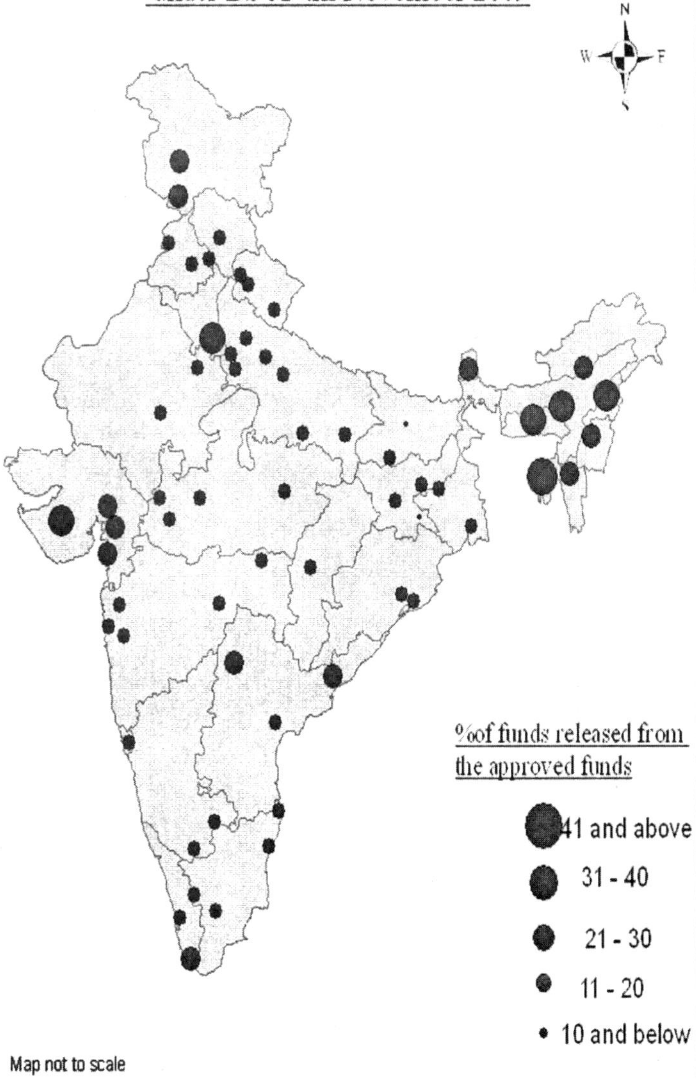

Source - JNNURM Website BSUP- Basic Services for the Urban Poor

Map 2.15

highest in case of the third category cities. When the ratio is 1.37 in case of the third category, the ratios are 0.70 and 1.17 in case of the first and the second categories. It has to be noted that, the smaller cities are also able to avail adequate share of funds in relation to the share of the urban poor population that they constitute.

In spite of constituting more than half of the urban poor population covered under the Mission, the low ratio of the category one cities (0.70) shows the poor performance of the Sub Mission in mega cities compared to the other two categories. The respective ratio of the first category cities under the Urban Infrastructure and Governance Sub Mission is 0.87. It means that the mega cities are performing better in case of the UIG Sub Mission in comparison to BSUP. In comparison to the large urban infrastructure projects, the projects for the urban poor were unable to attract private investment. This is the reason for the poor progress of the projects for the urban poor in most of the large cities. It is clear from the fact that even in cities like Delhi with huge chunk of urban poor population, the funds for the poverty alleviation through JNNURM remain unutilized, while other remunerative construction projects are completed on or before time with Public Private Partnership (PPP).[29] S. Mitra, D. Mahadevia(ed), (2008).

Urban governance reforms under JNNURM

The reforms under the Mission can be classified broadly into two categories, ie Mandatory and Optional reforms. Within the broad categories, there are reforms which are to be implemented at various levels. The implementation of the various reforms under the Mission can be analyzed both at the city and the state level. There are ten urban governance reforms under the state level and the level of implementation of these reforms across the states is as follows :

- *Implementation of the 74th CAA (transfer of the functions in the 12th Schedule),*

The states which have achieved this are Andhra Pradesh, Bihar, Chhattisgarh, Gujarat, Kerala, M.P., Maharashtra, Tamil Nadu, Tripura and West Bengal.

- *Reform of rent control* : The states which have achieved this reform are Karnataka, Manipur, Mizoram, Nagaland, Orissa, Rajasthan and West Bengal.

- *Constitution of District Planning Committee or DPC, 74th CAA* : In addition to the states which have achieved the first reform the states which have achieved this are Assam, Goa, Haryana, Jammu and Kashmir, Karnataka, Orissa, Rajasthan and UP.

- *Constitution of Metropolitan Planning Committee or MPC, 74th CAA* :The only three states which have achieved this reform is Andhra Pradesh, West Bengal and Gujarat.

- *Transfer of city planning functions* : The states which have achieved this reform are Andhra Pradesh, Assam, Chhattisgarh, Gujarat, Himachal Pradesh, Kerala, M.P, Maharashtra, Tamilnadu and West Bengal.

- *Transfers of water supply and sanitation reform* : All those states which have achieved the city planning functions, have achieved this reform except in case of Assam. In addition to these states the states which have achieved this reform are Bihar, Chandigarh and Haryana.

- *Stamp duty rationalization (up to 5 percent)* : The states that have achieved this reform are Goa, Gujarat, Jharkhand, Maharashtra, Sikkim, Pondicherry and Tripura.

- *Repeal of ULCRA (Urban Land Clearance Regulation Act)* : All the states barring Delhi, Jharkhand, and West Bengal, have achieved this reform.

- *Enactment of the Community Participation Law* : Except Andhra Pradesh, Assam and Gujarat no states have achieved this reform.

- *Enactment of the Public Disclosure Law* : In this case also, only a few states have achieved the reform. These states are Andhra Pradesh, Assam, Gujarat, Maharashtra, Tripura and Uttar Pradesh.

The reforms under JNNURM have to be achieved within the time frame of seven years and the Memorandum of Agreement (MoA) to implement these reforms has to be signed between the Ministry of Urban Development (MoUD), State government, and the Urban Local Body (ULB). Except Jamshedpur, all the Mission cities have signed MoA to implement the reforms. The implementation of governance reforms vary widely across the cities. Among the 23 reforms to be implemented under the Mission, there are cities like Vishakhapatnam, Rajkot, etc where except a few, all other reforms were implemented during the first half of the Mission period. At the same time, there are many cities such as Aizawal, Ludhiana and Ujjain where not even a single reform under the Mission was achieved during the last four years of the Mission period.

Table 2.12 Implementation of pro-privatization reforms under JNNURM

No. of Cities	*No. of Reforms Implemented Among 8 Pro-market and ULB Strengthening Reforms*	*Name of the Cities*
10	6 and above	Vishakhapatnam, Rajkot, Hyderabad, Vijayawada, Chennai, Ahmadabad, Vadodara, Surat, Coimbatore, Madurai
10	4 – 6	Jaipur, Kolkata, Indore, Mumbai, Bhopal, Nagpur, Nasik, Pune, Bangalore, Mysore
42	below 4	Rest of the Mission cities
20	No reforms implemented	Cities falling in J&K, Uttarakhand, Bihar, North-Eastern states, Chhattisgarh, Jharkhand and Goa

Source- Author's own assessment.

It has to be observed that most of the ULB level reforms are to encourage private sector participation in urban areas. The analysis of the implementation of the city level reforms under the Mission given in Table 2.12 (giving equal weight for the important reforms considered), the cities of Andhra Pradesh, Gujarat and Tamilnadu are ahead of rest of the states. The data analysis in the first part of this chapter had shown that these are also the cities which have performed well under the Mission. Thus, the argument that the institutionalization of various fiscal, financial management and governance reforms as the basis for success of the Mission, has to be accepted.'[30] The slower implementation of pro-liberal reforms in most of the Mission cities is a major threat for determining the level of success of the Mission as a whole. The slower achievement of the Mission governance reforms will delay the release of the funds under the various projects and in turn will not improve the functioning of the urban local bodies.

Critical Evaluation of the Mission Reforms

There is no common agreement about the urban governance reforms introduced under the Mission. One stream of literature on the Mission appreciates these reforms as the basis for the success of the ongoing Urban Development Mission in the country. Quite contrarily, the other stream observes that the Mission reforms as a means by the external funding and bilateral agencies to push in the agenda of neoliberal strategies of urban development. They doubt that the Mission reforms are part of the larger neo-liberal strategies which by means of various institutional reforms in the urban governance aim at maximizing economic growth and to create contemporary spaces for capitalistic expansion.[31] Nonetheless, from the first glance itself, it can be understood that there are several contradictions in the objectives of various Mission reforms.

One of the important mandatory reforms under JNNRUM is the full implementation of the 74th Constitutional Amendment Act. At the same time, there are many aspects about the mission which brings in the top down functioning of the Mission. The conditionality that the ULBs should implement minimum number of reforms to be considered as eligible to get the GoI funds under the Mission projects is a good example. This in fact should be considered as an indirect step to curb the powers of the grass root level governance bodies, ie ULBs and contradicts the attempt to fully decentralize urban governance through the Mission. The enormous official formalities which every project has to overcome in various stages of its implementation, further dampens the participation of the elected representatives under the Mission.

Though the Mission stresses on the need to ensure the common man's participation in decision making, the Mission has many hidden chains with which it has taken over the full control of the functioning of the ULBs. The signing of the Memorandum of Agreement between the Central-State Governments and the ULB as the first step to avail the fund from the GoI is another instance of the carrot and stick policy of the center. Thus, it is clear that the recent push for the urban governance decentralization in the neoliberal period is only a tool in the hand of local, political and economic elites to promote their own agenda in urban development.[32] Similarly, it is right that the Mission reforms have to be seen as part of large urban development projects which are characterized by the selective middle and upper class democracy and by less democratic and more elite driven participation.[33]

The thrust to promote the private sector investment in urban infrastructure through the Mission reforms also has to be carefully examined. Through these reforms, a clear attempt is done to facilitate the real estate business (which is the basis for the growth of cities in the globalised world) to flourish in the urban areas of the country. Many of the reforms including the repeal of ULCRA (Urban Land Ceiling Regulation Act), revision of bye-laws to streamline the approval process for construction of buildings, development of site, etc. and simplification of legal and procedural frameworks for conversion of land from agricultural to non-agricultural purposes are few examples. This will further marginalize the economically weaker sections residing in these urban centers. The Mission also gives thrust on the private sector participation in the provision of urban infrastructure and basic amenities and on full cost recovery for the services provided. In India, a country with huge chunk of its urban population living in poverty, the role of public sector in the provision of the basic amenities is still very crucial. The rolling back of private sector from the provision of these services while leaving everything open to the invisible hands of capitalistic market will make the urban poor more vulnerable.

Taking consideration of social welfare and public interest, public sector management of the urban amenities cannot be generalised as less efficient than the private sector counterpart which solely aims at the maximum returns.[34] Delimiting the supply of these services based on purchasing power will further narrow down the provision of basic amenities for the urban poor. The reform to implement full cost recovery is contradicting with the second Sub Mission to provide basic urban services to all the sections of urban population irrespective of their economic condition. None the less, it has to be accepted that any service provided will be unsustainable in the long run unless the cost for its production is recovered. When the stress is on full cost recovery, the economically backward areas of the city will be left behind the richer areas in terms of urban amenities. These set of Mission reforms introduced by the GoI, mark the green signal shown to the private sector approving an exclusive growth model in urban areas. It is rightly stated that the Mission will not substantially benefit the poor and the middle class as they are not interested in investing in basic services but only in the huge projects which will give them huge sum of profit.[35]

Another aspect which needs to be examined is the push for introducing urban governance restructuring. It has given stress on adopting efficient urban management techniques like GIS for mapping the entire urban areas including each property of the residents in the cities. Though it is assumed that the ULBs will be able to open many new sources of revenue through this, any doubt that it may once again push the agenda of demolition of squatter and slum settlements inhabited primarily by the urban poor is not out of place. Thus, this is an indirect measure to erect unseen walls around the cities and thus to curb down the flow of the poor and less skilled rural migrants who otherwise find a home in these slums. The strategies implemented to achieve the vision 'to make slum free cities', is the modified form of the 'bulldozer strategy' of urban renewal prevailed in the 1960s. This is clear from the fact that under majority of the slum development projects, the ULBs had been pushing the option of group housing within or outside the slums, rather than to provide the legal ownership of the land to the households at affordable price. On the one hand, the center exerts enormous pressure on the ULBs to implement the market oriented reforms, but on the other, center follows a very lenient attitude towards the ULBs for the implementation of the reforms to ensure complete decentralization. A good number of ULBs and states were not able to implement majority of the reforms aimed at decentralizing governance. For example, some of the major states like UP, Rajasthan, Punjab, Karnataka, Tamil Nadu, etc failed to transfer the functions mentioned in the 12th schedule to the ambit of ULBs. Ironically, the fact is that transfer of these functions to the ULBs itself is the crux of Urban Governance Decentralization Amendment passed in 1993.

Quite contrarily, except Jharkhand and West Bengal, all the states have implemented 'repeal of Urban Land Ceiling Regulation Act (ULCRA)', whose indirect objective is to boost up the private sector investment through real estate business. Since the Mission stresses on the market based funding of the urban projects, it is natural from the side of ULBs that they will give more weight for the implementation of market oriented reforms than decentralization oriented reforms. Thus, the Mission reforms in general have evoked the suspicion that these are the new tools to open the doors of capitalistic market for investing in urban areas in a large way, and in turn to achieve a quantum jump in economic growth of the country. Though, the betterment of the urban poor is included as the second Sub-Mission, the objectives and the probable impacts of the Mission reforms prove that empowering the urban poor is of least priority in the market oriented urban development strategy propagated through JNNURM.

Challenges of the Mission

The Mission was initiated with an objective to transform our cities and to raise them to the level of important centers of global economy. The Mission is constrained by the following factors :

- Slow project implementation : When half of Mission period is over, the number of projects approved is close to 930. On the other hand, the number of completed projects throughout the country is only less than 100. This shows a long time lag of the cities in course of projects designing and implementation.

- The poor reporting from the state governments in turn is another problem which has hindered the effective monitoring and implementation of Mission projects and reforms. The state governments are needed to give more detailed and timely reports on project progress under the Mission.[36]

- The expectations that funds sanctioned under JNNURM will leverage market funds did not materialize. Only a few projects could leverage market funding.[37] The lack of profitability through urban infrastructure investment, became the major reason which prevented the private investors investing in urban infrastructure.

- There are many issues that the ULBs face in the stage of reform implementation. Though all the cities have signed the Memorandum of Understanding with the Government of India, opposition from the common people and various political reasons make it very difficult for the ULBs to fully implement various reforms. Sustaining the enthusiasm and momentum among the States and Cities to implement the reforms is a critical challenge[38].

- Capacity Constraints : An ambitious national level program of this scale necessitates much greater capacities and management frameworks at all levels of Mission management. The inadequacy of the technically qualified people can be seen from the various monitoring agencies in the central level to the ULBs and parastatal agencies. This results in long delays in various stages of project implementation. A sudden shift from our outdated governance mechanisms to the efficient means like e- governance, property title certification system, etc. requires additional technically qualified staffs in huge numbers. Unfortunately, who are entrusted with these works currently, are either not experienced or are few in numbers, which ultimately delays the projects. Thus, ULBs and parastatal institutions face serious capacity constraints in undertaking such wide scale of investments that are much larger than earlier projects. The additional workload on ULBs through JNNURM will only further loosen their functioning, unless there is adequate technical and manpower support to implement the various projects and reforms under the Mission.[39]

Conclusions

The following conclusions can be drawn from the analysis of the data regarding the Mission projects.

- At state level, there is wide variation in the level of performance under the Mission as a whole and under the Sub Missions. Those states which were able to achieve the market oriented development governance reforms were able to attract huge foreign and private capital investments, while those cities which lagged in achieving the pro-privatization reforms were left behind. This is clear from the fact that most of the cities which have got the best performance awards under the Mission, are either from Gujarat or from Maharashtra. Maharashtra, Gujarat and Andhra Pradesh together have received more than half of the total Mission funds released. But the conclusion that only few large states are benefitting from the Mission is meaningless as it is natural that the larger states and the larger cities will get larger share of the funds than the smaller states.

- The difference in the performance under the Mission projects is clearer at the city level than at the state level. Within the category of large cities, the cities which were able to implement the market based reforms (like repeal of ULCRA, user charge collection, easy conversion of agricultural land to other uses, etc.) through various means, perform better than those cities which could not implement them. This is clearly proved by the fact that Surat, which has succeeded in a large way in implementing the reforms, was awarded the best performing city award under UIG Sub-Mission.

- JNNURM can be considered as a major step in reducing regional disparities across the country. The data analysis shows that North East India, which had been always out of major urban development initiatives in the past, are also able to get the funds through the Mission. The major problem of the cities in this region is the narrow revenue base. But this does not affect their performance under the Mission as the ULBs of these states do not have to deposit its share under the projects.

- The narrow revenue base of the small and medium towns is a major obstacle in the Mission progress as no projects will be initiated unless the funding share of the ULB is deposited first. The restructuring of the funding pattern of the group 'B' cities was done when this reality of the ULBs was felt widely. Still, the poor financial capacity continues to be one of the main reasons for the slow progress of the Mission projects in many of the Mission cities.

- The urban infrastructural sectors which were able to attract private investment easier than other sectors have got large chunk of the funds released under the Mission. These sectors are water supply, sewerage, drainage, etc.

Besides this, the Mission has given priority for the implementation of the projects in the crucial urban service areas like water supply, sewerage, etc, which have huge impact on the standard of living of the population.

- The division of the funds between the first and the second Sub Missions is less skewed as compared to the pattern of CDP investment layout of most of the Mission cities. The analysis of data shows that roughly 25 percent of the total released fund under the Mission was invested in BSUP projects. But the performance of the cities and states under BSUP varied widely.

- Urban Governance reforms initiated under the Mission can be considered as the potent tool with which GoI has attempted to promote the market based development of urban areas. While promoting the interest of elites who form a very minute fraction of city's population, these reforms will harm the decentralized governance and the economically weaker sections of urban society. In a country like India with large share of its urban population living in poverty, the privatization of the basic amenities will further delimit their access to basic amenities. Thus it is obvious that the implementation of market oriented reforms will only further deteriorate the living conditions of the poor and economically weaker localities in general.[40]

- A close look at the implementation status of the Mission reforms reveals that in comparison to the reforms meant for fuller decentralization of urban governance, ULBs were keen to implement market supportive reforms. The main reason for this tendency of the ULBs is because of their ultimate need to attract private investments in urban infrastructure and basic amenities. Few Mission reforms like the property entitlement certification, mapping of each and every corner of the Mission cities through GIS, etc. will lead to the raising of unseen walls around the Mission cities. This will enable the urban elites and the middle class to live in a city free of slums and squatters which are always perceived as the nuisance in their lives.

- The very low share of the projects completed in comparison to the total projects approved is a matter of grave concern and it puts a doubt on the success of JNNURM in the country. Long delay of the Mission projects has to be solved through capacity building initiatives and recruitment of adequate number of technically qualified man power in the ULBs.

References

1. It refers to a transition or interaction zone, where urban and rural activities are juxtaposed, and landscape features are subject to rapid modifications, inducing by human activities (Douglas, 2006).
2. Census of India considers these as the areas contiguous to the city or town, but most often falling in the statutory limits of village. Since such areas are already urbanized, it is not considered realistic to treat such areas lying outside the statutory limits of a town as rural units, although a few of them may not satisfy some of the prescribed eligibility tests to qualify themselves as independent urban units.
3. A number of city centers of various sizes are becoming connected along the transportation routes in linear development. They are the areas which experience very high population growth rates and most rapid urban transformation.
4. Swyngedouw, E., Moulaer, F., Rodriguez, A. (2002), "Neoliberal Urbanization in Europe: Large Scale Urban Development Projects and the New Urban Policy", *Antipode*, Vol. 34, Issue 3, p. 550.
5. It is the path breaking initiative passed by the Parliament to strengthen the ULBs in the country in 1992. It provided Indian constitution, recognition to the constitution, powers and functions of the urban local bodies for the first time in the history of India.
6. It is a loan with a below-market rate of interest. Soft loans are usually provided by governments to projects they think are worthwhile.

7. It can be defined as the use of technology to enhance the access to and delivery of government services to benefit citizens, business partners and employees.
8. It is an agency through which the state works indirectly. It can be a fully or partially state-owned corporation or government agency.
9. Asian Development Bank, (2008), "Country Assistance Evaluation Project for India", Operations evaluation department, p. 47.
10. It is a charge for the use of a product or service. A user charge may apply per use of the good or service or for the use of the good or service.
11. The Act passed by parliament in 1976 to facilitate the availability and affordability of urban land by increasing its supply in the market and by establishing an efficient land market.
12. It is a tax that is levied on documents. It has to be cut down to 5% in seven years and aims to establish an efficient real estate market with minimum barriers on property transfer so as to put them in more productive use.
13. The law passed to institute transparency and accountability in the functioning of municipalities through publication of information related to various facets of urban governance.
14. The law aimed at strengthening citizen participation by involving them in various functions of urban governance.
15. It aims to ensure easy accessibility and proper management and records of all property holdings within the city.
16. It is defined as a government service or private business venture which is funded and operated through a partnership of government and one or more private sector companies.
17. Cezayirli, G., Basu, K. (2008), "Two years of Jawaharlal Nehru National Urban Renewal Mission", ADB, p. 20.
18. "Proto type interactive public questions and answers", JNNURM Directorate, http://mhupa.gov.in/PQAS/jnnurm.pdf, p. 16.
19. Idelovitch, E., Ringskog, K. (1997), 'Private sector participation in water supply and sanitation in Latin America', Published by World Bank, Washington, p. 3.
20. 'Fund allocation and utilization: Summary statements, BSUP', Ministry of Housing and Urban Poverty Alleviation, https://jnnurmmis.nic.in/jnnurm_hupa/index.html, p. 4.

21. Swyngedouw, E., Moulaert, F., Rodriguez, A. (2002), 'Neoliberal Urbanization in Europe: LargeScale Urban Development Projects and the New Urban Policy', *Antipode*, Volume 34, Issue 3, p. 4.

22. Kundu, A. (2000), "Globalising Gujarat: Urbanization, employment and poverty", *Economic and Political Weekly*, Vol. 35, No. 5/36, p. 3172.

23. Miraftab, F. (2004), "Public Private Partnerships; The Trojan horse of Neoliberal Development", *Journal of Planning Education and Research*, Vol. 24, No. 1, p. 98.

24. Kundu, A., Bagchi, S., Kundu, D. (June 1999), "Regional Distribution of Infrastructure and Basic Amenities in Urban India: Issues concerning Empowerment of Local Bodies", *Economic and Political Weekly*, Vol. 34, No. 28, p. 1898.

25. Conner, K.R. (1991), "A Historical Comparison of Resource-Based Theory and Five Schools of Thought Within Industrial Organization Economics: Do We Have a New Theory of the Firm?", *Journal of Management*, Vol. 17, p. 147.

26. Banerjee-Guha, S., Sita, K., Phadke, V.S. (1988), *"The declining city-core of an Indian metropolis: A case study of Bombay"*, Published by Concept Publishing Company, New Delhi, p. 178.

27. Mukherji, S. (1995), Poverty Induced Migration and Urban Involution in ESCAP Countries, Paper presented at UN-ESCAP, Expert Group Meeting on Poverty and Population in ESCAP Region, Bangkok, Sept 1995, pp. 37.

28. Kundu, A., Lalitha, N. and Arora, S. (2001), "Growth Dynamics of Informal Manufacturing Sector in Urban India: An Analysis of Interdependencies", (with Lalitha, N. and Arora, S) in Kundu, A. and A.N. Sharma, (eds.), *Informal Sector in India*, Institute of Human Development, New Delhi, pp. 118.

29. Mitra, S., Mahadevia, D. (ed), (2008), "Financing urban development in Delhi: Towards inclusive Globalisation?", in *Inside the transforming urban India: Processes, policies and public actions,* Published by Concept Publishing Company, New Delhi, p. 619.

30. Asian Development Bank, (2008), 'Country Assistance Evaluation Project for India', Operations evaluation department, p. 47.

31. Brenner, N. (2004), 'New state spaces; Urban governance and the scaling of statehood', Published by Oxford University Press Inc, New York, p. 3.
32. Brenner, N., Theodore, N. (2002), "Preface; From the 'new localism' to the spaces of neoliberalism", Published by Blackwell Publishers Limited, UK, p.17.
33. Swyngedouw , E., Moulaert, F., Rodriguez, A. (2002), "Neoliberal Urbanization in Europe: Large Scale Urban Development Projects and the New Urban Policy", *Antipode*, Volume 34, Issue 3, p. 572.
34. Lobina, E., Hall, D. (2000), "Public sector alternatives to water supply and sewerage privatization: Case studies", *International Journal of Water Resource Development,* Vol. 16, Issue 1, pp. 33.
35. Baindur, V., Kamath, L. (August 2009), "Reengineering Urban Infrastructure; How the World Bank and Asian Development Bank shape urban infrastructure finance and governance in India", Asian Development Bank, p. 47.
36. Cezayirli, G., Basu, K. (2008), "Two years of Jawaharlal Nehru National Urban Renewal Mission", ADB, p. 23.
37. *Ibid.*, p. 23.
38. *Ibid.*, p. 25.
39. Vaidya, C., Vaidya, H. (2008), "Innovative Municipal resource mobilization in India", Paper presented at workshop on resource mobilization for urban poverty alleviation, Hyderabad, p. 6.
40. Kundu, A. (2000), "Globalising Gujarat: Urbanization, employment and poverty", *Economic and Political Weekly*, Vol. 35, No. 5/36, p. 3179.

3

Urbanization, Urban Infrastructure and Urban Governance in Kerala

Kerala : A brief introduction

Kerala, the small state located in the south western part of the country, ranks first in terms of the various human and social developmental indicators. The state caught the attention of the international academic community, owing to its unparalleled successful experience of achieving high human development unaccompanied by a matching rate of economic development which often was considered as a paradox in itself. At a time, when the policy makers worldwide had been hunting for a development model which could be successfully replicated on the large number of newly independent countries plagued with variety of socio-economic tensions, "Kerala model of development" captured the attention as an effective solution (T.N. Krishnan, 1980). With a total population of 3.2 crore, 3.1 percent of the total population of the country resides in the state. According to Census 2001, 26 percent population of the state lived in urban areas of the state and is the third most densely populated state in the country after West Bengal and Bihar.

The role of the state government in Kerala in achieving a level of human development is widely appreciated not only within the country but also at the international level. While proceeding with its welfare oriented development model, the sustainability of social development in spite of the weak economic performance is the most important question before the state.[1] Similar to the poor economic performance of the state, the physical infrastructure in the state also presents a very poor picture. It is often criticized that the predominance given for the improvement of the social sector by the state limits the ability of the state to make fresh investment in infrastructure.[2] The changing scenario in the post globalization period and the various loopholes in the existing system make the introduction of the reorientation of the government policies necessary in the social sector of the state.[3]

Another area where the state is ahead of rest of the country is in the area of decentralization in the planning process. Given the fact that the bureaucratic planning and implementation machinery is alienated from the people, decentralized planning makes the tapping of local resources possible by ensuring greater participation of the people in the developmental process.[4] Though it was a difficult task as in any other state, through a variety of acts and other necessary steps, the state has succeeded in decentralizing governance in an appreciable manner.[5] 'Kerala has a long and celebrated history of social mobilization and a dense and vibrant civil society, which make the decentralization task slightly easier than everywhere else.'[6] Urban areas of the state play very vital role in the economy of the state.

Constituting an urban population of 8.1 million, the state has roughly 2.8 percent of the urban population of the country. Thiruvananthapuram and Kochi are the two cities which are covered under JNNURM from Kerala. This chapter aims to examine the performance of Kerala under the ongoing Urban Development Mission; JNNURM with special focus on the Sub-mission of Urban Infrastructure and Governance (UIG). According to Census 2001, Kochi, which is otherwise known as the commercial capital of the state has a population of 5.96 lakhs and Thiruvananthapuram, the administrative capital of the state has a total population of 7.45 lakhs. Thus, the two cities together cover more than 16.5 percent of the urban population of the state.

With 13.5 lakhs and 8.9 lakhs population in the City Development Plan area, Kochi and Thiruvananthapuram fall under second and third categories of cities under the Mission. The first part of the study attempts to understand the general pattern and urbanization processes experienced in the state. While the second part deals with the performance of the Mission cities under the first Sub-Mission of Urban Infrastructure and Governance. The data for the analysis are taken from City Development Plans of the cities, Detailed Project Reports and JNNURM official website.

Urbanization patterns and processes in Kerala

According to the Census 2001, in the state as a whole, 25.97 percent of the population lives in urban areas which is lower than the level of urbanization at the national level. Urban population of the state is spread across 159 urban centers including five corporations and fifty-three municipalities. The low level of economic development in the state supports the widely accepted fact that the level of urbanization that a society has reached is a good indicator of the level of economic development. As in case of the social development history, the urbanization processes experienced in the state also are quite different from the rest of the country. They have to be studied from the point of view that entire state except for the highly rugged parts of the state is a part of the rural urban continuum.[7] This means that unlike in case of any other states, the clear cut boundaries between the urban and the rural areas cannot be drawn in the case of Kerala. Thus, the stratification of the urban areas in the states should be done and has to be understood from the point of view of the mixed rural and urban settlement pattern.[8]

The dispersed settlement pattern of the state from the historical times and a liking for the homestead type of

Table 3.1 Level of urbanization and Growth rate of Urban Population in India and Kerala from 1901-2001

Year	*Percentage of Urban Population- Kerala*	*Percentage of Share of Urban Population-India*	*Decadal Growth Rate of Urban Population- Kerala*	*Decadal Growth Rate of Urban Population- India*
1901	7.11	10.85	-	-
1911	7.34	10.29	15.44	36.15
1921	8.73	11.18	29.77	8.26
1931	9.64	11.99	34.57	19.12
1941	10.84	13.86	30.47	31.98
1951	13.48	17.29	52.71	41.40
1961	15.11	17.97	39.88	26.41
1971	16.24	19.91	35.72	38.23
1981	18.74	23.34	37.64	46.14
1991	26.3	25.71	60.96	36.47
2001	25.97	27.8	7.64	31.11

Source- Census of India, 1901-2001.

development, comparatively developed infrastructure in rural and the urban areas availability of the Sub soil water almost everywhere in the state are some of the factors behind the peculiar urbanization pattern experienced in the state. As a result of this the rural to urban migration which accentuates urban poverty and other problems is almost absent in the state.[9] The state has very low share of its population living in poverty both in urban and rural areas. This is very true in the case of slum population in the state. Urban population in the state is spread throughout and there is no urban area which crosses the mark of million population.

Figure 3.1

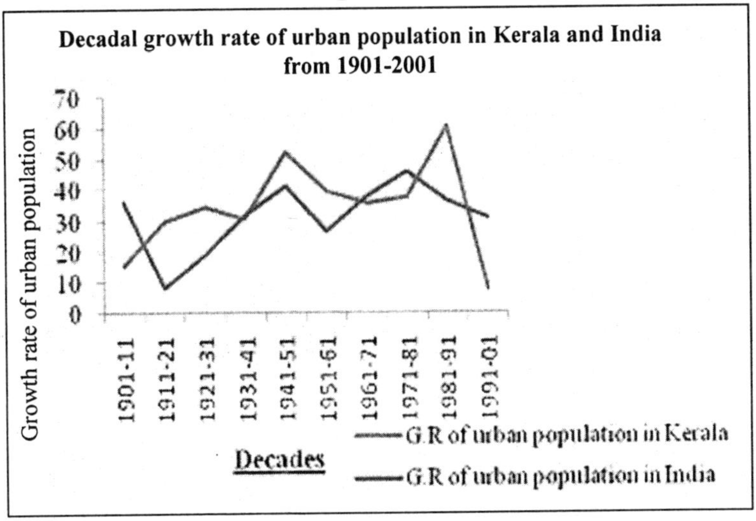

From the beginning of the twentieth century itself, the level of urbanization in the state was lower than that of the national level. From 1901 there had been a continuous increase in the share of urban population in the state until 1991, when the level of urbanization in the state reached at its peak level of 26.3 percent. It was only in 1991 that the share of the urban population in the state was higher than that of the national average. As a result of the declassification of certain Municipalities in 2001, the share of urban population in the state fell down as compared to the previous decade. In 2001

Figure 3.2

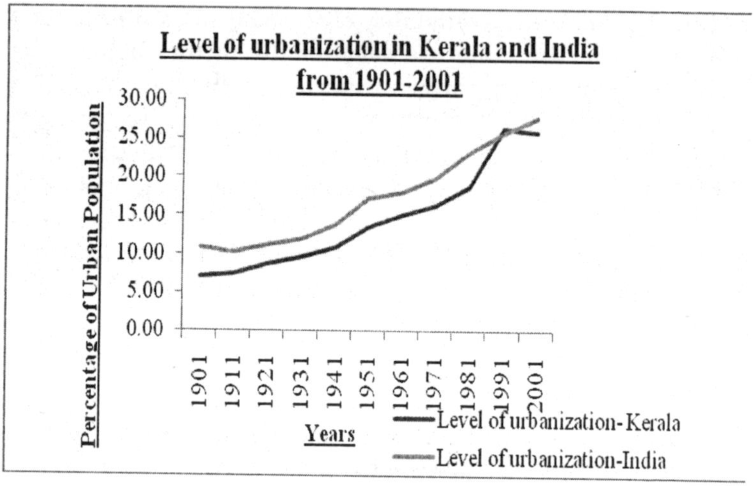

there were 17 urban agglomerations in the state which were located in all the districts of the state except in the three hilly districts. In terms of the actual numbers, the number of urban centers had declined from 197 in 1991 census to 159 in 2001. The main reason for this reduction is the expansion in the jurisdiction of a few urban settlements by including the

Figure 3.3

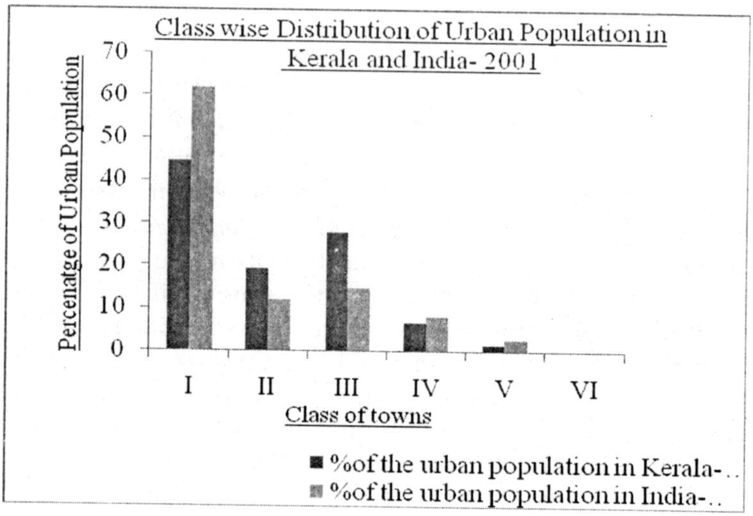

neighboring Panchayats. The formation of the urban agglomerations through this process led to the reduction in the number of the towns and cities in 2001 in comparison to 1991.[10]

From the analysis of the distribution of urban population across the various classes of urban area, it can be understood that there is no primate city in the state. In the total urban population, close to 45 percent live in the Class one cities which are nine in number, while the respective share of the Class one cities at the national level is close to 62 percent. The five municipalities of the state, namely Thrissur, Kozhikkodu, Kollam, Thiruvananthapuram and Kochi comprise about 35 percent of its urban population. In terms of numbers, majority of the towns fall in the small or medium categories. The medium towns in the state have much larger share of urban population than at the national level. But the share of urban population in the last two categories of very small towns is lower in the case of Kerala than at the national level. It is also interesting to note that a good number of villages in the state have much larger population than many small and medium towns. In spite of the larger population of these villages, they remain to be considered as villages as they do not fulfill other criteria to be classified as 'urban'. Another interesting fact is that the rural urban continuum pattern of settlement prevalent in the state has resulted in the non availability of large vacant areas for major organized development. This has led to the expansion of urban areas contiguous along the arterial corridors resulting in urban agglomerations.[11]

The distribution pattern of urban areas in the state clearly shows that majority of the urban areas are located either in the low coastal plains or in the midland sandwiched between the coastal plain and Western Ghats. The urban population of the state is distributed quite unevenly across its fourteen districts (See Table 3.2). The share of urban population ranges from 3.8 per cent in the hilly Wayanadu district to 50.4 per cent in Kannur district. Other districts with high level of urbanization are Ernakulum (48.7per cent), Kozhikode (38.3 per cent), etc. Apart from Wayanadu, the districts with low level of

Table 3.2 Urbanization in Kerala at District Level in 1991 and 2001

Name of the District	*Percentage of Urban Population in 1991*	*Percentage of Urban Population 2001*	*Percentage of Share of Urban Population in the State*	*Location Quotient*
Thiruvananthapuram	33.88	33.78	10.16	1.30
Kollam	18.53	18.03	8.12	0.69
Pathanamthitta	13.05	10.03	3.87	0.39
Alappuzha	30.46	29.36	6.61	1.13
Kottayam	17.55	15.35	6.13	0.59
Idukki	4.72	5.07	3.54	0.20
Ernakulam	48.74	47.65	9.73	1.83
Thrissur	26.31	28.21	9.35	1.09
Palakkad	15.72	13.62	8.22	0.52
Malappuram	9.12	9.81	11.40	0.38
Kozhikkodu	37.62	38.25	9.04	1.47
Wayanadu	3.41	3.76	2.47	0.14
Kannur	50.87	50.46	7.58	1.94
Kasaragod	8.94	19.42	3.78	0.75
Kerala	26.39	25.97	100	1.00

Source- Census of India, 1991 and 2001.

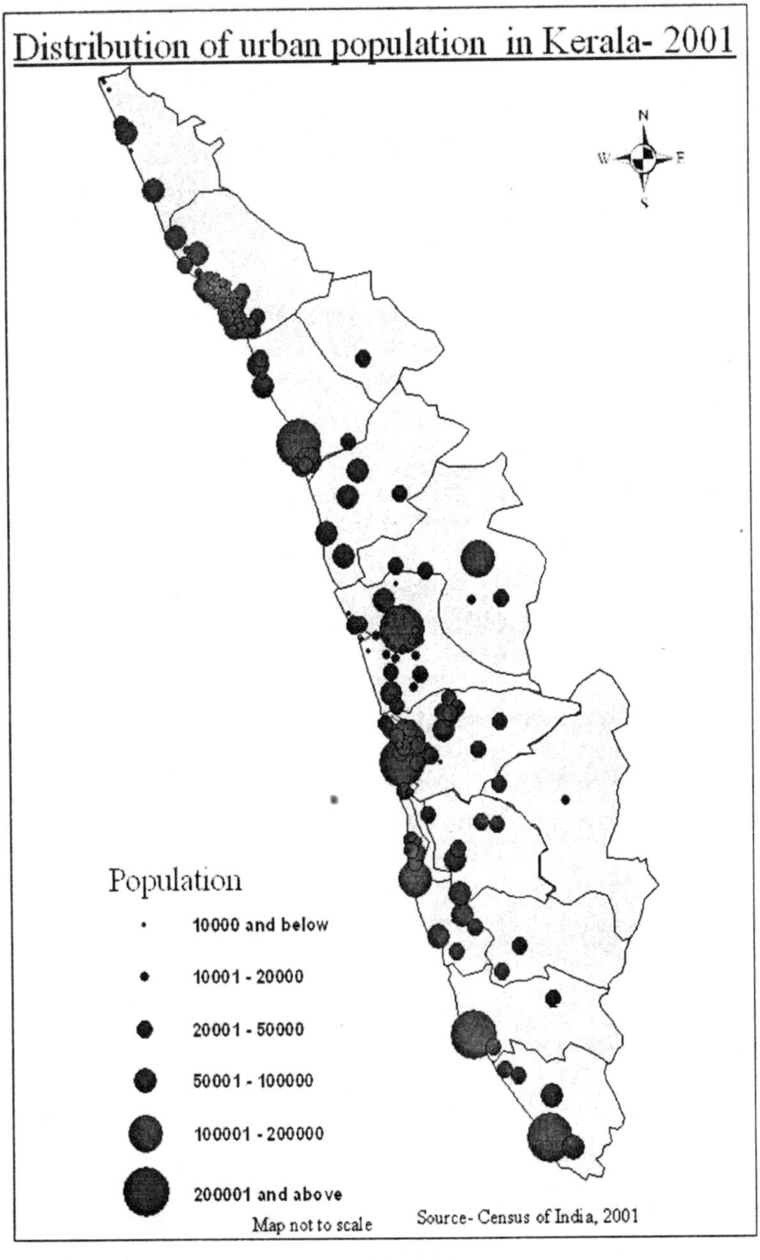
Distribution of urban population in Kerala- 2001
N
W
E
S
Population
10000 and below
10001 - 20000
20001 - 50000
50001 - 100000
100001 - 200000
200001 and above
Map not to scale
Source- Census of India, 2001

Map 3.1

urbanization are Idukki (5.1 percent), Malappuram (9.8 percent) and Pathanamthitta (10 percent). In 2001 all the districts except Kasaragod have followed the same ordering of 1991 in terms of the level of urbanization. The sudden rise in the level of urbanization in Kasaragod district from mere 8.9 percent in 1991 to as high as 19.4 percent was different from the experience of the rest of the state where the shares of urban population had either increased or decreased only marginally.

The uneven distribution of urban population across the districts is evident from Map 3.1 and becomes clearer from the location quotients of urban population which ranges between 1.94 in Kannur and 0.14 in Wayanadu. Wayanad is followed by Idukki (0.20) Malappuram (0.38) and Pathanamthitta (0.39). Except Malappuram, the other three districts with very low levels of urbanization are located on the Western Ghats. The unfavorable topography has made these districts unattractive for investment and thus they have very few urban centers in spite of their large size. Districts like Kannur, Ernakulum, and Kozhikode which have a very high concentration of urban population are located in the coastal areas of the state. This enabled the growth of several urban centers in close proximity to one another in these districts. Thus, the strong control of the physiographic factors on the distribution pattern of urban population in the state is evident from the historic times. Apart from the geographical factors the urbanization pattern in the state is also influenced by its unique socio-cultural and historical settings and the interplay of these factors have resulted in the evolution of a peculiar urbanization pattern in the state. It is widely accepted that the urbanization processes in Kerala is not associated with accelerated industrialization, but is the result of the development of tertiary activities.[12]

Urban development in Kerala

In comparison to many major states in the country, the level of physical infrastructural development in Kerala shows a poor picture, especially in the urban areas. The poor mechanism of cost recovery for the services provided in the state has made the provision of various urban services unsustainable in the long run. It is also accepted that the long history of state funding in important areas of urban basic amenities (which used to provide various services at minimal cost or without any cost) have created a kind of mental set up in the population and the lack of willingness to pay for the services.[13] This is very clear from the fact that any hike in the user charges often leads to mass strikes and interruption of the normal life. The unwillingness of the people to pay the user charges will not be changed unless new institutional mechanisms are introduced. It is widely accepted that the wide gap in the demand and supply of the urban basic amenities can be filled up only through the active participation of private sector in infrastructure creation.[14]

In the urban development strategy Kerala formulated in 1996, the state government has given differential priorities for the development of urban centers in the state. The major criteria taken into consideration while giving the differential priority are density of population, functional linkage with present settlement, functional dependency of surrounding Panchayats, corridor development along major arterial roads, level of transportation facilities, land use, and the functional category of town in the region. Kochi Urban Agglomeration was given the first priority in urban development in the state. Second and third priorities were given to Thiruvananthapuram and Kozhikode urban agglomerations. Kochi and Thiruvananthapuram are the two cities which are included under JNNURM from the state. Kochi is the largest commercial center in the state, and Thiruvananthapuram is important because of its administrative functions as the capital city of the state.

Other than JNNURM, the state has one more large scale urban development project namely Kerala Sustainable Urban Development Project (KSUDP). It has covered five cities in the state including the two cities covered under JNNURM. The other three cities are Kozhikkodu, Thrissur and Kollam. The main objective of this ADB funded urban development initiative in the state is the infrastructural development of the selected cities in a sustainable manner. There are many areas of functional overlaps in the cities which are covered both under JNNURM and KSUDP (ie Kochi and Thiruvananthapuram). The 11th Five Year Plan is a milestone in the urban planning history of the state as two large scale urban development schemes, i.e. JNNURM and KSUDP are in operation during this plan. The following are the ongoing urban development initiatives during the Eleventh Five Year Plan in the state :

- Jawaharlal Nehru National Urban Renewal Mission (JNNURM)
- Kerala Sustainable Urban Development Project (KSUDP)
- Special packages for planning and development of selected towns
- Urban Infrastructure Development Scheme for the Small and Medium Towns
- Preparation of heritage plans for Alappuzha and Thalassery
- Swarna Jayanthy Shahari Rozgar Yojana (SJSRY)
- Integrated Housing and Slum Development Programme (IHSDP)
- Development authorities, Kochi, Thiruvananthapuram and Kozhikodu
- Clean Kerala Project and finally Capital City Development Project

Level of urban infrastructural facilities in Kerala

In order to assess the contribution of JNNURM in improving the urban infrastructural facilities in the Mission cities of the state, it is very essential to examine the level of infrastructural facilities available in the cities before the Mission. The non-reliability of the data available on urban amenities itself is the major crisis in such an analysis. The level of the basic amenities in the urban areas of the state can be analyzed to some extent from the housing amenities data published by Census of India.

Among the housing amenities and infrastructural facilities available given in Table 3.3, there are some aspects which are much more crucial than the rest in determining the quality of life. Some of these are availability of water within the premises,

Table 3.3 Urban Housing and other basic amenities - 2001

Housing and Other Infrastructural Amenities	*India*	*Kerala*	*Kochi*	*Thiruvananthapuram*
Coverage of Banking Facilities	49.5	54	55	49
Owns no assets	19	19	16	18
Access to drinking water in the premise	65.4	78.9	59.7	83.2
Latrine Facility in the households	73.7	92.2	92.1	92.3
Coverage of electricity connections	87.6	84.3	92.3	88.3
Firewood, cow dung etc for cooking	31.4	59.4	27.5	45.9
Availability of separate kitchen	76	95.3	95.1	95.5
Bathroom facility within the house	70.4	78.9	90.3	78.1
Coverage of the drainage facility	77.9	30.9	59.1	35.4
Good condition of the house	64	64.9	68.2	62.5
Houses in non dilapidated condition	96.4	97.7	96.2	88.2
Share of houses with kutcha roof material	7.1	7.3	2.3	15.5
Houses with concrete roofs	44.4	41.4	32.8	49.3
Share of houses with Kutcha wall material	6.7	5.8	4.1	5.7
Share of the owned houses	66.7	87.5	79.9	80.5
Share of houses with only two rooms and below	37.4	10.2	8.0	13.6
Share of the houses with room density 3 and above	14.2	1.4	.9	1.8

Source- Housing Tables, Census of India, 2001.

latrine facility within the house, coverage of electricity connections, coverage of drainage facilities, ownership of any assets etc. Barring few cases like drainage and electricity connection, the urban areas of the state have better living environment than at the national level.

Housing amenities in the Urban area of India and Kerala - 2001

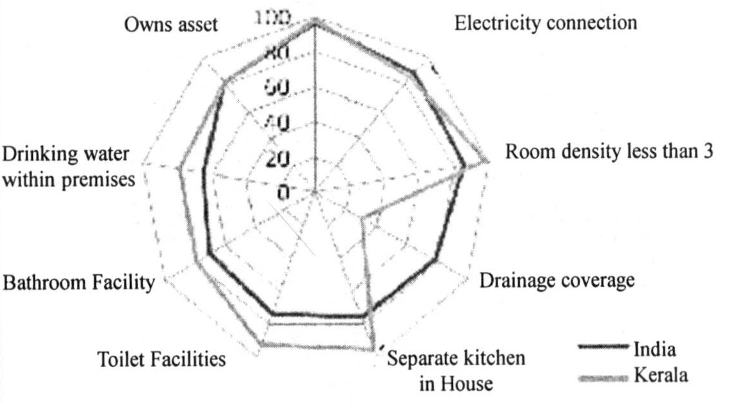

Figure 3.4

Housing amenities in the cities of Kochi and Thiruvananthapuram - 2001

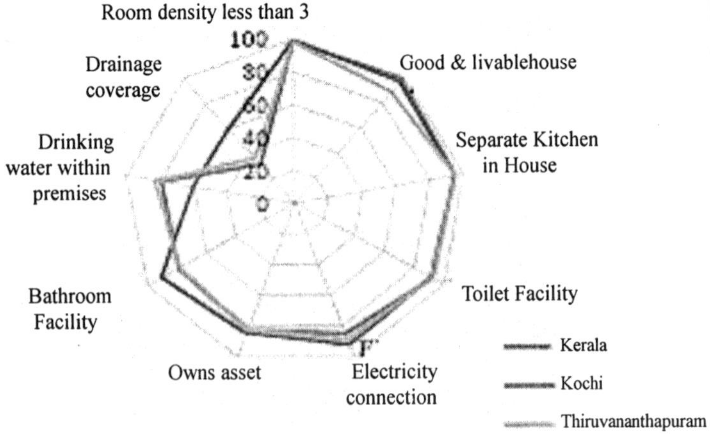

Figure 3.5

The analysis of urban housing amenities in the state and of the two Mission cities reveals that the most important challenge of the urban areas in the state is the acute shortage in the coverage of drainage facilities. The downpour during the rainy seasons floods many important urban centers of the state especially Kochi and Thiruvananthapuram. The coastal location of most of the cities of the state makes them more prone to flash floods in the rainy season. This is very clear in case of Thiruvananthapuram, the capital city of the state which has only 35 percent of its households covered under the drainage network as compared to the 79 percent coverage at the national level. Kochi is ahead of the state and Thiruvananthapuram in terms of coverage of drainage facility. The share of the houses with drinking water within the premises is only 60 percent in Kochi while it is as high as 83 percent in Thiruvananthapuram. Kochi presents a very poor picture in the coverage of the drinking water facilities in comparison to the state as well as the country as a whole. It was also noticed that the share of the houses in dilapidated condition is much higher in Thiruvananthapuram than in Kochi and the state as a whole.

JNNURM in Kerala

The two cities which are covered under JNNURM from Kerala are Kochi and Thiruvananthapuram. This part of the chapter attempts to analyze the CDPs of both the Mission cities as well as the progress made by the cities under the Sub-Mission of Urban Infrastructure and Governance (UIG).

Table 3.4 Funding pattern for the Mission projects in Kerala

Name of the City	*Share in Percentage*		
	GoI	*State Government*	*ULB*
Thiruvananthapuram	80	10	10
Kochi (initial allocation)	50	20	30
Kochi (Revised allocation)	50	40	10

Source- Ministry of Urban Development, India.

Table 3.5 Investment Plan Kochi and Thiruvananthapuram under JNNURM -2006

Sections/ Subsections	*Important Sectors*	*Kochi*		*Thiruvananthapuram*	
		Investment (Rs in Crores)	*Sectoral Share in Percent*	*Investment (Rs in Crores)*	*Sectoral Share in Percent*
(A) UIG	Water Supply	1216.7	11.12	1041.41	14.04
	Sewerage	2629	24.03	1081	14.57
	Storm Water Drainage	902	8.24	175.75	2.4
	Environment	291	2.66	24.33	.32
	Solid Waste Management	152.4	1.39	51	.68
	Traffic and Transportation	4252	38.87	3786.54	51.05
	Urban Renewal	295.5	2.7	200	2.7
	Heritage and Tourism	360.85	3.3	322.4	4.34
(A) UIG-TOTAL	Investment under Urban Infrastructure and Governance	10053.5	91.91	6839.73	92.22
(B) BSUP	Basic Services for the Urban Poor	885	8.1	577.2	7.78
TOTAL (A+B)	Total investment under JNNURM	10938.5	100	7416.93	100

Source- CDPs of Kochi and Thiruvananthapuram, 2006.

Investment Plans under JNNURM

CDPs of the Mission cities have clearly explained the strategy for urban development through the Mission in various sectors, and also the expected pattern of investment in various sectors. The structure of investment plan under the Mission reveals the skewed allocation of funds in the investment plan between the first Sub Mission of Urban Infrastructure and Governance and the second Sub Mission to ensure basic urban amenities to the poor. Financial layout across the various infrastructural sectors in the cities as stated in the CDPs of the cities is given in Table 3.5.

Examining the patterns of fund allocation in the CDPs of the Mission cities shows that the Sub-Mission for the urban infrastructure and governance were given very low priority as compared to the second Sub-Mission for the urban poor. When the shares of UIG in Kochi and Thiruvananthapuram were 91.9 percent and 92.2 percent respectively, the shares of BSUP in the investment project were mere 8.1 percent and 7.78 percent. In the background of the statistics given in the CDPs, the shares of the urban poor were as high as 35 percent and 17 percent in the two cities, the fund allocated under BSUP as per the plan is quite inadequate.

Population Distribution within the CDP areas of Mission cities

The city development plans of both the Mission cities in the state were submitted in 2006. The CDPs have not only covered the core city area but also the adjacent Municipalities and Panchayats which are expected to merge with the core city in the near future. The CDPs of Kochi and Thiruvananthapuram under JNNURM are analyzed separately.

Kochi

The city which is known as the commercial capital of the state is located on the shore of Arabian Sea. The emergence of the city as a commercial center in the South at present is closely linked with its historical background as an administrative center on the Malabar Coast. The history of the city as an

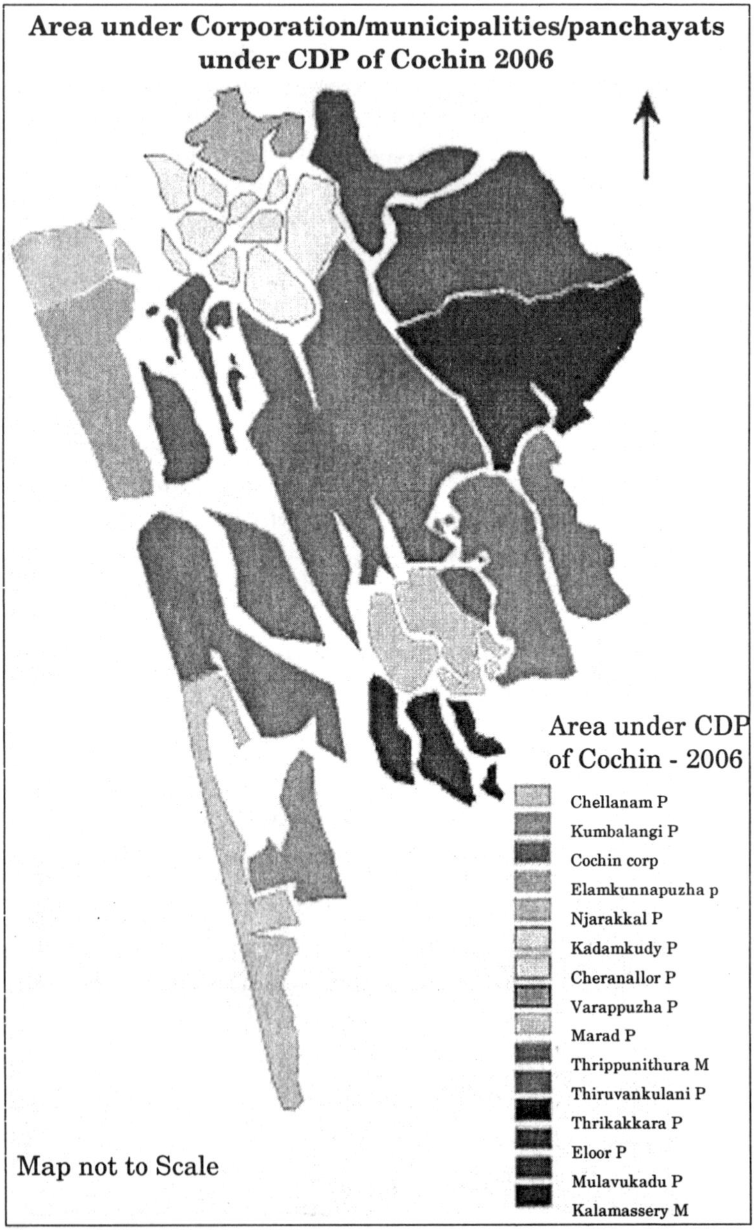

Source- CDP of Cochin 2006

Map 3.2

important center for trade and commerce can be traced well back to 1341 AD, when Kochi port came into existence. It gradually emerged as a major commercial center in South Asia. Kochi Municipal Corporation came into existence in 1967, incorporating the Municipalities of Fort Kochi, Mattanchery and Ernakulam. The first comprehensive plan for the city was prepared in 1976 which included the scientifically delineated plan for Kochi region. As expected, the secondary urban centers could not absorb the continuously growing population in the core city. The latest development plan for the city was prepared in 2006 under JNNURM.

Apart from the core Kochi Corporation area, the City Development Plan (CDP) prepared under JNNRUM for the city has included two adjacent Municipalities and thirteen adjacent Panchayats. This excludes few Municipalities and few Panchayats which are included under the Kochi Urban Agglomeration area. It is assumed that the thirteen Panchayats and two Municipalities which are included under the CDP will become a part of the core city in a decade or two. The distribution of population within the CDP area of the city and the decadal growth rate of population in each unit is given in Table 3.6

Thiruvananthapuram

Thiruvananthapuram erstwhile 'Trivandrum' is well known for its importance as an administrative center from the historical times dating back to 1000 BC. The name of the city which means 'the city of Lord Anantha' shows the religious importance of the city. With 7.5 lakh population residing in the city, it is the largest urban center in the state. As in the case of Kochi, Thiruvananthapuram is also located on the Coast of the Arabian Sea. The city is famous for its beaches like Kovalam and is one of the well known tourist destinations in the country. The geography of the city is characterized by undulating low coastal hills. Since the city was not an important commercial center in comparison to Kochi, Thiruvananthapuram benefitted very little from the British rule in terms of urban infrastructural development. At present, Thiruvananthapuram is a fast growing city and is well connected to all the important cities of the region.

Table 3.6 Distribution of Population within the CDP area of Kochi- 2001

Serial No:	*Name of the Administrative Unit*	*Population in 2001 (in 000s)*	*Population Growth Rate During 1991-2001*	*Density in per Hectare Area*	*Percentage Share in the Total Population in CDP Area*
1.	Kochi corporation area	596.5	5.65	63	51.9
2.	Kalamassery municipality	63.2	16.1	23	5.5
3.	Tripunithura municipality	59.9	17.2	32	5.2
4.	Thrikakkara Panchayat	66.0	28.9	21	5.7
5.	Thiruvankulam Panchayat	21.7	17.9	33	1.9
6.	Maradu Panchayat	41.0	17.2	13	3.6
7.	Mulavukadu Panchayat	22.8	2.3	28	2.0
8.	Kadamkudy Panchayat	15.8	7.9	13	1.4
9.	Varapuzha Panchayat	24.5	8.9	29	2.1
10.	Cheranalloor Panchayat	36.2	22.9	25	3.2
11.	Eloor Panchayat	35.6	3.2	25	3.1
12.	Elamkunnapuzha Panchayat	50.6	5.6	29	4.4
13.	Njarakkal Panchayat	24.2	8.2	19	2.1
14.	Kumbalam Panchayat	27.6	14.1	17	2.4
15.	Kumbalangi Panchayat	26.7	11.9	12	2.3
16.	Chelanam Panchayat	36.2	9.6	24	3.2

Source- CDP of Kochi, 2006.

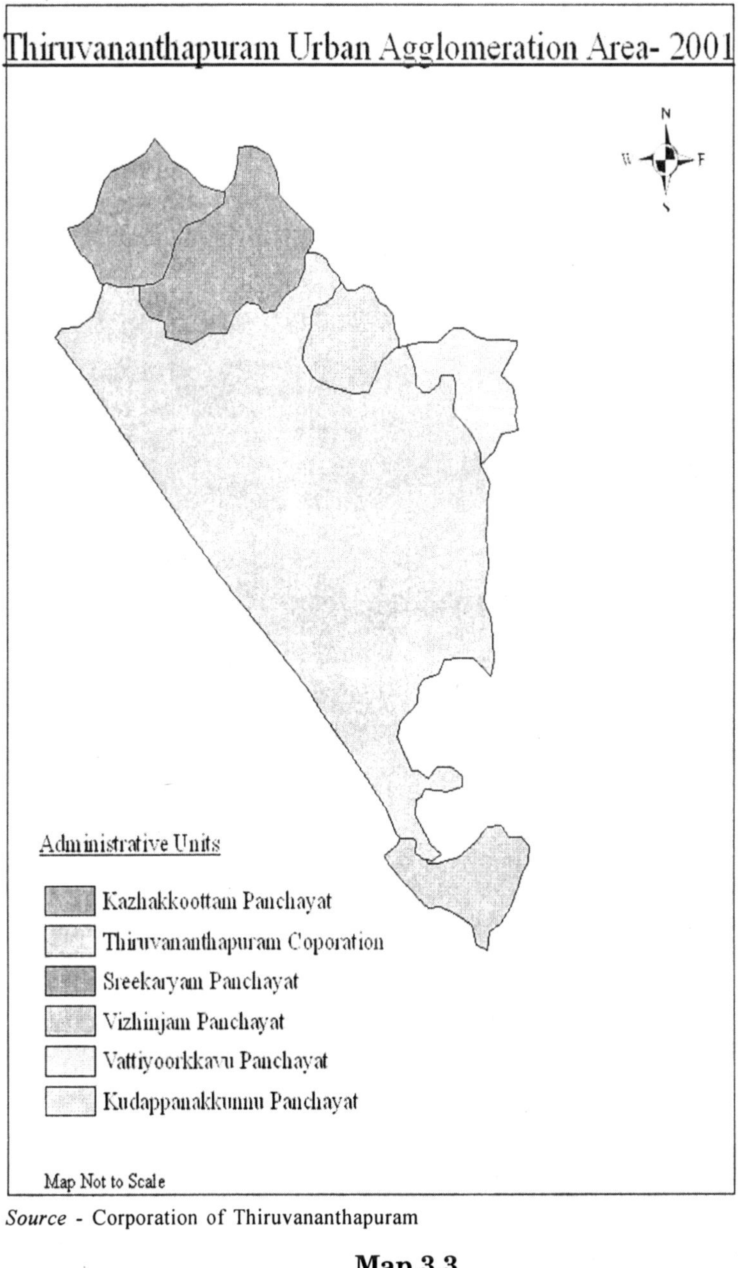

Source - Corporation of Thiruvananthapuram

Map 3.3

Table 3.7 Distribution of Population in the CDP area of Thiruvananthapuram in 2001

Sl No.	*Area*	*Population (in 000s)*	*Area (in sq km)*	*Density of Population (per sq km)*	*Share in the Total CDP Population*
1.	Thiruvananthapuram City	745	141.74	5256	83.7
2.	Kazhakkottam (Outgrowth)	14.4	5.03	2865	1.6
3.	Kudappanakkunnu (Outgrowth)	38.2	7.69	4964	4.3
4.	Sreekaryam (Outgrowth)	21.4	8.87	2416	2.4
5.	Vattiyoorkkavu (Outgrowth)	41.9	1.11	37739	4.7
6.	Kovalam (Outgrowth)	28.8	3.33	8632	3.2
	Total	889.6	177.77	5004	100

Source- CDP of Thiruvananthapuram, 2006.

Table 3.8 Distribution of Population in Thiruvananthapuram Urban Agglomeration-2001

Sl No:	*Name of Local Body*	*Total Population in 2001(0000s)*	*Density of Population (per sq km)*	*Population Growth rate during 1991-2001*
1.	Thiruvananthapuram Corporation	74.5	5256	5.68
2.	Kazhakkoottam Panchayat	3.4	1753	15.99
3.	Kudappanakkunnu Panchayat	3.8	4964	13.73
4.	Sreekaryam Panchayat	4.9	2071	16.9
5.	Vattiyoorkkavu Panchayat	4.2	3948	24.7
6.	Vizhinjam Panchayat	4.7	3738	11.09

In the recent decades, apart from the administrative importance of the city, it has gained importance as a major commercial center of the state. Setting up of Technopark in 1995, Construction of Mega Deep Water Trans-shipment Port at Vizhinjam, increasing military establishments, etc are some factors which have notably contributed to the growth of the city in the recent years. Realizing the fast growth of population, the first master plan for the city was prepared in 1966. Afterwards many modifications had to be introduced to the earlier plans to cope up with the fast growing population in the city core. The latest plan for the city was prepared under JNNURM in 2006. The area under the CDP of the city prepared under JNNURM coincides with the area of Thiruvananthapuram Urban Agglomeration.

Table 3.8 shows that the CDP area of Thiruvananthapuram consisted of the Corporation area and five outgrowths namely Kazhakkoottam, Kovalam, Sreekaryam, Kudappanakkunnu and Vattiyoorkkavu. Including the population in the outgrowths, the total population covered under the Mission in the city is 8.89 lakhs. The large share of the population covered under the Mission is from the core city itself, while the share of the peripheral region is only 16.3 percent. Instead of including the entire Panchayat areas in which outgrowths of the city fall in, the CDP has included only the outgrowths.

Density of population within Thiruvananthapuram Urban Agglomeration was highest in the core area and was followed by the Panchayats of Vattiyoorkkavu, Vizhinjam and Kudappanakkunnu. A close look at the density of population in the CDP area reveals that in spite of covering only 1.1 sq km area, the urban outgrowth named Vattiyoorkkavyu had the highest density and was several times higher than the density of the core city. Beside Vattiyoorkkavu outgrowth, the outgrowth in Kovalam also had experienced a higher density of population as compared to that of the Thiruvananthapuram Corporation area. Other three outgrowths of the city also had high density of population in 2001. The population growth pattern within the CDP area has revealed the increasing concentration of population in the peripheral areas of the city rather than in the core area.[15]

Progress of Urban Infrastructure and Governance (UIG) in Kerala

Under the Sub-Mission of Urban Infrastructure and Governance various sets of projects were undertaken in the state. The total number of the Detailed Project Reports (DPRs) submitted by the state was 23 in which only 10 projects were approved by the GoI. In both the Mission cities, no projects were completed in the first four years of the Mission. For better understanding, the progress of the urban infrastructure projects under the Mission can be analyzed separately for Kochi and Thiruvananthapuram.

Progress of Urban Infrastructure and Governance (UIG) in Kochi

The city is one of the fast growing urban centers in the state. The progress of the infrastructure projects in the various sectors can be briefly explained as follows :

Solid Waste Management : Under JNNURM, a solid waste treatment plant was completed at Brahmapuram, while the Refused Derived Fuel (R.D.F) plant is under construction. The other projects undertaken in this sector include sanitary land filling, fence construction, effluent treatment plant, laboratory construction, etc. In order to maintain these services, many instruments, trucks, etc. also were purchased. Two DPRs in the same sector for Thripunithara and Kalamassery Municipalities had been already sent for approval.

Urban Transportation : Under this sector, the projects which got approval are urban road transport (4 stretches), stadium-link road and rail over bridge (3 points). Prior to the preparation of the DPR, city mobility plan (a well comprehensive study on the urban transport of the CDP area) for Kochi was prepared by Water and Power Consultancy Services India Limited (WAPCOS). The construction of the various stretches of roads is in the initial stages that the surveying did not begin until the end of 2009. To modernize the urban transport, ULB has got the approval from the center to purchase 200 Volvo, A.C and low floor buses. The DPR of this project was prepared by (National Transportation Planning and Research Center (NATPAC)[16] and the project has reached only the tendering stage.

Drainage : There are 18 stretches of the drainage network which are included in the first phase of drainage development. In this, construction of four stretches is over while those of some other stretches is under progress.

Water Supply: The first DPR in water supply sector has got the approval of Government of India (GoI). The projects under the water supply sector are fully under the supervision and the guidance of the Kerala Water Authority. The first phase of the project includes the subcomponents to improve water supply in selected parts of the city and also in case of the surrounding Panchayats like Maradu, Kumbalangi, Kumbalam, Chellanam, etc. The project which is divided into twelve parts is mostly in the stage of tendering while five parts have already got the tenders successfully.

*Sewerage :*The projects in this sector mainly concentrate on the methods to improve the sewerage facilities in Central part of the city and it is estimated to benefit 1.9 lakhs of people. In this project, the waste water of the houses from the domestic underground sewerage pipes will be collected and pumped to the sewerage treatment plant. The project has got the approval from the central government and is in the stage of retendering.

Heritage : One DPR of this sector is under preparation by the private agency C-Hed. The DPR of the 30 crores project was submitted to the GoI in the beginning of 2009 and even after almost one year, it did not get the approval from the centre. This shows the long delay in the implementation of various projects because of the long official formalities associated in each stage of project progress.

E-governance : Kochi is one of the 37 cities under the Mission which were chosen by the GoI for e-governance. The DPR of the project got the approval from the central government. The project which was undertaken by M/S Wipro aims to modernize accounts related to eight major areas of urban governance in the first phase and to modernize the rest in the later stages.

Fund Allocated under UIG in Kochi

The share of the fund allocated under the Sub-Mission of Urban Infrastructure and Governance (UIG), in the City Development Plan of the city is 91.9 percent. The investment plan in the CDP of the city shows that close to 10000 crores was planned to be invested in various sectors of urban infrastructure in the city during the Mission period.

Figure 3.6 shows that among the various urban infrastructural sectors, solid waste management has the highest share of the funds allocated in comparison to the planned investment. The share of the approved fund was very low in the case of sectors like storm water drainage, sewerage, etc. At the same time, it has to be also noticed that no fund was approved in the sectors like environment, urban renewal and heritage and tourism, etc.

Table 3.9 Fund Allocation under Urban Infrastructure and Governance in Kochi till November 2009

Areas of Urban Infrastructure and Governance	*Fund Allocation Under UIG in Kochi City (in Rs. Crores)*				
	Total Fund Allocated Under CDP (for seven years)	*Funds Planned to be Invested as per CDP in First 4 years*	*Approved Cost*	*Funds Utilized*	*Percentage of Fund Utilisation*
Water supply	1216.7	333.96	201.17	0.13	0.06
Sewerage	2629	804.3	78.41	0.13	0.16
Storm Water Drainage	902	534.4	9.78	2.21	22.6
Environment	291	135.95	-	-	-
Solid Waste Management	152.4	113.77	88.12	22.34	25.35
Traffic and Transportation	4252	2826	180.64	6.74	3.73
Urban Renewal	295.5	155.5	-	-	-
Heritage and Tourism	360.85	201.45	-	-	-
Urban Governance Reforms	5	3.2	8.71	-	-
Investment under Urban Infrastructure and Governance	10053.5	5136.14	566.83	31.53	5.56

Source- Kochi Corporation Office, 2009 November.

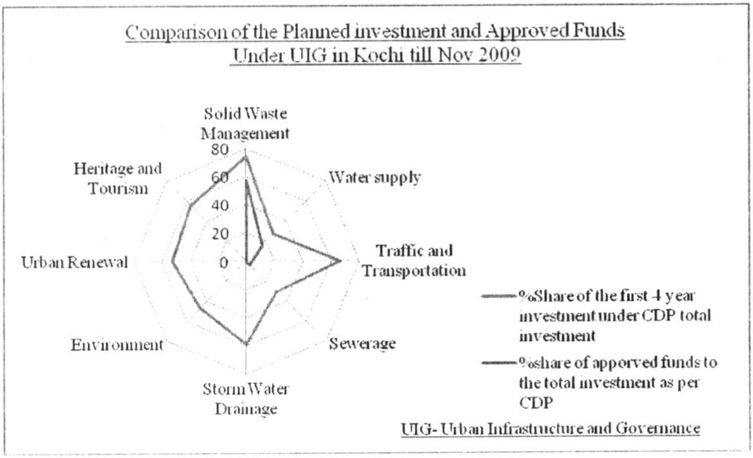

Figure 3.6

Figure 3.7 illustrates that the level of fund utilisation from the approved funds was very low across all the infrastructural sectors in the city. This is in spite of the fact that the share of the approved funds in comparison to the investments as per the CDP within four years itself was very

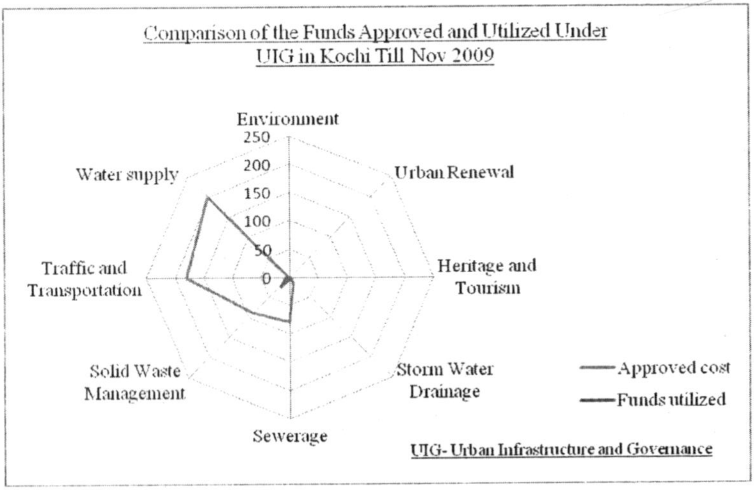

Figure 3.7

low. The percentage share of the funds utilized from the total approved funds was close to 5.6 percent. In comparison to the rest of the sectors, the level of fund utilization was highest in the case of solid waste management (26 percent) and is followed by storm water drainage (23 percent). Despite being the sector with the highest share of the funds released under the Mission, fund utilization was the lowest in case of water supply sector (0.06 percent) and is followed by sewerage sector (0.16 percent). On the other hand, in the sectors like environment, urban renewal, heritage and tourism etc., no DPRs were approved in the first four years of the Mission.

In general, the above analysis of the financial status of JNNURM projects in Kochi shows that the progress of the various infrastructural sectors varied widely within the city. Under JNNURM, Solid Waste Management sector could make remarkable progress in the city while the sectors like Urban renewal, environment, heritage and tourism could not make investments through the Mission. These sectors did not have any project approved until the end of 2009.

Progress of Urban Infrastructure and Governance (UIG) in Thiruvananthapuram

The city is well known from the historical times mainly in terms of its religious and administrative importance. The sector wise progress of the urban infrastructure projects undertaken through JNNURM is given below.

Solid Waste Management : The thrust areas of the project under this sector are primary waste collection and storage, transfer station, transportation, basic infrastructure and finally treatment and disposal of the waste. The amount approved for the project was 40.4 crore. The main projects included under this sector are leech ate plant, Refused Derived Fuel (RDF) plant and Landfill. The work of the leech ate plant has already begun and the Corporation officials said that the work is expected to finish by the end of 2009. But it has to be also noticed that as per DPR of the project, the work was estimated to be finished in March 2009. The other projects in the sector have not begun till date.

Sewerage : The progress of the projects under this sector is undergoing two phases and both the phases have got the approval of the central government. The sewerage treatment plant is under construction in Muttamthura coastal area. The area which will be covered under the sewerage network in the first phase is close to 64 sq km. The land will be acquired from various parts of the CDP area to construct sub pumping stations from where the waste water will be pumped into the main plant. The owners of the land will have to lease the land to the Corporation for the next 50 years and will be paid back not in money but in kind. The first phase of the project will cover the areas like Attippara, Kadamappally, Karimanal, Poonthura, Beemappally, Pappanam code, etc. which are not covered in the present sewerage network.

Storm water drainage : The main areas which are covered under the storm water drainage project are Aamayizhanjan thodu, Pazhavangadi thodu, Thampanoor and East fort area. Drainage facility is very poor in the city as a whole. The Thampanoor area where the central railway station is located in the city gets flooded very frequently in the rainy season. Though many other projects were there earlier in the sector, none of them were successful. The main problem while undertaking any storm water drainage project in the city especially in the Thampanoor area is in terms of the inclusion of the various stake holders.

Traffic and transportation : No DPRs for urban transport were approved in the city during the first four years of the Mission. Though the first DPR for the sector was prepared and submitted in the second half of 2008, it has not got approval from the Central Government. The DPR for the second phase has yet not got finalized though it had been first prepared in 2008. To modernize urban transport in the city 150 low floor and air conditioned buses were approved by the central government. The routes for the buses were decided with the consultation of ward representatives and taking into consideration factors like road width, traffic flow, etc. But until November 2009 no companies have bid the project.

Water supply : The nodal agency for the implementation of the schemes in this sector is Kerala Water Authority (KWA). The components under the project are strengthening the distribution system and rehabilitation works. In this 60 percent of the strengthening of the distribution system is completed while the tendering and negotiations are going on in the case of the other projects. In the twenty-three total contracts in the first phase of the project, only nine were already awarded. The project as a whole is expected to be completed within July 2010. The length of the pipe connection in the CDP area in 2006 was only 413 km and JNNURM water supply project in the first phase is estimated to add another 692 kilometers of water supply services in the existing area. Other projects which were under revision or waiting for approvals were Traffic and transportation, Social infrastructure project (Market), heritage and tourism, etc. In case of the later three sectors, the agencies which prepared the DPRs were asked to revise the DPRs as per JNNURM norms. Though the DPR for the tourism sector was submitted to GoI in 2008, it did not get the approval until the end of 2009.

Fund Allocated under UIG in Thiruvananthapuram

Under the Sub-Mission of UIG, the share of the total funds allocated as per the CDP in the city was 92.22 percent. During the Mission period of seven years, roughly 6900 crores was planned to be invested in urban infrastructure and governance reforms in the city. Figure 3.12 illustrating the share of the funds approved in four years in comparison to the investment planned under CDP shows that solid waste management sector could make remarkable progress under JNNURM as compared to all other sectors. Within the first four years, close to 65 percent of the total planned investment in the sector during the Mission period was approved. The other sectors which have received noteworthy share of the funds approved in comparison to the investment plan in CDP are sewerage, water supply and storm water drainage.

The sectors like Environment, Heritage and Tourism, etc had planned to release roughly 90 percent of the total

Table 3.10 Fund Allocation under Urban Infrastructure and Governance in Thiruvananthapuram till November 2009

Areas	*Fund Allocation Under UIG in Thiruvananthapuram*				
	Total Fund Allocated Under CDP for Seven Years, (Rs in Crores)	*Funds Planned to be Released as per CDP in First 4 Years (Rs in Crores)*	*Approved Cost (Rs in Crores)*	*Funds Utilized (Rs in Crores)*	*Percent of Fund Utilization*
Water supply	1041.41	533.35	87.16	15.70	18.0
Sewerage	1081	931.5	336.56	3.80	1.12
Storm Water Drainage	175.75	155.41	40.39	.12	0.29
Environment	24.33	22.73	-	-	-
Solid Waste Management	51	38.92	24.56	1.69	6.86
Traffic and Transportation	3786.54	2289.26	53.40	5.07	9.5
Urban Renewal	200	NA	-	-	-
Heritage and Tourism	322.4	285.9	-	-	-
Investment under Urban Infrastructure and Governance	6839.73	4357.07	542.07	26.37	4.86

Source- Thiruvananthapuram Corporation Office, November 2009

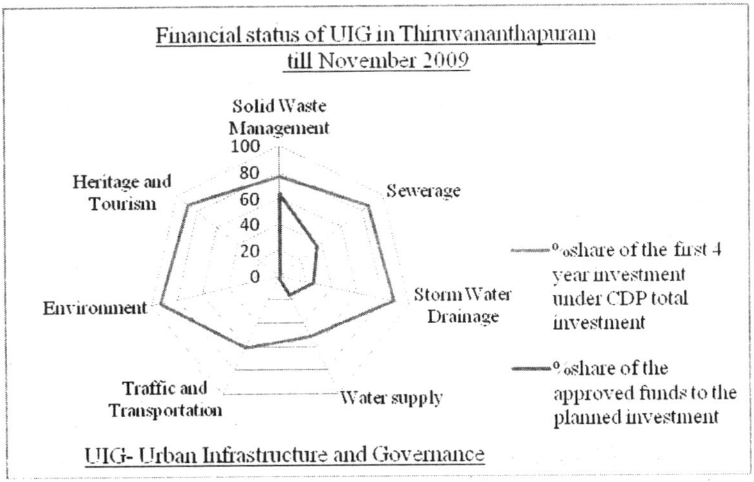

Figure 3.8 Comparison of Planned Mission Investment and Approved Fund- Thiruvananthapuram till November 2009

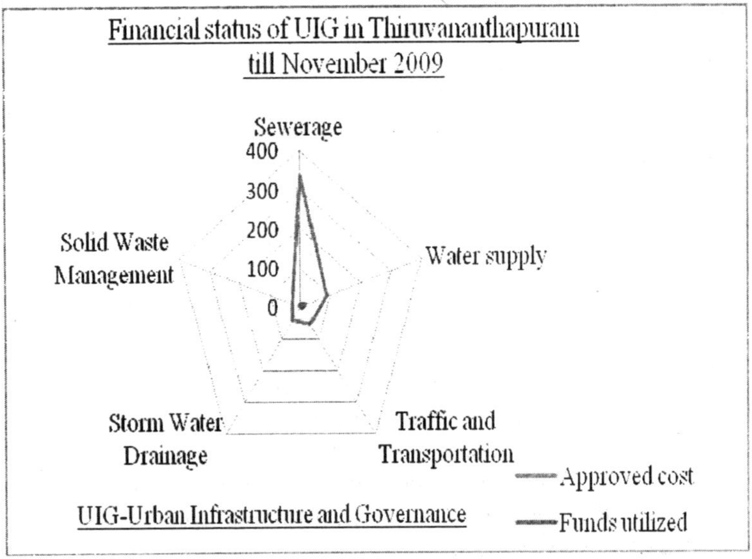

Figure 3.9 Comparison of approved and utilized funds UIG in Thiruvananthapuram till November 2009

investment through the Mission in the first four years. Quite disappointingly, these sectors could not have funds approved under the Mission until the end 2009. This reveals the very poor progress of the projects in most of the sectors. It also hints towards the fact that in comparison to the CDP vision of the city regarding the sectors like environment, tourism, heritage, etc the chances to materialize the Mission aims are not bright.

The level of fund utilization under the Sub Mission as a whole was close to 5 percent in city which shows the very poor progress of the Mission projects. The corresponding share was the highest in case of water supply (18 percent) and was followed by traffic and transportation (9.5 percent) and solid waste management (6.8 percent). The sectors like environment, urban renewal and heritage and tourism did not have any projects approved in the first four years of the Mission. Despite being the sector with the highest approved fund, sewerage has very low level of fund utilization. Similarly, solid waste management, the sector with comparatively high share of the funds approved in comparison to the CDP investment plan, had one of the lowest levels of fund utilization. The analysis of the various projects and fund allocation under the Urban Infrastructure and Governance Sub-Mission in Thiruvananthapuram city proves the very slow progress of the Mission projects. The sector which could make appreciable achievements under the Mission is Solid waste management. Though not remarkable, the other sectors which were able to make investments through the Mission were water supply, sewerage and traffic and transportation.

Comparative progress of UIG in the Mission cities of Kerala

A comparative assessment on the performance of the Mission cities in the state under the Sub-Mission for urban infrastructure and governance can be done from the data given in Table 3.10. It has included various aspects through which the degree of success of the city in implementing the Mission projects can be evaluated.

The statistics on the fund allocation under UIG clearly shows that the actual investment which was made in both the

Table 3.11 Various Aspects on the Progress of Urban Infrastructure and Governance in the Mission Cities of Kerala till November 2009

Various Aspects on UIG	*Mission Cities*		
	Kochi	*Thiruvananthapuram*	*Kerala*
Projects undertaken under UIG	5	5	10
Percentage share of city in funds released to total funds released in the country under UIG	0.56	0.41	0.97
Percentage share of population covered in the CDP area of the city to total population covered under Mission	1.26	0.83	2.09
Ratio between the funds released and the population share	.45	0.50	.45
Percentage share of funds utilized to the CDP investment layout for 4 years	0.61	.60	.61
Percent funds approved as share of the CDP layout for 4 years	11.03	12.44	11.68
Percentage of funds utilized from the approved funds	5.56	4.86	5.22
Investment actually made in urban infrastructure per 1000 population in four years (Rs in lakhs)	2.75	2.96	2.84
Investment planned to be made in urban infrastructure per 1000 population in four years (Rs in lakhs)	447	489	465

Source- CDPs 2006 and Corporation Offices of Kochi, Thiruvananthapuram.

cities in urban infrastructure through JNNURM was negligible as compared to the planned investment as mentioned in the CDPs. When we take into account the share of the approved funds in the total amount of the funds to be invested (as per the CDPs), Thiruvananthapuram performed better than Kochi. In the total funds which had to be invested within the first four years of the Mission, 12.4 percent of the funds were approved in the case of Thiruvananthapuram while the corresponding share was close to 11 percent in case of Kochi. The share of the invested funds in urban infrastructure in comparison to the planned investment is roughly 0.6 percent in both the cities. The Mission cities in the state covers more than 2 percent of the total population covered under the Mission, while the share of the state in funds released under the Mission was only 0.94 percent. The very low ratio of the state between the share of the funds allocated under UIG and the share of population covered under the Mission shows the slow progress of UIG projects in Kerala.

According to the CDPs of the cities, it was expected that Rs 4.47 crores and Rs 4.89 crores will be invested per 1000 population in Kochi and Thiruvananthapuram during the first four years of the Mission. But the actual investment made in urban infrastructure in the four years is abysmally low, only 2.75 lakh rupees and 2.96 lakh rupees per 1000 population. The share of the funds which were actually invested in comparison to the total planned share of the funds which had to be invested within the first four years of the Mission is very low, i.e. close to 0.6 percent. If we assume that the proposed investment as given in the CDPs is essential to overcome the current shortages in urban infrastructure, it cannot be expected that the Mission will be able to solve the major portion of the shortages in urban infrastructure in these two cities.

Figure 3.10 clearly illustrates that the funds approved as compared to the planned investment through the Mission varied widely across the sectors. This share was highest in solid waste management. They were as high as 78 percent and 63 percent in Kochi and Thiruvanathapuram. Though, it may not appear

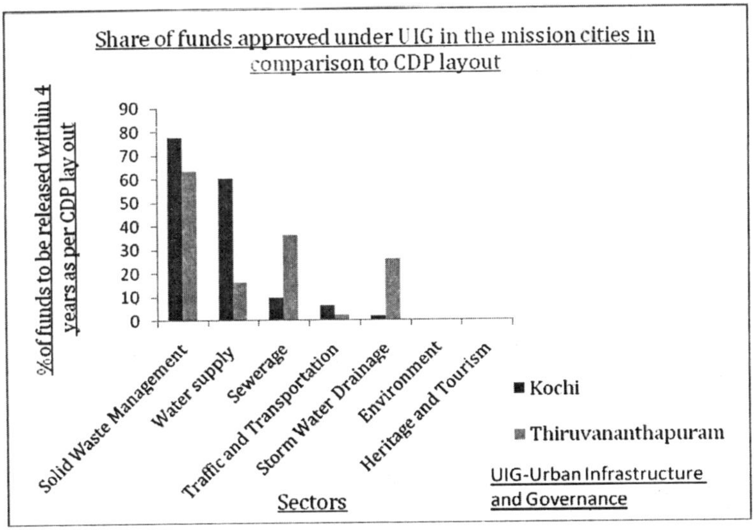

Figure 3.10

to be appealing, in consideration to the share of the funds released in comparison to the investment plan in other sectors, solid waste management sector has made remarkable achievement. Kochi is ahead of Thiruvananthapuram in the case of sectors like solid waste management, water supply, traffic and transportation, etc. On the other hand, Thiruvanathapuram is ahead of Kochi in the sectors like sewerage and drainage. In the state as a whole, no projects in the sectors like 'environment', 'tourism', 'heritage', etc. were approved in the first four years of the Mission. The low share of the funds approved as compared to the planned investment in both the cities points out the various capacity constraints of the ULBs.

The progress of the cities under the Sub-Mission can also be analyzed in terms of the share of funds utilized from the approved funds. The Solid Waste Management sector had the highest level of fund utilization in the case of Kochi while it is water supply sector in the case of Thiruvananthapuram. Figure 3.16 shows that the utilization of the approved funds varied widely across the sectors as well as across the cities. This can

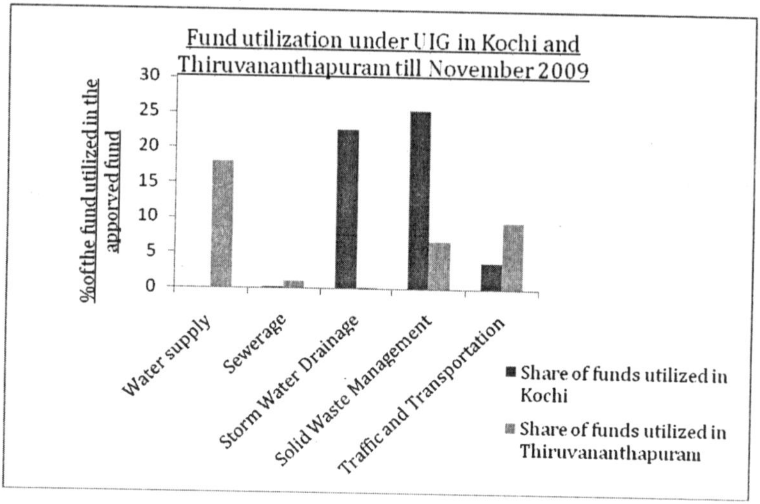

Figure 3.11

be clearly understood from the fact that when storm water drainage sector had one of the highest level of fund utilization in Kochi (22.6 percent), the corresponding fund utilization was abysmally low (0.29 percent) in case of Thiruvananthapuram city. Similarly, the level of the fund utilization in Thiruvananthapuram was highest in the case of water supply sector (18 percent) whose corresponding fund utilization was almost negligible (0.06 percent) in Kochi. Sewerage sector had very low level of fund utilization of the approved funds in both the Mission cities. (0.16 percent and 1.12 percent) and was followed by traffic and transportation sector.

Perhaps the best way to assess the overall success of any program is to examine the actual fund invested against the funds planned to be invested within a specific time period. This shows the extent to which the ULB was able to make real investments in specified areas as against the investment plans. Figure 3.14 illustrates the percentage share of the utilized fund as compared to the CDP layout. It shows clearly the fact that in both the cities, the actual investment in the urban infrastructure was very low in all the sectors. The only exception to this is the solid waste management sector. There is a wide

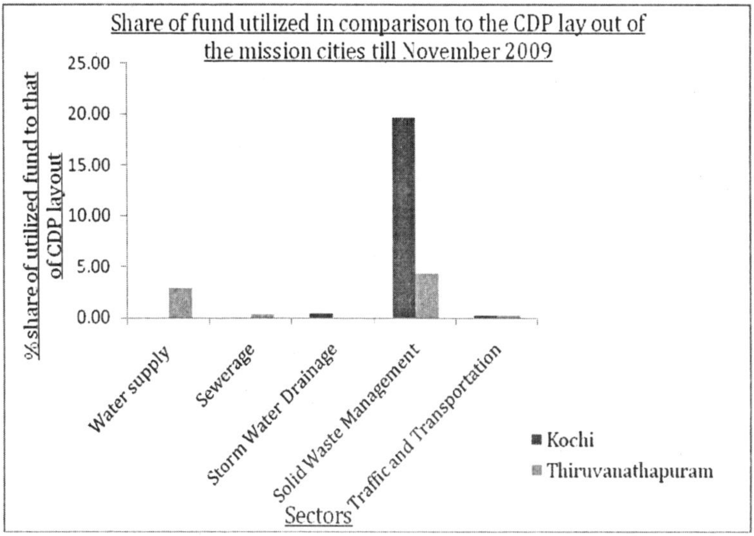

Figure 3.12

gap between the cities as well as across the various infrastructural sectors in the level of investment made through JNNURM.

The sector wise assessment of the investment under the Mission shows that in case of both the Mission cities, the highest investment through the Mission in comparison to the planned investment was made in solid waste management. Under the same sector, the investment made in Kochi is much higher than that of the investment made in Thiruvananthapuram. Except in the case of solid waste management (in the case of both the cities) and water supply (only in the case of Thiruvananthapuram), the actual investment in urban infrastructure through the Mission in the state is very negligible in the first four years.

From the above analysis it is clear that solid waste management sector could make remarkable progress through the Mission in both the cities. This can be traced to the active involvement of the local people in the various activities especially in service delivery. The waste is collected from the various parts of the city every day by the *Kudumbasree* workers. It enabled the active participation of the common people especially women in the provision and management of this service. The most important aspects of this kind of an arrangement for waste collection is that along with improving cleanliness of the urban area, it has economically empowered the women from the lower strata. An amount of Rs.30 per household has to be paid to the ULB for providing the service from which the wages of the women engaged in the collection of waste are paid. This user charge is paid by the users on a monthly basis. In Thiruvananthapuram city itself, around 850 women are engaged in the collection of the waste on a door to door basis at present. However, all the households in the city are not covered under this service as either they are not willing to pay for the service or they have some other option for waste disposal. The field observations and the analysis of the field work data shows that even a good number of people from the lower income categories were also covered under the paid services as they desperately want to improve the living

Performance of Kochi and Thiruvananthapuram under UIG Till November 2009

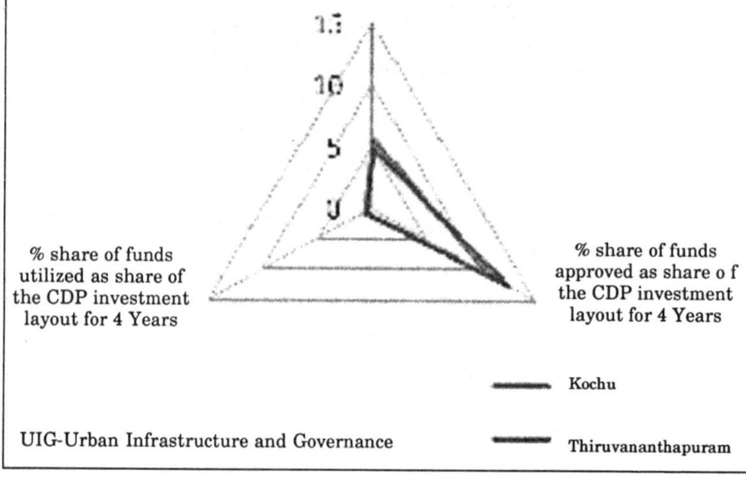

Figure 3.13

conditions in the slums. But when there was open space available for waste disposal near the slums, most of the households did not avail of the service. The best example is of Ernakulam Railway Goods colony.

The above analysis on the progress of the Sub-Mission of Urban Infrastructure and Governance in the state has revealed the very slow pace of the Mission projects. The very low ratios between the share in total funds released and the share in the population covered under the Mission, shows that the cities were unsuccessful in getting investment in proportion to their population size. A balance ratio show a value close to '1', but the ratios are only 0.45 for Kochi as well as for the entire state and 0.50 for Thiruvananthapuram. It has to be also remembered that the cities like Pune, Surat, Vadodara, etc. have a ratio above two. At the state level also, the large states like Gujarat, Andhra Pradesh and Maharashtra have a ratio well above 1. Thus, it is clear that in comparison to many other states, Kerala has performed disappointingly in the creation of urban infrastructure under JNNURM during the first four years of the Mission.

Challenges of UIG in the Mission cities

There are numerous challenges that the state is facing at present under the UIG Sub-Mission. Some of them are the following :

- The high cost of construction materials especially of sand in the area (costs around 55000 per truck). This is the most important challenge in getting the tender at the approved cost. Since most of the projects were approved far back, tendering is one of the major problems at present. The prices of the materials used for construction have gone very high as compared to that of the prices when the project funds were approved. Due to this problem no agencies are coming forward to accept the tender at the approved rates. For eg., in the water supply scheme in Thiruvananthapuram the tender excess was as high as 180 percent. In some projects in Kochi, the tender excess is as high as 400 percent. Due to this problem many of the projects which were approved by the Government of India (GoI) far back could not pass even the tender stage.

- Lack of technically qualified staff for the implementation and for other related works is a major reason for the long delays in the project under UIG in the state. For instance, though the number of engineers needed for JNNURM wing in Thiruvananthapuram Corporation is 20, only 3 engineers are there.

- Lack of technical knowledge of the available staff in the ULBs is another constraint in the various stages of project implementation.

- Lack of initiatives from the private investors or contractors due to various reasons like low profitability and the long delay of the projects is another reason for the slow progress of the projects. For e.g., sewerage scheme in Thiruvananthapuram city was tendered twice with no response. In both the cities, many projects had got the approval from the center far back. But due to the long delay in getting the tender from the private companies after the approval of the projects, only few projects have begun in the state.

- Land acquisition issues in the implementation of various projects are other problems in the Mission cities especially in Kochi where even a small piece of land costs several millions of rupees. The land which has to be acquired even for a single project costs many crores.

Conclusion

The analysis of the Sub-Mission of Urban Infrastructure and Governance (UIG) in the Mission cities of Kerala leads to the following conclusions :

- Taking consideration of the population growth pattern in the Mission cities, the area included under the CDP of Thiruvananthapuram is found to be inadequate to plan for the city in a sustainable manner. Along with the core city, the CDP has included only the outgrowths of the city which have already experienced high population growth in the last decades.

- The peripheral areas have also benefitted from the Mission projects to a large extent especially in the sectors like water supply, transportation, drainage, etc. But the degree to which these areas have got the benefits through JNNURM could not be studied due to paucity of data.

- The analysis of the data proved that there is wide inter city and intra city variation in the pattern of fund allocation under JNNURM. Kochi is ahead of Thiruvananthapuram in the degree of utilization of approved funds as well as in the share of actual investment made in urban infrastructure as compared to the planned investment given in the CDPs. The main reason for the better performance of Kochi is because of its ability to attract private investments as it is the center of commercial activities in the state, standing much ahead of Thiruvananthapuram.

- The performance of the cities in Kerala under UIG is appalling in comparison to many other Mission cities. The share of the invested funds in urban infrastructure as compared to the planned investment is roughly 0.6 percent in both the cities. Because of the various capacity constraints, both the cities could utilize only 5 percent of the total released funds under the urban infrastructure Sub-Mission. At the present level of progress, it cannot be expected that the cities will be able to overcome the present challenges in urban infrastructure delivery through JNNURM.

- In both the cities, solid waste management sector has performed far ahead of the other sectors. Though not significant. The other sector where investment could be made under JNNURM in the cities is water supply. The investments in other infrastructural sectors which were mainly dependent on private sector investment were negligible or absent.

- Irrespective of the economic conditions, a good number of the slum households are covered under the solid waste management service in both the cities. They are willing to pay for the service as they believe there are no other options to better their living condition than to get the paid service. It was also noticed that irrespective of the level of income, the families residing in slums located near vacant public land, do not avail the paid service as they have the option to dump the waste in the open space.

- The main reason for the success of solid waste management sector in the state is the active participation of the common people in various activities involving service delivery. Besides creating numerous low skilled jobs, these activities have also empowered the women economically and socially. Door to door waste collection by these women has made the service delivery efficient.

- Severe shortage in the number of technically qualified staff in the JNNURM wing of the ULBs is another problem the Mission cities in Kerala are facing at present. This further delays the project implementation making it more difficult to get the bids successfully from the private investors for various projects.

References

1. Kannan, K.P. (Sep. 1-8, 1990), "Kerala Economy at the Crossroads?", *Economic and Political Weekly,* Vol. 25, No. 35/36, p. 1958.
2. Urban Policy, 2002, Government of Kerala, http://www. 'kerala.gov.in/annual profile/urban.htm.
3. 'Annual plan 2007-2008', Kerala State Planning Board, p. 412.
4. Charvak, (July 2000), 'From decentralization of planning to people's planning; Experiences of the Indian states of West Bengal and Kerala, CDS, Discussion paper No. 21, p. 57.

5. Sharma, R. (Sep. 6-12, 2003), "Kerala's Decentralisation: Idea in Practice", *Economic and Political Weekly*, Vol. 38, No. 36, p. 3847.
6. Heller, P. (2000), "Degrees of democracy: Some comparative lessons from India", *World Politics*, Vol. 52, No.4, p. 512.
7. Sreekumar, T.T. (1993): "Urban Process in Kerala", CDS, Thiruvananthapuram, p. 127.
8. Epen, M. (1999), "Economic deiversification; A spatial analysis", Working paper no. 293, CDS, Thiruvananthapuram, p. 30.
9. *Ibid.*, p. 5.
10. Economic Review of Kerala, (2006), Kerala State Planning Board, http://www.keralaplanningboard.org/, p. 295.
11. City Development Plan of Kochi prepared under JNNURM, (2006), Prepared by the Corporation of Kochi, p. 34.
12. Economic Review of Kerala, (2006), Kerala State Planning Board, http://www.keralaplanningboard.org/, p. 298.
13. 'Special evaluation study on urban sector strategy and operations', (June 2006), Asian Development Bank, p. 38.
14. Kannan, K.P. (Sep. 1-8, 1990), "Kerala Economy at the Crossroads?", *Economic and Political Weekly,* Vol. 25, No. 35/36 p. 1955.
15. CDP, (2006), Thiruvananthapuram Corporation.
16. A State Public Sector Enterprise for undertaking research and consultancy works in the various fields of traffic engineering and transportation planning, including their impact on environment and population.

4

Basic Services and Urban Poor in Kerala

Introduction

Poverty is a major constraint which has direct control over the capabilities that one possesses and the freedom he enjoys. It delimits the functions that one can perform at various realms of life and thus acts like a strong chain which restricts personal development.[1] Thus, poverty alleviation measures are regarded as of crucial importance for the overall development of a nation of state. From the beginning of the five year planning, poverty alleviation was one of the areas of major stress in the country. Over a period of six decades numerous changes have come up in the nature of these poverty alleviation programmes, especially in the mechanisms and the agencies involved. Through several schemes, Government of India has succeeded to a great extent in reducing poverty through out the country, especially in the urban areas.[2]

Incorporating provisions to meet the basic amenities for urban poor in the urban development strategies is a major challenge in the developing countries.[3] It is explicit that poverty alleviation schemes improve the living of the poor only if these schemes enable them to expand their capability through ensuring minimum access to positive resources needed to develop these capabilities.[4] In the recent years, in order to achieve the highly ambitious 'millennium development goals' by 2015, Government of India as well as many state governments have taken several steps to achieve a faster decline in poverty in which Basic Services of the Urban Poor (BSUP) initiated by the Government of India is a major one. BSUP attempts to ensure the minimum standard of urban amenities to the entire urban population and thus to enhance their capabilities.

Kerala is well known for its peculiar development model for which we cannot find an equal match anywhere in the country. From the First Five Year Plan, the share of the funds allocated for social services in the state had been close to 1/4th of the entire outlay, while in the country as a whole it ranged from 14 percent-17 percent.[5] The high social development achieved by the state, in spite of its poor economic development caught the attention of researchers and policy makers even at the international level. The 'Kerala model' is often compared with the development model adopted by the countries like Sri Lanka.[6] From the time of the formation of the state on 1st November 1956, the state is known for the various initiatives it has taken in the area of poverty alleviation and to improve the standard of living of the less privileged groups of the society. The recent studies show that the state stands ahead of rest of the country in terms of effective implementation of the anti poverty schemes.[7] The success of the Public Distribution System is a good example for this. The share of the population living below the poverty line in the state as a whole is 15 percent (49.6 lakhs). The percentage shares of the urban and the rural poor separately are 20.2percent (17.2 lakhs) and 13.2percent (32.4 lakhs).[8]

The high priority that the social development sector gets in the development strategy adopted by the state is clearly visible from the pattern of sectoral investment in the state. It is mainly in the area of housing that the state has initiated various schemes for the betterment of the urban poor. 'The statistics shows that about 80 percent of the financial support that the state government had provided has gone to the Economically Weaker Sections (EWS). Despite this, presence of a large number of houseless population in the state shows the failure of the state in the implementation of the housing schemes. It proves that the present structure of the housing schemes is unsuitable to the needs of the urban poor. Without supporting the poor to empower themselves with entitlements for procuring inputs from the market it is unlikely that these housing schemes with the present system of partial financial support will achieve goals.'[9]

The urban poverty alleviation programs in the state were mainly funded by the central or by the state governments or in combination of both. Some of the important urban poverty alleviation programs in Kerala are National Slum Development Program (NSDP), Valmiki Ambedkar Aavaas Yojna (VAMBAY), Urban Basic Services for the Poor (UBSP), 20 point program, Mythri housing scheme, EMS housing scheme, Bhavanasree housing scheme, Matsyafed housing scheme, Department for International Development (DFID) of UK funded project. The first four programs were sponsored by the GoI, the latter four are fully sponsored by the state government and the last project is sponsored by the Department for International Development (DFID) of UK government. Compared to these programs for urban poverty alleviation, BSUP has the following merits :

(a) Under BSUP every beneficiary gets 120000 for building an individual house. Against this, the money that the beneficiaries were given under National Slum Development Program (NSDP) and Valmiki Ambedkar Awas Yojana (VAMBAY) were only 30000 and 40000 respectively which were meager in comparison to the actual construction cost.

(b) Under BSUP, the lower levels of governance institutions have much more decision making power in the structuring of various developmental programs. Under the programs like NSDP and VAMBAY, the minimum and maximum shares of the funds used for upgrading the houses and for other activities were clearly defined. There is not such strict direction from the center in case of BSUP in utilizing the funds.

(c) BSUP has tried to capture a wider perspective of urban poverty than the previous programmes. It is neither merely an urban housing programme, nor merely a slum development programme.

(d) It enables very active participation of the common people in the various stages of project implementation, beneficiary selection, etc. Under BSUP, the power to make the major decisions on fund utilization and to prioritize various projects to improve the living condition is mainly entrusted with the ULBs, the urban governance body at the grass root level.

(e) In all the previous schemes for alleviation of urban poverty, the Subsidy part of the housing and other loans to improve the income of urban poor was comparatively much lower than that in BSUP. The National Slum Development Programme which had collaboration with NABARD had very little impact in achieving the objectives of the programmes. The *Kudumbasree* officials held that in most of the instances, the beneficiaries were not in a position to repay the loans and their economic condition was further worsened.

(f) BSUP does not enforce the ULBs across the country to accept a common method for beneficiary selection. For example, beneficiary selection under VAMBAY which was an urban housing programme in the slums, the GoI had strictly defined "slum" as given in 2001 census. This kind of a definition for slum will not fit in case of slums in many states like Kerala where the slums are very small in size and difficult to demarcate. Thus, there were very few slums which were covered under the programme. This problem does not arise in BSUP, as the responsibility and criteria to be applied to select the beneficiaries is vested on the State and ULBs.

In Kerala, every beneficiary of individual or scattered housing project under BSUP should have an account in Syndicate Bank. For making the money transactions easier, all the transactions under BSUP are done through the Syndicate Bank. The beneficiary has to deposit his or her share in housing (12 percent for OBC and general and 10 percent for SC/ST) in their own accounts. The Bank offers insurance coverage for the house and the individuals on very minimal charges. Kudumbasree, the state poverty alleviation Mission of the State Government of Kerala is the nodal agency for the implementation of BSUP in the state. Thus, the next part of the chapter deals with the Kudumbasree Mission in details with special reference to the beneficiary selection under BSUP.

Kudumbasree and Poverty Alleviation in Kerala

Though the State government has initiated several poverty alleviation schemes, it was from the middle of 1990s that the state government started taking initiative to organize the urban poor women into neighborhood groups with the aim of alleviating poverty and to empower the women from the economically backward sections of the population. With the primary objective to eradicate poverty, '*Kudumbasree*' was launched by the State Government in 1998 under the Poverty Eradication Mission (PEM) of Government of Kerala which is directly administered by the Local Administration Department. The Mission is implemented both in the urban as well as in the rural areas of the state. In 1991, Government of Kerala along with UNICEF initiated a community based nutrition program in Alleppey town whose success led to the replication of a similar scheme in the rural areas of Malappuram district in 1994. The success of these schemes through community based organization both in rural areas and urban areas led to the state wide launching of '*Kudumbasree*', the poverty alleviation Mission in 1998.

At present a lion's share of the schemes of central and the state governments for poverty alleviation is implemented through *Kudumbasree*. The central governments schemes like National Slum Development Program (NSDP), Valmiki Ambedkar Awaas Yojana (VAMBAY) and the state government schemes like Maythri housing scheme etc were implemented through the Mission. At present the earlier urban poverty alleviation schemes funded by the GoI were merged with the second Sub Mission of JNNURM, ie., Basic Services for the Urban Poor (BSUP) and Integrated Housing and Slum Development Programme (IHSDP). The State Government has chosen *Kudumbasree* as the nodal agency for the implementation of various schemes under BSUP. The Mission gives thrust on community participation in decision making and empowerment of women. 'The methodology adopted by the Mission is to build community structures of women drawn from poverty stricken families and to facilitate them to overcome the tide of poverty through social and economic empowerment.'[10]

Structure of *Kudumbasree*

Kudumbasree, the poverty alleviation Mission has a three tier structure. At the grass root level, every family below poverty line is a member of the neighbourhood groups which cover 20-40 families in the area. The thrift and the credit societies exist at this grass root level. The NHGs have weekly meetings in which each member has to deposit a minimum amount of money into the common fund. The mobilized fund by the members is deposited by the members in charge in Commercial Banks.

The amount is lent to the members of the NHG in case of any need. In case there are more needy members of money at the same time, then the lottery method is opted to decide to whom the available money will be lent. The lent money has to be paid back by the borrower within a limited period of time. The main difference between NGOs and *Kudumbasree* in lending money is that the former mainly depends on the Commercial Banks to borrow money whereas the common deposits of the members is the main source of borrowing in case of the latter.The thrift and credit system of the Mission helps the poor families to overcome the economic difficulties and acts as an informal banking system for the poor which is

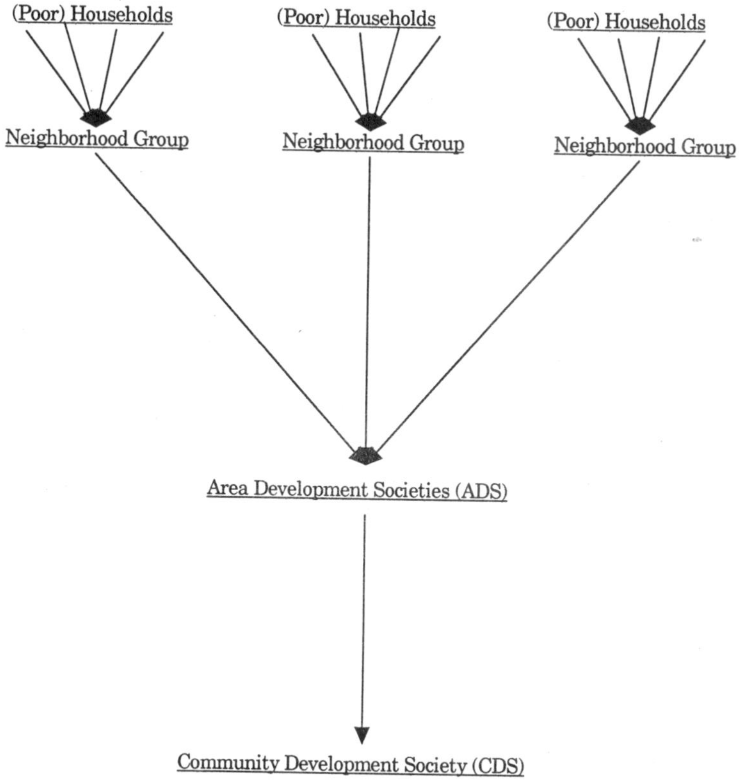

Figure 4.1 Structure of *Kudumbasree.*

free of the lacunae of formal and other forms of informal sources of credit giving institutions. At present, *Kudumbasree* is the largest micro finance scheme in the world.[11] Every neighbourhood group or NHGs has five members who are in charge of its functioning. They are Community health volunteer, Community infrastructure volunteer, Community income generation volunteer, Secretary and President. At the ward level NHGs are combined to form Area Development Societies (ADS). Community Development Society which combines ADSs is the apex order in the restructuring of *Kudumbasree*. The strength of the Mission can be recognized from the fact that the number of NHGs in Kochi city is as high as 1302 and the families covered under this are close to 42000.[12]

Role of *Kudumbasree* in providing Basic Services for the Urban Poor (BSUP)

Basic Services for the Urban Poor is the second Sub Mission of JNNURM. *Kudumbasree* is the nodal agency which implements the Sub Mission in the state. '*Kudumbasree* is conceived mainly as an urban employment generation program through active involvement and participation of women for eradication of urban poverty.'[13] The main projects included under BSUP are development of slum infrastructural facilities *in situ*, slum rehabilitation, individual housing and miscellaneous schemes for the other categories of urban poor like street vendors, mentally challenged persons, orphans etc. The share of the funds allocated for the urban poor under BSUP in Kochi and Thiruvananthapuram are 8.1 percent and 7.8 percent, the share of the urban poor population as per CDPs of these cities are 35 percent and 16.4 percent respectively.

The responsibility to identify the urban poor families in the Mission cities is assigned to *Kudumbasree*. The following are the criteria used for identifying the poor under BSUP projects in the state :

1. Women headed households
2. Presence of Unwed mother / Divorcee / Widow / Abandoned lady
3. Chronically ill member in the family (suffering from cancer, paralysis, HIV-aids, going under treatment for kidney problems, heart problem etc).
4. Presence of illiterate/ illiterates who are below the age of 65.
5. Presence of person/persons who left schooling before matriculation (applicable only to those who are below 20 years at the time of survey)
6. Presence of elderly members who are above 65 in the family.
7. Presence of mentally or physically challenged persons.
8. Belongs to traditional fisherman family/ Scheduled Caste or Scheduled Tribe family

All the eight criteria are given equal weights of 5 marks each. Thus, the maximum mark that a family can get under the criteria for giving preference is 40. Other than these eight criteria, there is another set of criteria to understand the current living conditions of the family and these are given varying weights on the basis of the importance of the criteria. The weights given for each criterion are given in brackets.

1. No land to construct own house (10)
2. House built illegally in 'purambokku' land (15)
3. The condition of the house
   (a) No house (15)
   (b) Hut (10)
   (c) Sheet / thatched roof (7)
   (d) Dilapidated / uncompleted (5)
4. No latrine facility (10)
5. No access to safe drinking water within a distance of 500 meters (10)
6. No electricity connection (10)

   Total marks that one family can get (60)

Thus, the total number of marks that a poor family can get under the two sets of criteria for beneficiaries selection under BSUP is 100 (i.e. 40+60).

Slums in Thiruvananthapuram and Kochi

Slum population is generally considered as the synonym of urban poor population. If we examine the various schemes for the urban poor at the state and the central level in the country, they mainly focus on the improvement in the living and the economic condition of the slum population. In order to understand the various facets of life in slums (indirectly urban poor) in the cities of Kochi and Thiruvananthapuram, a field survey was conducted by the researcher in the fourteen slums of these two cities, covering seven slums each from a city. The slums covered for the survey fall in various categories like notified, non-notified, small, large, and fisherman colony. Though all slums have some common characteristics, every slum has some characteristics which are unique to it.

Among the fourteen surveyed slums in the two cities, seven are covered under BSUP projects in various phases. The survey aimed to analyze the infrastructural facilities, economic condition of the slum population, the extent of their participation in decision making and above all, the perception of the population living here about their life in the slum and popular demands for their betterment of life. In the field survey, the samples were selected through non random judgment sampling (non probability judgment sampling) as there was no prior knowledge about the slums. Another aim of the field survey was to assess the changes which are brought by the Mission projects in those slums through BSUP. From the fourteen slums, two hundred samples were collected for the field work.

Slums in Thiruvananthapuram

In order to have a broader view of the slum population who constitute a substantial portion of the urban poor in both the cities, seven slums in the city were taken for the field survey. Among these, three slums namely Karimadom, Rajiv Nagar and Poonthura are covered under BSUP. The basic characteristics of the surveyed slums are given below :

Karimadom

It is one of the well known and very large slums in the city. Located very close to the busy Chhalaai market area the slum is connected to the city through motorable road. The houses are arranged in highly congested manner in the slum. The slum has very high proportion of the poor population. Another important aspect to notice is that none of the slum dwellers has the legal ownership of land where the house is located. In spite of this, there have been lots of improvements in the slum facilities in the past years. In order to improve the life of the slum population through BSUP, it is mainly the 'Flat model' which is being implemented. This can be due to the central location of the slum in the city. Along with this, renovation works of selected few houses also will be undertaken. The most important problem that the residents here are facing is lack of proper drainage. The slum is infamous for the large number of crimes associated with the residents.

Chenkalchulah

The slum is located at the center of the city. The slum has been here for more than four decades. It is generally accepted that this area was first settled by the migrant population from Tamilnadu who came to the capital city for the construction work of state secretariat. In their long waiting for the delayed payment from the government, they became the permanent settlers in the city. Most of the residents have the legal ownership of land. The geographical importance of the slum in the centre of the city can be the reason for the fact that it had been covered under various previous urban poverty alleviation schemes and slum development schemes. In spite of this, the slum has poor infrastructure facilities in terms of the road, drainage and sanitation facilities.

There are many flats within the slum which were constructed and distributed to the slum dwellers as part of the earlier programs. Though these houses were distributed in 2003-04 these flats do not have power connection and water supply even at present. Because of this lacuna, the expected improvement in the living condition of the beneficiaries could not be achieved. Several residents of the slum complained that the flats were distributed not to the needy or eligible people but to the economically better off people with strong political background especially bachelors. One case of flat allotment is undergoing trial in the State High Court at present which indicates the malfunctioning of the allotment pattern. Because of its large size, the slum is considered as a vote bank in the city. Many of the residents here told that they do not believe in any particular political party as both Communists or Congress Governments could make visible progress in their standard of living.

Gundukad

Gundukad colony is located away from the city center. Though it had been a notified slum in the past in the government records, at present it is a non notified slum. The slum is approachable through motorable road. The slum settlement gives the appearance of a well planned and neatly managed rural settlement. There are very few households which fall in the very low income category. The slum had been covered under previous slum improvement schemes. In general, the infrastructural facilities in this slum are much better than in other slums in the city. This is further proved through the fact that this is the only slum where all the surveyed households expressed satisfaction in the available infrastructural facilities.

Poonthura

It is a large fisherman's colony located in the city. The physical infrastructure in the slum is very inadequate. The slum is seen with fear by the outsiders, because of the recent violent clash between two communities and the incidents that followed. In majority of the cases, all the male members of the family are fishermen. Since income through fishing depends both on the seasons and the very unpredictable weather conditions in the coastal area, their daily life is less smooth than in the rest of the colonies. The interview with the local fishermen and their wives in the slum revealed the fact that a good share of their income from fishing goes in drinking toddy, the locally prepared drink from coconut and in gambling. Though the wives of the fishermen are illiterates or have very low level of education, they engage in various economic activities like fish selling, tailoring, etc. The economic participation of the female family members is very important to run the family, especially in the rainy season, when the fisherman will not be able to go for fishing in the rough sea. The slum is one of the three slums covered under JNNURM- BSUP for slum improvement. Though many of the basic civic amenities are in shortage in the slum, the most serious shortage is in case of drainage. Majority of the households do not have drainage facility and for those who have the facility, overflow of the drains is very frequent as the drains are narrow and very shallow.

Rajiv Nagar

In spite of the fact that the slum is much better off than many other surveyed slums, it is covered under the slum housing and infrastructure upgradation project under BSUP. The most noticeable fact about the slum is that there is quite a wide gap in the economic conditions of the residents. Comparatively much better off households and poor households are located adjacent to one another often separated by walls. In fact, it will be very difficult to accept it as a 'slum colony'. Except in the case of few households who live in the rented houses, all have the legal ownership of land. The main reason for the inclusion of this slum under the Mission project can be due to its location close to the airport and also due to the pressure from the middle class population settled in the slum.

The slum had been covered under the previous schemes like VAMBAY, while a large number of slums in much worse condition had not received any attention of the corporation and the state government. Since the monthly income as told by the respondents is often far understated from the reality, the actual economic condition of the families here was understood through the housing amenities which can be easily observed. Some households who live in very poor environment complained that there are clear discrepancies in the selection of beneficiaries. Since they do not believe that the selection method is transparent, they have stopped going for the NHG meetings. The field observation that some of the very poor families living in fully dilapidated houses are not covered under the BSUP housing scheme clearly approves this fact. It was also noticed that some families with better facilities than many others and whose members are actively involved in beneficiary selection mechanism in the slum are already covered under the housing scheme.

Chaakka

The slum is also known as 'Puthuval colony' and 'Wireless colony'. It is a comparatively small slum located near the Thiruvananthapuram airport. After independence, the freedom fighters were gifted land here and became the permanent residents. Some others were allotted this land by the state government when their land was acquired by some industrial units in another part of the city. Though the land here had been allocated by the State Government to the residents, few people are also staying in the rented houses. There are few houses in satisfactory condition, while the majority are dilapidated. The very low share of the population staying in the slum for more than 15 years shows that it is in the recent years the population in the slum has increased. The most important problem that the residents face is lack of proper drainage. The residents are also afraid of a forced resettlement to another area since there are numerous construction activities coming up in recent years around the airport area, especially by the large private companies.

Shinkarathoppu

This is a non notified slum located away from the core of the city. The name of the slum comes from the myth that in the old times the local ruler or "Raajaavu" used to come to this particular place to meet his lovers. Middle class families are almost absent in the slums. Most of the residents here are working as construction laborers. There are no adequate drainage and sanitation facilities in the slum and the majority of the households do not have electricity connection. Illegal electricity connection or electricity theft is very common in the slum. The slum is well connected by roads on both the sides. A road passes through the slum dividing it into almost equal halves. A good number of households had received some or the other kind of economic benefit from the state.

Slums in Kochi

Seven slums were surveyed in the city in which four slums namely Padiyathukulam, 24 Mury, Kissan and A.K.G Colony are covered under BSUP projects. The basic features of these slums are the following :

Padiyathukulam

It is the slum which is located at the center of the city adjacent to the state highway. This slum is located in two units. One part of the slum is adjacent to the state highway with 10-12 households located in a highly congested manner. The other part is located on the other side of the road, slightly cut off from the first part. This part of the slum covers much more households than the previous one. It is the former part of the slum which is covered under the program for slum resettlement project. The second part of the slum is much better off than the smaller part in all the infrastructural aspects and thus is not covered under BSUP projects. Location of the previous portion of the slum adjacent to the wide and open drain with hardly a distance of 2 feet in between is the most important problem for the people here. It is due to the high price of the land here that the ULB is not agreeing to the demand of the residents to provide proper drainage facility rather than to relocate them to another place as decided at present by the ULB. The residents complained that the flats that they will get through BSUP are much more congested than their present dilapidated or semi dilapidated houses.

E.R.G Colony (Ernakulum Railway Goods Colony)

It is a notified slum located adjacent to the railway junction. Though the slum is well connected with the rest of the city and is located almost at the city center, it faces acute shortage in sanitation and drainage facilities. Except few houses, the majority do not have latrine facility. Whoever has latrine facility, it is 'pit latrine' which is generally considered as unhygienic and those who do not have latrine, have to use the railway land adjacent by to attend nature's call. Another problem of the slum is that some of the households face the problem of overflow of the drains especially in the rainy season. All the surveyed households had been here for more than fifteen years and this shows that this is not a growing slum. Majority of the households do not have the legal ownership of the land. Another important point to notice is that almost the entire slum households have received economic benefit from the ULB in the past for constructing latrine, (i.e. 5000 rupee per family). In spite of this, majority of the households do not have latrine facilities here. This points out the fact that the money was used by the households for meeting needs other than for the purpose for which it was given. It was also observed that there are few families of Kodagu (Karnataka) origin settled in the slum.

Maariyathu

This is a small non notified slum located at the core of the city. All the houses of the slum are located parallel to the main road and a closed drain runs adjacent to these parallel houses. Very few households only have the legal ownership of the land in the slum. The houses are very small and are very congested. The contrasting nature of the slums in Kerala to that of the slums in any other states can be understood from this slum. The slum enjoys much better basic civic amenities than the majority of the surveyed slums. Since it had never been a notified slum, till present no household has received any economic benefit from any governing institution.

Tatapuram

The slum is also known as the 'Mathai Manjuran road colony' and falls in the category of 'notified slums'. Barring few, all the houses are in dilapidated condition and are very poor. Majority of the surveyed households in the slum fall in the very poor category and no household has the legal ownership of land. The fact that all the surveyed households had been living in the slum for more than 15 years shows that this is a very old slum. Most of the households do not have sanitation and proper drainage facility. The low terrain of the area causes the drainage water to enter their houses even on a slightly rainy day. It was noticed that few aged people live alone in houses, in spite of the fact that they have sons or daughters who are ready to take the responsibility to look after them. Some of them revealed the truth that they live here as they may be economically benefitted from the various urban poverty alleviation schemes. They believe that they will be covered under housing programs sooner or later and if they leave the slum to live with other family members, they will miss the opportunity.

24 Mury colony

This is one of the slums selected for resettlement under the Mission. Though it is considered as a slum, it enjoys much better basic infrastructural facilities than any other surveyed slums in the city. The slum was settled at first by the 24 families who came for the construction work of a State Government building. Once the work had begun, the workers were given the quarters by the center and became the permanent settlers. These 24 houses are located in six long lane houses with four houses each in a single lane and share a common bathroom and toilet. But adjacent to the lanes, more houses were built in the later years by the earlier settlers and also by the outsiders. The slum had been covered under various schemes undertaken by the ULB and State Government. Many of the households have got their floors tiled with the ULB fund. At present, the residents do not agree with the ULB option of flat construction and their resettlement in the same location. They believe that the flats will be much more congested than the condition in which they live at present and they do not want to leave their present houses which are in good condition. Few families residing in the slum are of 'Tamil' origin.

Kissan Colony

This is one of the very large slums in the city and is covered under BSUP. The most noticeable aspect which makes this slum different from rest of the surveyed slum which are covered under the Mission is that this is the only slum where the ULB has agreed to give the '*patta*' or the legal ownership of the land. All the beneficiaries will not be given *patta* in a single stretch and beneficiaries or households to which the '*patta*' will be distributed are selected through lottery system. As cost of '*patta*', the beneficiary will have to pay 2000 rupess to the ULB which is quite meager in comparison to the current land prices in the city. The first stage *patta* distribution for six people was done recently. The very low share of the households falling under the very low income category shows the better economic condition of the people in the slum. It was also noticed that some people in the slum had more than one house in the same slum. The owner and family live in one house while the other is often rented to outsiders. Better condition of the infrastructural facilities is clear from the high level of satisfaction of the respondents in the available facilities.

A.K.G. Colony

This is a very large slum located away from the center of the city. The slum is covered under the slum infrastructural improvement project under BSUP in the second phase. Except the few households who live in the rented houses, all the households have the legal ownership of land. It can also be seen that there are some families which have bought the house here in the recent years. The main problem of the slum is that, as the slope of the drain is in the wrong direction, a part of the slum is facing the problem of drainage overflow during the rainy season. Except this, the infrastructural facilities in the slum are very satisfactory. The slum altogether gives the look of a 'clean village transplanted in the Corporation area'.

Socio-Economic Analysis of Slums in Thiruvananthapuram and Kochi

In this part of the study, important aspects about the life in the slums of the mission cities are analyzed. This includes the data analysis of the field work as well as the observations of the researcher and facts revealed from the interactions with the slum population.

Economic Condition of the Slum Population

The monthly per capita income of the family is categorized into four, the first category with income above Rs.1500 and above, the second category with Rs.1000-1500 income, the third category with Rs. 500- 1000 income and the fourth category with income of Rs. 500 and below. The economic condition of the population differs widely across the slums. At the city level, the level of slum population falling in the lowest income category is roughly double in Thiruvananthapuram (59 percent) than in Kochi (30 percent). It is widely accepted that the longer one stays in the slum, the more he gets adjusted to the slum environment and will learn to get a living out of the available circumstances. As the nature of slums varies widely from one to another in both the cities, we cannot generalize this argument. The main exception to this behavior is that of Tatapuram colony where majority of its surveyed households fall in very low income group in spite of the fact that all the surveyed households had been staying in the slum for more than 15 years. This slum is very small in size and is very poor in the infrastructural facilities. The poor facilities in the slum may be because of its small size which makes it less attractive for being covered under the slum infrastructural developmental projects.[14]

The poor infrastructural facilities in the slum make the slum unattractive for the new migrants to the city. The assumption that longer stay in the slum is improving the economic condition of the resident is proved right at the city level also. Thiruvananthapuram city with 59 percent of its slum population falling in the very low income category, has 75 percent of its slum population staying in the slum for more than 15 years while in case of Kochi which has only 30 percent of its slum population in the very low income group, has 94 percent of its slum population staying in the slums for more than 15 years. This supports the fact that those who have lived for a longer time in the slum, will have better economic conditions than those who settled comparatively later.[15] The poor economic condition of the households also has to be understood from the fact that only very small proportion of the slum population owns any assets elsewhere. It is true in case of few migrants from Tamilnadu presently residing in these slums.

Legal ownership of land

Legal ownership of land in slums can have several implications on the level of infrastructural facilities available and the housing conditions. Except in case of few slums, majority of the slum population do not have the legal ownership of land where the house is located. It is only in Poonthura where all the residents have the legal ownership of the land while there are four slums namely Karimadon, Tatapuram, Kissan colony and 24 Mury colony where no residents have legal ownership of land. One of the provisions included under the Mission BSUP is to provide '*pattas*' or the legal ownership of land to the tenants. Kissan colony is selected under this scheme and six families were given *patta* in the first phase of *patta* distribution recently. It has to be noted that, in most of the cities where the residents do not have legal ownership of land, are located in the important parts of the city. Only exception for this is that of Chenkalchulah slum which is located at the center of Thiruvananthapuram and a good number of its population had legal land ownership. This can be due to the fact that the slum had existed here for the last several decades and was covered under earlier slum development projects.

It is widely believed that the slums with high proportion of households with legal ownership of land are better covered under the services, especially in case of waste disposal. It means the slums with higher share of the households with legal ownership of land will have larger share of the households paying user charges. The case of Poonthura fisherman colony can be seen as an exception, which can be mainly due to the relatively low and high instability in the income of the fisherman. The lack of permanent source of income can be due to the reason that some households are not being covered under waste disposal service by the NGOs or ULB. It has also to be noted that all those who pay user charges are paying it for waste disposal except in case of Chenkalchulah slum, where the residents have to pay user charge also to ensure proper drainage in given time periods.

At the city level also this assumption is proved right. Kochi, with only 22.3 percent of its slum households with legal ownership of land, has 43.5 percent of its households paying user charge. But in Thiruvananthapuram city, where the share of the households with legal ownership of land is as high as 68.2 percent (which is more than three times than that of Kochi) has 86 percent of the slum population paying the user charges. The fast soaring land values in Kochi because of its commercial and economic importance, is the main reason for the very low share of slum households with legal ownership of land. The slum housing can be improved in different ways firstly through improving the same structure, secondly through giving financial support to the households to construct the new house at the same place and thirdly the 'flat model' which involves the construction of 2-3 storey flats for the slum households. These flats can be either in the same place or in another place.

Despite the strong resistance from the residents, it is the 'flat model' which is going to be implemented under BSUP and the only exception is Kissan colony. The people believe that their life will be far better if they are given the legal ownership of the land where the houses and other basic facilities are located than by relocating them into the congested flats. The respondents told that the houses which are under construction and are to be distributed under BSUP are very small in size often much more congested than their present houses and believes that they will not get privacy in such flats. The exceptional consideration given to in the case of Kissan colony can be because of its large population. The slum is much larger than any other slums visited by the researcher in the city. This is a proof for the 'crucial role of vote bank politics' in decision making.

In order to flatter the large number of voters, the political parties and the elected representatives exert pressure on the ULB and the higher authorities that the demand of the slum residents is accepted. It is widely accepted that the less privileged and the poorer sections of the urban society are always pushed from the center to the corners through various reasons like 'slum improvement', 'slum development', etc.[16] Thus, resettling the slum population from the center of the city elsewhere in the name of slum housing and development rather than financially supporting them to construct the houses at the same place or slum development has to be considered as a policy of deliberate marginalisation. This kind of a slum housing program will only add to their problems rather than solving them in an easier manner.

Common people's participation in decision making

Kudumbasree is the poverty alleviation initiative established by the state government in 1998. The self help groups under *Kudumbasree* are well organized and work according to fixed rules and regulations. The better performance of *Kudumbasree* compared to other self help groups run by other NGOs is clear from the low drop out ratio in the former.[17] The level of participation of the people in developmental activities can be evaluated through the proportion of membership of the households in *Kudumbasree*. As the Sub-Mission for urban poor is implemented through *Kudumbasree*, this is obvious in case of JNNURM projects. Above all, the studies show that more than 70percent of the funds allocated under poverty alleviation schemes reach the beneficiaries through the medium of *Kudumbasree*.[18]

The participation of the households in developmental activities varies widely which is clear from the fact that all the surveyed slum households in the slums like Poonthura, A.K.G colony and Tatapuram have membership in it, and they believe in the ability of the organization to improve the living condition of the poor. On the other hand, very poor participation of the households is seen in the slums like Chenkalchulah, Karimadom, and Gundukad. The reason for the poor membership of households in these slums is because of the lapses in the finance management by the self help groups in these slums. The lack of coordination between the members in the SHGs became the sole reason behind the loss of trust in the scheme and also for the drop out in the membership. The disagreement between the various members is also due to the conflicting interests of the various members within SHGs. This is clearly evident under BSUP as *Kudumbasree* and the NHGs have the full power to prepare the beneficiary list on the basis of the various criteria.

It is generally assumed that the poorer the people, the more important will be the role of SHGs in their life.[19] In case of the poor, especially of the women from poor families, self help groups can play a vital role in improving their standard of living by means of involving them in economically productive activities. But there is no correlation between the proportion of the households with membership in *Kudumbasree* and the level of monthly per capita income of the family. Karimadom colony which has a large share of the surveyed households under the urban poor category has very poor membership in *Kudumbasree*. This is vice versa in case of 24 Mury Colony. Thus, it is wrong to assume that it is only the poorer sections of the slum population who are dependent on are getting benefits from *Kudumbasree*.

This is proved at the city level also. Kochi, which has only 30 percent of its surveyed households under the urban poor category, has 91 percent of its households covered under *Kudumbasree*. In contrast to this, Thiruvananthapuram, where 59 percent of the surveyed slum households are in the urban poor category, but only 58 percent of its households are covered under the *Kudumbasree* scheme. The mismanagement of the thrift amount by the elected members of the NHGs was the main reason given by those who have dropped the *Kudumbasree* membership after enjoying it for some time. Few also alleged that there is personal bias by the elected members in the selection of beneficiaries under various poverty alleviation programs including BSUP. Thus, the selection of beneficiaries by *Kudumbasree* NHGs at the local level has to be strictly monitored by government agencies so that the poorest families will be benefitted first rather than benefitting the politically and economically stronger people. As the major share of the funds under the poverty alleviation is implemented through *Kudumbasree*, the high drop out in its membership in some of the slums has to be taken seriously.

User Charge Payment

The concept of user charge, though not very new in the country as a whole, it is a notion of relatively recent origin in the state. The increasing importance of the growth of sustainable cities in the globalised world, and the intervention by the international monitoring agencies in directing the urban development in the country are the main reasons behind the increasing stress for 'user charge'.[20] Kerala with a unique development model is different from the rest of the country in terms of its peculiar political environment. The state government had always given priority to public sector in providing the basic services, so that the poor will also be able to avail them at very nominal prices which were often strikingly lower than the cost of providing these services, and thus unsustainable in long run. The studies have proved that this kind of development without aiming at the economic development will be unsustainable.[21] The compulsion on the ULBs to implement the reforms and to follow the guidelines under the externally funded projects in urban development was a major turning point in the state policy for service charge collection.

Though JNNURM is not funded by the external funding agencies, it recommends the ULBs to go for 100 percent cost recovery for all the infrastructural projects and services provided under the Mission. The implications of the transformation in the cost recovery mechanisms for urban services in these cities are clearly visible in the slums also. Among the slums surveyed, except one, all are covered by some or the other services for which user charges are collected. When there are slums where all the surveyed households pay user charge, there are also slums where majority of the surveyed households do not pay it. The normal assumption that the economically better off population will be more willing to pay the user charges than the poorer ones is proved wrong in this case.

The slums like Poonthura and Tatapuram, which have very poor infrastructural facilities have majority of the surveyed households falling under the urban poor category. In contradiction to the normal assumption, all the surveyed households of these slums are covered under the paid waste disposal service. This shows that to some extent, the urban poor are also willing to pay for the civic amenities if they are ensured adequate and efficient service supply.[22] But this cannot be concluded as the generalized picture as there are many households in these slums which are not covered by the service due to various reasons. The lack of space in these slums to dump the wastes generated leaves no other option for the residents than to depend on the service provided by *Kudumbasree*. They view this as the only way through which they can keep their living environment in a better condition. This positive attitude of the slum population is evident in case of the Chenkalchoolah colony, where the residents pay user charges both for waste disposal as well as for drainage system maintenance.

Coverage of the households under previous developmental schemes

The studies have revealed that the state government spends a noticeable portion of its resources for social development.[23] There are numerous schemes for poverty alleviation and for the economically and socially deprived categories both in the urban and rural areas of the state. It is only in A.K.G colony, that the entire surveyed households were covered by one or the other Government welfare schemes in the past. At the same time, there are colonies like Maariyathu, Tatapuram, etc where no surveyed households have benefitted yet from any welfare schemes of the government. Most of these households got the financial support for the creation of private toilets which in majority of the cases were not used to meet the purposes meant.

In spite of the fact that E.R.G colony is very small in size in comparison to many other slums surveyed, majority of the surveyed households have got the financial support from the ULB. Each household was given Rs. 5000 each to construct toilets. This does not agree with study findings by NIUA (1993) that the bigger slums will be always preferred for the developmental projects, as larger number of people will be benefitted from them than in case of smaller slums.[24] But this can be proved to be right in case of small slums like Tatapuram and Maariyathu, which were not covered by any other development schemes. At the city level, Kochi with 43 percent of its surveyed households covered under any previous anti poverty and housing scheme in the past, stands ahead of Thiruvananthapuram city whose corresponding share is 37 percent.

Preference of the households for 'in situ' slum development

A large majority of the surveyed households prefer 'in situ slum development'. They believe that the equilibrium that they have developed with the slum environment over long periods of stay will be totally disturbed once they will settle in the flats constructed within or outside their slum. The beneficiary households under BSUP housing scheme who will be allotted the flat rooms soon, complained that the flat rooms that they will be given are much smaller than the size of their present dwellings. In those slums which have poor infrastructural

Table 4.1 Socio-economic Aspects of Slum Population in the Mission cities of Kerala

Various Aspects	*Percentage Share of Surveyed Households in Various Socio-economic Aspects*											
	c-1	*c-2*	*c-3*	*c-4*	*c-5*	*c-6*	*c-7*	*c-8*	*c-9*	*c-10*	*c-11*	*c-12*
Thiruvanantha-puram	97.6	58.8	68.2	90.6	75.3	94.1	57.6	80.0	85.9	36.5	91.8	45.9
Kochi	97.4	29.6	22.6	97.4	93.9	65.2	91.3	66.1	43.5	42.6	83.5	65.2
Total	97.5	42.0	42.0	94.5	86.0	77.5	77.0	72.0	61.5	40.0	87.0	57.0

Source- Field work in the slums of Kochi and Thiruvananthapuram.

Codes-

(c-1) Native state -Kerala

(c-2) MPCI 500 and below

(c-3) Has legal ownership of land

(c-4) No other private property

(c-5) Stay in slum for 15 years and above

(c-6) Found betterment in slum facilities

(c-7) Has membership in *Kudumbasree*/ SHGs

(c-8) Not satisfied with the slum facilities

(c-9) Pay user charges

(c-10) Has received economic benefit from Govt

(c-11) Wants the new house at the same place

(c-12) Family size 5 and below

Table 4.2 Socio-economic Aspects of Slum Households with MPCI below Rs.500

Various Socio-economic Aspects of Slum Population for Households with MPCI below Rs.500	*Percentage of Share in Surveyed Households*		
	Total	*Kochi*	*Thiruvananthapuram*
Family size below 4	57.1	76.5	44.0
Has legal ownership of land	48.8	23.5	66.6
No other private property	96.4	100.0	94.0
Length of stay in slum for more than 15 years	79.8	94.1	70.0
Observes betterment in slum facilities	79.8	52.9	98.0
Membership in *Kudumbasree*	76.2	94.1	64.0
Satisfied with the facilities	19	26.5	14.0
Pays user charges	67.9	35.3	90.0
Good interaction with ULB	34.6	55.9	52.0
Received any benefits from Govt:	44	44.1	44.0
Wants the new house in the same place	90.5	82.4	96.0

Source- Field work in the slums of Kochi and Thiruvananthapuram.

Table 4.3 Cross Tabulation of Status of Land Ownership and MPCI of Household

Status of Land Ownership	*Per capita Percentage of Households with income of Rs.*				*Total*
	500 and below	*500-1000*	*1000-1500*	*1500 and above*	
Has no legal ownership of land	43	32	15	26	116
Has legal ownership of land	41	21	8	14	84
Total	84	53	23	40	200

Source- Field work in the slums of Kochi and Thiruvananthapuram.

facilities, noticeable share of the households prefer to be resettled in flats as they believe that it is the only way through which they can escape from their present deplorable condition. It was also noticed that some of the surveyed households do not have preference between flat and separate house, but are willing to accept any option in case they are covered under such schemes. This shows the disappointment of these people in their present living conditions and the desperateness to live in a better environment.

Table 4.4 Cross tabulation of coverage under previous schemes and MPCI

Coverage under previous schemes	*Per Capita Percentage of Household Run on Household.*				*Total*
	500 and below	*500-1000*	*1000-1500*	*1500 and above*	
Has not got financial aid from govt.	47	34	12	27	120
Has got financial aid from govt.	37	19	11	13	80
Total	84	53	23	40	200

Source- Field work in the slums of Kochi and Thiruvananthapuram.

Table 4.5 Cross tabulation of payment of user charge and MPCI of household

Payment of user charges	*Per Capita income of Percentage of Households with Per Capita Income of Rs.*				*Total*
	500 and below	*500-1000*	*1000-1500*	*1500 & above*	
Does not pay user charge	27	20	11	19	77
Pays user charge	57	33	12	21	123
Total	84	53	23	40	200

Source- Field work in the slums of Kochi and Thiruvananthapuram.

Interesting facts were revealed from the cross tabulation of important indicators. Some of the tables of cross tabulation between various aspects are given below :

From the above tables, the following conclusions can be drawn.

1. Monthly Per Capita Income (MPCI) of the household does not have any influence in determining the ownership of the land occupied by the household. The analysis shows that among the surveyed urban poor households, almost half of the households have legal ownership of the land while in the category of households with MPCI of Rs.1500 and above, close to about 26 percent of the households do not have legal ownership of the land.

2. There is no correlation between the membership in *Kudumbasree* and the level of household income. Out of the 46 households not covered under the scheme, 20 households fall in the urban poor category while out of the 40 households falling in the highest income category 25 households have membership in the *Kudumbasree*. This disproves the normal assumption that it is mostly the lower income groups who participate in the initiatives like SHGs as they act as an additional source of family income.

Table 4.6 Cross-tabulation of MPCI and Length of stay in the slum

Length of Stay in the Slum	*Per Capita income of Percentage of Households (in Rs.)*				*Total*
	500 and below	*500-1000*	*1000-1500*	*1500 and above*	
4 years and below	2	1	1	1	5
4-7 years	0	0	0	1	1
7-14 years	15	2	3	2	22
14 years and above	67	50	19	36	172
Total	84	53	23	40	200

Source- Field work in the slums of Kochi and Thiruvananthapuram.

Table 4.7 Cross-tabulation of MPCI and Size of the family of slum households

Size of the Household	*Per Capita Income of Percentage of Households with Rs.*				*Total*
	500 and below	*500-1000*	*1000-1500*	*1500 & above*	
Family size 5 and below	48	25	12	29	114
Family size 5-8	32	28	11	11	82
Family size 8 and above	4	0	0	0	4
Total	84	53	23	40	200

Source- Field work in the slums of Kochi and Thiruvananthapuram

Table 4.8 Cross-tabulation of MPCI and Kudumbasree membership of the household

Status of Kudumbasree Membership	*Per capita income of Percentage of Households with Rs.*				*Total*
	500 and below	*500-1000*	*1000-1500*	*1500 and above*	
Do not have *Kudumbasree* membership	20	7	4	15	46
Has *Kudumbasree* membership	64	46	19	25	154
Total	84	53	23	40	200

Source- Field work in the slums of Kochi and Thiruvananthapuram.

3. The payment of user charges for the services does not depend on the income level of the household. The share of the households who do not pay the user charges in the lower income category is only less than 1/3rd of the total. In contradiction, close to half of the total households in the highest income category do not pay user charges. It is believed that the lower income categories are also willing to pay for the services if there is assurance in the quality and efficiency of the services provided.[25] The interaction with the people revealed that the readiness shown by the poor households to pay the user charges in spite of their low income is because of their desperateness to improve their living conditions.

4. The financial aids channelised through the earlier poverty eradication schemes for the slums were not limited to the poor households but also to the better and high income category. Though close to half of the beneficiaries of these schemes were from the lowest income group, roughly 66 percent of the households in the highest income category have also benefitted from these schemes. It points out the discrepancies in the selection of beneficiaries in the previous poverty alleviation and housing schemes.

5. In the case of a slum housing project, irrespective of the income of the household, majority prefer to construct the new house in the same place than to be shifted to flats offered within or outside the slum.

6. It is generally assumed that income and family size are negatively correlated as the better educated will prefer to have small families.[26] In spite of the very low income, majority of the households in the poorest category opt for small family. Out of the total households with five members and below, close to 42 percent are from the lowest income category. It is also to be noticed that in total, the proportion of the households with five members and below is 57 percent while that of households with

family size of 8 and above is only 2 percent. This proves the fact that in spite of the low income level, the slum households are aware of the merits of the small family and prefer to have small families.

7. The cross tabulation between the *Kudumbasree* membership and the user charge payment, show that the membership in it is not a prerequisite to be covered under various services in which *Kudumbasree* is actively involved.

8. Those households which have benefitted from the previous slum developmental schemes were not always the members of *Kudumbasree*. Among the benefitted households 84 percent were members of *Kudumbasree*.

Most of the normal assumptions regarding income level and other related aspects are proved to be wrong in the case of both the cities. This can be due to the highly varying nature of slums in the state. It is almost impossible to draw a generalized picture about the various aspects of slums life. There are slums with highly developed infrastructural facilities; often very difficult to be recognized as slums by the outsiders. Slums also vary greatly in size. There are slums with hundreds of households and slums with hardly ten households.

BSUP in the Mission Cities of Kerala

The CDPs of the Mission cities shows that by the end of Mission period, nearly Rs.1460 crore will be invested in the two Mission cities under the various projects for urban poor, close to 62 percent of which was to be invested during the first four years of the Mission. BSUP projects in the state are implemented through the state appointed agency for poverty alleviation, '*Kudumbasree*'. Besides the slum population, the categories which comprise the urban poor population are fishermen, street vendors, house less population, mentally and physically challenged people, orphans etc. Housing programs are one of the most important components of BSUP, and are divided into group housing and individual/ scattered housing projects. If group housing projects are preferred in case of slum population, individual housing is preferred in case of the urban poor families which are lying scattered in the city. The various components included under the group housing projects in both the Mission cities are the following:

- Group housing or 'flat housing'
- Provision of infrastructural facilities like, storm water drainage, water supply, solid waste management, sewerage, electric connection, street lighting, bio gas plants, construction and repair of roads etc.
- Landscaping (beautification of the area through tree planting and other means)
- Other civic amenities (Angan waadi, community hall etc.)

Beneficiary contribution is needed for the individual housing programs under BSUP. The amount to be paid by the beneficiary is Rs.12,000 in case of Scheduled Caste (SC) or Scheduled Tribe (ST) families, while it is Rs.14,400 in case of families belonging to Other Backward Castes (OBC) and general categories. Thus, the structure of funding for the housing programs under BSUP is as follows.

- 50 per cent - Central government
- 30 per cent - State government
- 8 per cent - Urban local body
- 12 per cent - Beneficiary contribution (Rs.14,400)

Thus, it is assumed the construction of a house will be completed in Rs.1,20,000. The amount given to the families for the construction of houses under BSUP is much higher than that of any other earlier urban housing and slum development programs like VAMBAY, NSDP, etc. Thus, the official accounts show that all the families which applied for the funds in the recent years, prefer to apply under BSUP. Under the individual housing programs, the fund is given to the households in four installments as follows :

- First installment : Rs. 10,000 is given after land clearance for house construction.
- Second installment : Rs. 50,000 is given after the completion of the basement of the house.
- Third installment : Rs. 40,000 is given once the construction reaches at the lintel level.
- Fourth installment : Rs. 20,000 is given once the house construction is completed.

The photo of the house at each construction stage will be taken. This is a pre-requisite condition to get the funds allocated at every stage. The size of the house constructed through BSUP should not be less than 300 sq feet and not more than 600 sq feet. Each house to be constructed should have a kitchen, one bedroom, a hall, toilet and bathroom, etc. Even if the land where the house will be constructed is owned by a male head, the fund in various installments will be allocated in the name of the female member in the family. The house will be given in the account of male member, only if there are no adult female members in the family. Regarding the implementation of BSUP housing projects, the Government of Kerala has directed ULBs to strictly stick to the following guidelines :

- Before choosing the beneficiaries, the areas for the housing project should be selected and the areas with large number of poor population should be given priority.
- In the total houses to be constructed, 30 percent and 3 percent of the houses should be reserved for SC/ST and physically handicapped categories. The legal ownership of the new house built under BSUP, will be given to the adult female member in the family and the male member will get the ownership right only if there is no adult female member in the family.
- The applications should be invited through *Kudumbasree* and the beneficiaries should be well aware of the loan

amount, installments, etc. While applying the marks that each family has got in the vulnerability marking also has to be written. The application forms thus got have to be again scrutinized through the CDS of the *Kudumbasree* organization, so that the discrepancies in beneficiary selection can be reduced. The final list of the beneficiaries will be prepared once the ULB and the ward committee members come to an agreement after discussions on the beneficiary list.

- In case of the integrated slum development, all the families residing in the selected slums should be given new houses. The beneficiary share of those who are covered under the Asraya project[27] will have to be taken by ULB.

- While the beneficiary list is prepared, it should be in accordance with the list accepted at the ward level. After this, the list of the beneficiaries can be displayed and the other needed details and documents about the beneficiaries have to be sent to the ULB for further processes. Each beneficiary should submit the original copy of the land ownership document with the ULB for the next seven years. This is to prevent the beneficiaries from selling their land and house to the outsiders and thus to prevent them from claiming houseless status once again. In case the original documents are not with the beneficiary (with the Bank), then the Bank signs an agreement with the Corporation, to ensure the handover of the original land documents of the beneficiary to the corporation in case he or she completely repays the loan before seven years.

Both Kochi and Thiruvananthapuram Corporations have received thousands of applications for individual housing, a large portion will not be considered eligible to apply as they do not posses land ownership documents or '*patta*'. Thus, a large number of the urban poor population will not be able to get any benefit from the Mission. This is most evident in case of the traditional fisherman colonies where a large number do not have '*patta*', as the area in which they are settled fall under the 'Coastal Regulatory Zone'.

Progress of BSUP in Kochi

According to CDP of the city, the urban poor population in the city is approximately 2.13 lakhs while the slum population is 1.28 lakhs. The corresponding figures are 4.24 lakhs and 1.39 lakhs when the entire CDP area is considered. There are 280 slums within the city, thus taking the total number of slums within the CDP area to 411. Quite different from these data, the Census figures show that there are only 62 slums in the city. The city was covered under several urban poverty alleviation schemes including NSDP, VAMBAY. BSUP is the most recent scheme in this list. There are three phases of BSUP in the city, and the total approved funds for the three phases are Rs.135.65 crore. The private agency which has undertaken the preparation of Detailed Project report (DPR) under BSUP

Table 4.9 Projects Included Under Various Phases of BSUP in Kochi

Phase No.	*Name of the Colonies / Slums Phase 1*	*Phase 2*	*Name of the Colonies/ Slums Phase 3*
	(1) 24 Mury (2) Vennalappara (3) Padiyathukulam (4) Mundamveli (5) Perandoor (6) Fisherman colony (7) Kissan (8) Palluruthy relief settlement (9) Individual housing	24 colonies will be selected under this. Work has not begun	(1) A.K.G Colony (2) Glass colony (3) Sahridaya Nagar (4) Panakkal (5) Valiyathura (6) Poonthura (7) Pambadithazham
Approved funds	26.6 crores	104.45 crores	4.6 crores

Source- DPRs-BSUP, Kochi Corporation.

in the city is C-Earth. The main components included under the various phases of BSUP in the city are given in Table 4.9.

In the first phase of BSUP in the city, besides the Palluruthy relief settlement and individual housing projects, there are seven slums where the slum housing projects were undertaken. Even after two years of getting the 1st phase of BSUP approved, the construction works have begun only in two colonies. Perandoor colony, which is located adjacent to the Perandoor canal, was recognized as a slum by the state government and the ULB. The slum is located in the core area of the city and is also included in the slum housing program. At present they are given accommodation in a corporation owned building in the nearby area and will have to reside there till they are given a newly constructed flat. As a result of the strong protest from the residents in Kissan colony against the decision to implement the 'flat model', ULB had to change this plan. It is the only slum covered in the first phase of BSUP in the city, where the "flat model" will not be implemented. The residents demand the renewal of the existing houses with the financial support of the government through the Mission. The Corporation officials held that the main reason behind the opposition from the residents against the flat model is because of the reason that at present many of the residents here own their own land which will be lost once they are given flats. At the present level of land price, the land that the residents possess costs several lakhs.

Though the tendering for the flat construction works is over in 24 Mury colonies, similar opposition against the "flat model" is coming from the residents. The colony initially consisted of quarters given by the ULB to the 24 laborer families for construction works. But in course of time more and more people started coming and settling in the colony illegally. Though it had been close to six decades since the colony came into existence, none of the families including the 24 families have ownership of the land. Most of the houses are spacious, the residents protest against the flat construction and demand for house renovation along with awarding of '*patta*', the legal ownership of land. Mundanvely is the second colony which has got the tender successfully, and the construction of two flats is already over. The group housing project which is supposed to provide houses to 200 families in this slum is in progress. Though the construction of these housing units was expected to be over by the beginning of the year 2009, (that is within a period of six months), in reality the construction has not completed due to many problems. The total money released under BSUP till November 2009 is Rs. 28.5 crores, in which Rs. 25.7 crore was utilized.

Individual housing

Individual housing is covered in various phases of BSUP in Kochi. It aims to provide a better living condition for the urban poor population living in the Municipalities and Panchayats covered under the CDP area. The money for individual housing is given in four installments to the beneficiaries. The number of the houses which were constructed till November 2009 within the Kochi Corporation area under the individual housing program is 1003. From the statistics, it can be easily understood that individual housing projects have made remarkable progress in the city than the group housing schemes. The main reason for the lagging of the group housing projects is mainly because of the lack of willingness of the private builders to engage in the project as the tender rates approved by the Government of India are much lower than the current market rates for the construction materials. In order to overcome this standstill, it was decided after long discussions with the organizations like Kerala Builders Forum, that the extra fund needed for the works will be sourced through Public Private Partnership mechanisms. As a positive response, the construction of the 12 units of group houses in Mundamveli had begun soon after this decision.

Progress of Basic Services for the Urban Poor in Thiruvananthapuram

The projects included under BSUP in various phases are given in Table 4.10.

At present, the Sub Mission of BSUP in the city is in progress under four phases. The fourth phase was initiated by

Table 4.10 Projects Included Under Various Phases of BSUP in Thiruvananthapuram

	Name of the slums covered			
	Phase 1	*Phase 2*	*Phase 3*	*Phase 4*
	(1) Two Cent colony (2) Rajiv Nagar (3) Kannanmoola	(1) Poonkulam (2) Karimadom Individual housing	(1) ManvilaHarijan colony (2) Manvila Lakshamveedu (3) Balanagar (4) Beemappally (5) Mannamoola (6) Kalladimugham (7) Fisherman colony Individual housing	Covers Infrastructural Development of 12 slums in the city
Funds approved	5.65 crores	37.29 crores	125.87 crores	125.88 Crores

Source-DPRs of BSUP, Corporation of Thiruvananthapuram.

the end of 2009. The number of projects taken up under the first, second, third and the fourth stages are 3, 2, 6 and 12 respectively. Excluding these four phases of group housing, there are projects for a large number of individual housing.

Group housing

Construction of the group houses/ flats in the five slums covered under first and second phases of BSUP, has begun in the city by government approved private agency. The construction of the flats has begun in the slums of Karimadom, Kannanmoola, Two Cent and Rajiv Nagar colonies. The MoU (Memorandum of understanding) between Thiruvananthapuram City Municipal Corporation (TCMC), *Kudumbasree* and the three contracting agencies was signed in January 2008. As the construction works were going at a snail's pace there were continuous protests from the residents. The main reason for the delay in starting the construction works was due to the demand for change in the structural design of the houses to be built under the program. The progress of the group housing schemes in Thiruvananthapuram city was much faster than in Kochi. This is evident from difference in the number of projects already initiated in both the cities under group housing.

Individual / scattered housing

The individual housing is included in the second and third phases of BSUP in the city. At first, 1000 houses will be built within the Municipal corporation area while in the second part another 1000 houses will be constructed which will be allocated equally between the four Pachayats in the CDP area (ie 250 houses each in Kazhakkoottam, Sreekaryam, Vattiyoorkkavu and Vizhinjam Panchayats). From the later group of 1000 houses, 218 houses will be given to the families of Scheduled Tribes and Scheduled Castes. The number of houses constructed through the Mission in the city is much lower than that of Kochi.

Comparative Progress of BSUP in the Mission Cities of Kerala

Various indicators can be used to measure the level of progress of the Mission in both the cities. The Table 4.11 is an attempt to summarize the comparative performance of the two Mission cities under BSUP. In the state as a whole, there are seven projects under the Sub Mission. These cover mainly the slum and individual housing for the urban poor. In order to analyze the performance of the Sub Mission in the two cities separately, aspects like fund utilization, share of the funds invested in comparison to the planned investment, etc are compared. Thiruvananthapuram with four phases of the BSUP projects stands ahead of Kochi in various aspects related to BSUP performance.

The share of the state, in the total funds released under the BSUP is 1.7 percent while it is 0.48 percent and 1.19 percent in case of Kochi and Thiruvananthapuram. This cannot be considered as poor performance of the state under the Mission, unless we compare it with the size of the urban poor population in the state. The ratio between the share in the BSUP funds released and the share in the urban poor population covered under the Mission proves this fact.

The share of the urban poor living in Thiruvananthapuram is only 0.5 percent of the total urban poor population covered under the Mission, while the share of the city in the funds released is 1.19, thus making the ratio between the two as high as 2.38. On the other hand, the share of the urban poor population in Kochi is as high as 1.76 percent. But, the share of the city in funds released under the Sub Mission is only 1.19 percent, thus keeping the ratio between the share of the city in funds released and urban poor population much lower than that of Thiruvananthapuram.

The wide gap in the two cities in the ratio between the funds released in relation to the urban poor population shows that Thiruvananthapuram city is performing much better than Kochi in case of BSUP. This is evident in all the other aspects related to the progress of the BSUP projects. On one hand, according to the CDPs, the amounts that were expected to be invested in BSUP in the four years for every 1000 urban poor

Table 4.11 Assessment of Progress under Basic Services for the Urban Poor in the Mission cities of Kerala

Various aspects on BSUP	*Mission Cities*		
	Kochi	*Thiruvananthapuram*	*Kerala*
Projects undertaken under BSUP	3	4	7
Percent share funds released to total funds released in the country under BSUP	0.48	1.19	1.7
Percent share of urban poor covered in the CDP area of the city to total urban poor covered under Mission	1.76	0.50	2.26
Ratio of the cities between the shares of the funds released under BSUP and urban population covered under Mission	0.27	2.38	0.75
Percentage share of funds released as share of CDP investment layout for 4 years	3.53	14.41	7.62
Percentage funds approved as a share of the CDP layout for 4 years	23.6	60.01	37.30
Percentage of funds released from the approved funds	14.94	23.98	20.42
Investment actually made in urban infrastructure per 1000 population in four years (in Rs. lakhs)	4.77	41.23	12.85
Investment planned to be made in urban infrastructure per 1000 population in four years (in Rs.lakhs)	135	286	168

Source- CDPs and Corporation Websites of Kochi and Thiruvananthapuram Corporations.

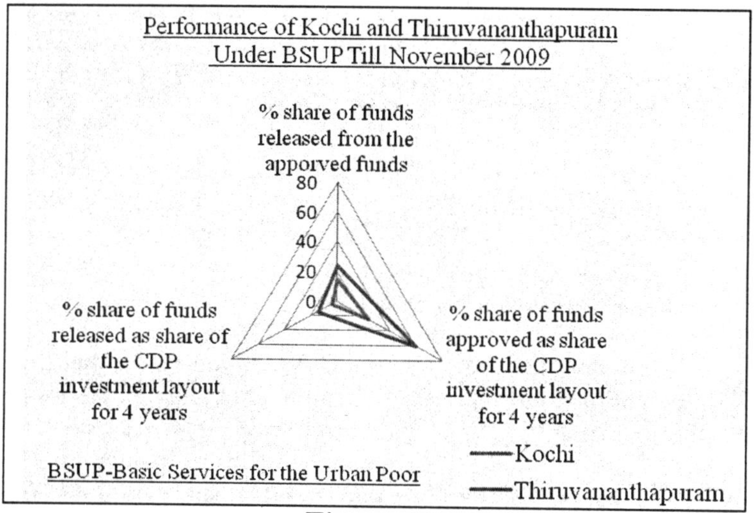

Figure 4.2

population were 1.35 crores and 2.86 crores in case of Kochi and Thiruvananthapuram. But on the other hand, the amounts which have actually been invested in the four years per 1000 urban poor population are 4.77 lakhs and 41.23 lakhs. Thus, it is proved that Thiruvananthapuram city has made much more progress in the BSUP than Kochi.

The percentage shares of the released fund to that of the CDP investment layout for the initial four years, also support this fact. If we assume that Rs.100 was planned to be invested under the Sub Mission during first four years of the Mission, the comparison becomes easier. In this plan, Thiruvananthapuram city was able to get more than Rs.60 approved and close to Rs. 14.5 was invested for the various projects. On the other hand, Kochi was able to get only Rs.23.6 approved and Rs. 3.5 was invested in various BSUP projects. Though the share of the urban population is much larger in Kochi in comparison to Thiruvananthapuram, the former one failed to make adequate investments in this area.

Challenges of BSUP in Kerala

The assessment of BSUP projects in the state shows that the Mission cities are facing several constraints in the various stages of project implementation. Some of them are as follows.

- Lack of reliable data on slums and urban poor is the biggest challenge that BSUP is facing at present in Kerala. This has led to wrong selection of slums and beneficiaries to be covered under the housing programs.

- Construction works could not be started in the colonies even after getting the project approval long back. This was because of the delay in the beginning of the projects due to the demand for the change in the structural design of the houses to be constructed.

- The resistance from the residents in accepting the 'flat model' is another hurdle in implementation of projects. Majority of the slum residents who will benefit from the Mission are against the 'flat model' as they believe that it will worsen their living conditions as the new flats are too congested in design and will be a major constraint on privacy.

- A large portion of the urban poor population in the city as well as the surrounding areas will not be benefitted from the Mission as they do not have legal ownership of the land, where the present house is located. This is very true in case of the fisherman families whose houses fall within the Costal Regulation Zone.

- Another problem is the high cost of construction materials especially of sand in the area (costs around Rs. 55,000 per truck). This makes it very difficult and almost impossible for the beneficiaries of individual housing to finish the house construction with the Rs.1,20,000 allotted under the program.

- Lack of technically qualified staff for implementation and for other related works leads to time lag in the entire processes. The Corporation officials stated that though the number of engineers needed for JNNURM wing is 20, only 3 engineers are available. This is one of the main reasons for the delay in the implementation of the projects.

- The residents complain that there is discrepancy in the selection of the beneficiaries. This has to be properly checked by the ULBs as the ward members have vital role in preparing the beneficiary list in the final stage. The same problem can be observed in case of the previous housing programs for slum population. In some of the cases, the residential flats constructed through these schemes, were allotted to non slum individuals with strong political background.

- Lack of initiatives from the private investors or contractors due to various reasons like low profitability and the long delay of the projects are other reasons for the slow progress of the projects. Because of the cumbersome official formalities before and after the approval of the projects, only few projects have begun till date.

- Since most of the projects were approved far back, tendering is one of the major problems at present. The prices of the materials used for construction have gone very high at present than compared to that of the prices when the project funds were approved. Due to this problem no agencies are coming forward to accept the tender at the current rates.

Conclusions

Kerala is a state well known for the various initiatives taken in the area of social development, especially in the area of poverty alleviation. The following conclusions can be drawn from the study on urban poor and basic amenities in the state with special focus on BSUP.

- Thiruvananthapuram is far ahead of Kochi in progress of projects under BSUP and has made remarkable achievements in urban poverty alleviation. This is clear from the fact that when Kochi could invest only 3.5 percent of the planned investments under BSUP while the corresponding share of Thiruvananthapuram city is 14.4 percent. But the state as a whole has not been able to get the funds under BSUP in proportion to the urban poor population.

- The two Mission cities of the state vary widely from one another in terms of size, settlement pattern, economic condition of the residents and availability of the infrastructural facilities. On one hand, there are slums with hardly 100 people living in, but on the other, there are slums with population well above 2000. Similarly, there are slums with well developed infrastructural facilities and slums with very poor infrastructural facilities.

- The interaction with the slum households disclosed the strength as well as the loopholes of the state sponsored poverty alleviation Mission, *Kudumbasree* in its functioning. Since it was initiated when the Communist Party was in power, it is often considered by many as a Marxist institution for poverty alleviation. Serious discrepancies were noticed in the selection of the beneficiaries under BSUP. The political intervention by various parties in the selection of beneficiaries as well as in the overall functioning of *Kudumbasree* is one major threat of BSUP in the state. This has made many of *Kudumbasree* members to be pessimistic about the beneficiary selection and its functioning. The drop out noticed in *Kudumbasree* has to be taken seriously as the increasing drop outs will spoil the entire objectives of the Mission in course of time. The impartiality in beneficiary selection can be ensured only if various steps are taken to guarantee transparency in its functioning.

- It was noticed that though 'giving tenure at affordable cost' is one option of slum housing under BSUP, the ULBs are least interested in implementing this. It is only in case of a large slum named 'Kissan colony' that the ULB has agreed to give land tenure to the households. It was also observed that the official formalities involved are taking very long time and only six families were given "*patta*" or legal ownership of land in the first four years of the Mission. The interview with the residents revealed that 'flat housing' is against the interest of the slum population. This will further deteriorate the life of the urban poor. The study also supports the fact that the grievances of the people should be properly channelized towards the authorities for the better performance of these programs in the future.[28]

- The lack of reliable data on the slums and urban poor in the cities is another problem in the implementation of the poverty alleviation schemes in Kerala. Besides this, there is serious shortage in the data available on slums in the cities. The long tussle between the Town and Country Planning Organization of the state and *Kudumbasree* in coming to an agreement on the number of slums in the Mission cities proves this problem. This has led to wrong selection of the slums under various schemes while the more needy ones were left behind. The responsibility to list the slums in these cities is vested on the ward members. This gives enormous scope for manipulation of the reality by the elected members to suit their political needs. Those who are more politically powerful than the rest will be able to bargain in the process to exaggerate number of slums and to get them covered under poverty alleviation schemes.

- There are a large number of slums which lack infrastructural facilities much acutely than the slums covered under the Mission. Thus, the argument that the slums under BSUP are selected on the basis of the intensity of shortage in the basic amenities cannot be accepted. The field observation has revealed the fact that the majority of the slums covered under the Mission are either located in the central parts of the city, or near to the strategic locations.

- The implementation of 'flat model' housing in the slums like 24 Mury colony with well developed infrastructural facilities and fully furnished houses will only deteriorate their living. Thus, the benefits and the losses that the slum families will get after the implementation of a housing program have to be compared before pushing for the 'flat model' in all the selected colonies. The push by the ULBs for the "flat model" has to be conceived as an attempt by the ULBs to evacuate huge expanses of urban land at many important locations of the city.

- It is mainly the housing projects which are taken under BSUP in both the cities. Within this, it is the individual or scattered housing projects which have progressed a large way than the group housing projects. The construction of more than 1000 houses was completed in both the Mission cities. Opposition from the slum population against the implementation of 'flat model' houses, lack of private contractors coming forward to participate in construction etc, have hindered the smooth progress of the group housing projects in the state. The urban poor households falling outside the core city area benefit from the individual housing projects to a remarkable extent.

- A large chunk of the urban poor will not be benefitted from the Mission firstly due to its small number of slums covered under BSUP and secondly, because of the disqualification of a good portion of urban poor to apply for the housing scheme. This is true in case of fisherman slums where the majority of the households do not have the legal ownership of the land which is necessary to apply for housing scheme under BSUP.

References

1. Sen, A. (1989), "Development as Capability Expansion", *Journal of Development Planning*, Vol. 17, p. 43.
2. Radhakrishna, R., Rao, K.H. (2006), "Poverty, Unemployment and Public intervention", India Social Development Report, Council for Social Development, p. 78.

3. Parnell, S., Robinson, J. (2006), "Development and Urban Policy; Johannesburg City Development Strategy", *Urban Studies*, Vol. 43, No. 2, p. 352.
4. Sen, A. (1989), "Development as Capability Expansion", *Journal of Development Planning*, Vol. 17, p. 48.
5. Government of Kerala, (2002), "Tenth Five Year Plan", Kerala State Planning Board, p. 159.
6. Casinader, R. (Dec 1995), 'Making Kerala Model More Intelligible: Comparisons with Sri Lankan Experience', *Economic and Political Weekly*, Vol. 30, No. 48, p. 3087.
7. NIUA (2005), "Local Economic Development and Poverty Reduction Strategies", Impact of the Constitution of 74th Amendment Act on the Working of Urban Local Bodies, p. 62.
8. National Sample Survey, 2003-04.
9. 'Annual plan 2007-2008', Kerala State Planning Board, p. 414.
10. Government of Kerala, (2003), "Economic Review of Kerala, 2002", Kerala State Planning Board, p. 308.
11. *Ibid*, p. 3.
12. *Ibid*, p. 12.
13. Government of Kerala,(2002), Urban Policy, http://www.kerala.gov.in/annualprofile/urban.htm
14. NIUA, (1993), "Evaluation of the Slum Upgradation Programs in Kerala; Case Studies of Kochi, Thiruvananthapuram and Calicut", p. 132.
15. Gupta, I., Misra, A. (2002), "Rural migrants and labor segmentation; Micro level evidence from Delhi slums", *Economic and Political Weekly*, Vol. 37, No. 2, p.167.
16. Wichester, H.P.M., White, P.E. (1988), "The location of marginalized groups in the city", *Society and Space*, Vol. 6, No. 1, p. 37.
17. Loyolla College of Social Sciences, (Dec 2004), "A comparative study of Self Help Groups organized and promoted by Non-Governmental Organization and *Kudumbasree*- A Government organized Non Governmental organization in Kerala, towards empowerment of poor women", Report submitted to Ministry of Human resource development, p. 15.
18. John, J. (2009), "*Kudumbasree* Project: A Poverty Eradication Program in Kerala: Performance, Impacts and Lessons for the other states", Planning Commission Report, p. 7.
19. *Ibid.*, p. 12.

20. Baindur,V., Kmath, L., (2009), 'Reengineering Urban Infrastructure; How the World Bank and Asian Development Bank Shape Urban Infrastructure Finance and Governance in India', Asian Development Bank, p. 27.
21. World Bank, (2009), "Improving Municipal management for cities to succeed; An Independent Educational Group special study", p. 17.
22. Ghosh, D., Ghosh, S., Bounsley, L. (2006), "Water and the Urban Poor", NIUA, Working Paper, 06-11, p. 23.
23. Government of Kerala, (2002), "Tenth Five Year Plan", Kerala State Planning Board, p. 158.
24. NIUA, (1993), "Evaluation of the Slum Upgradation Programs in Kerala; Case Studies of Kochi, Thiruvananthapuram and Calicut", p.148.
25. Ghosh, D., Ghosh, S., Bounsley, L. (2006), "Water and the Urban Poor", NIUA, Working Paper, 06-11, p. 23.
26. Kumar, N., Aggarwal S.C. (2003), "Patterns of consumption and poverty in Delhi slums", *Economic and Political Weekly*, Vol., No., p. 5297.
27. Asraya is a destitute eradication program started by the state government. It is the first integrated program for addressing issues affecting the poorest of the poor who generally are not covered by any of the designated poverty alleviation programs and who live in the margins of economy and society and polity. Destitute families will be identified according to the nine-point criteria evolved earlier by the *Kudumbasree* Mission.
28. Paul, S (1994)., "Public Services for the Urban Poor; Report Card on the three Indian Cities", *Economic and Political Weekly*, Vol. 29, No. 50, p. 3133.

5

Conclusions and Policy Suggestions

The tremendous increase in the role of urban areas in the economic growth of the country especially in the post economic reform period led to the introduction of several urban development initiatives both at the state and national levels. The first part of the study has attempted to analyze the progress of the states and the cities under the ongoing large scale urban development program in the country namely, Jawaharlal Nehru National Urban Renewal Mission (JNNURM), whereas the second part of the study deals with the progress of JNNURM projects in the two Mission cities in Kerala; i.e. Kochi and Thiruvananthapuram. Taking into account the factors of the number of cities covered, size of the investment and the nature of the reforms suggested in the field of urban governance, there is no doubt of the fact that JNNURM is a milestone in the history of urban development in the country. But, the question whether the Mission could progress satisfactorily as compared to the level of abysmally high expectations of the policy makers and the international agencies is a difficult one. This chapter summarizes the conclusions of the present study (which is done section wise for better understanding) in the first part while the second part deals with the policy suggestions to improve the progress of JNNURM projects. The following conclusions are drawn from this study.

JNNURM - Major conclusions at the state and city levels

- Both at the city and state levels the division of the released funds between the Sub-Mission for the urban infrastructure and governance and the Sub-Mission to improve the quality of life of urban poor is not very skewed as compared to the allocation of funds in CDP investment layout of most of the Mission cities. Roughly 25 per cent of the total released funds under the Mission were invested in the BSUP projects.

- Wide variation in the level of performance under the Mission as a whole and under the Sub-Missions was observed both at the state and city levels. Those states which were able to achieve the market supportive reforms were successful in getting huge private investments, while those states which lagged in implementing the pro-market reforms were left behind. It was also noticed that the narrow revenue base of the small and medium towns is a major obstacle in the Mission progress as no projects are initiated unless the share of the ULB in the project is deposited first.

- JNNURM can be considered as a major step in reducing regional disparities across the country. The analysis of the data on fund allocation proved that North East India, which had always been bypassed by the major urban development initiatives in the past were however, able to get funds through the Mission. The special considerations given to the cities of this region in the funding pattern under the Mission projects is an additional support given by the Government of India to enable them to better their poor physical infrastructure.

- The urban infrastructural sectors which were able to attract private investment easier than other sectors have got large chunk of the funds released under the Mission. These sectors are water supply, sewerage, drainage, etc. The Mission has also given priority for the implementation of the projects in the crucial urban service areas like water supply, sewerage, etc., which have huge impact on the standard of living of the population.

- Urban Governance reforms initiated under the Mission can be considered as the potent tool with which Government of India has attempted to promote the market based development of urban areas. Some of the Mission reforms will curb decentralized governance in urban areas and will further marginalize the economically weaker sections. In comparison to the reforms aimed to decentralize governance, ULBs were keen to implement market supportive reforms. The main reason for this tendency of the ULBs is their ultimate need to attract private investments in urban infrastructure and basic amenities.

- It is also revealed from the study that the Mission will not be able to improve the quality of life of a large proportion of the urban poor in these cities. The number of houses to be constructed through various housing projects under the Mission falls short of the actual need. Besides this, the Mission has given indirect signal for the demolition of the non notified slums by means of various reforms. This model of slum development is nothing but the modified form of the 'bulldozer' approach in urban renewal.

- The very small number of the projects completed as compared to the approved projects puts doubt about the degree of success of the Mission in transforming the urban areas of the country. One of the important reasons for the very slow pace of the progress of the Mission projects is the shortage of technically qualified staff needed for project implementation.

Progress of Urban Infrastructure and Governance (UIG) in Kerala

- The peripheral areas have also benefitted from the Mission projects to a large extent especially in the sectors like water supply, transportation, drainage, etc. But the degree to which these areas have got the benefits through JNNURM could not be studied due to paucity of data.

- The analysis of the data proved that there is wide intercity and intra city variation in the pattern of fund allocation under JNNURM. Kochi is ahead of Thiruvananthapuram in the degree of utilization of approved funds as well as in the share of actual investment made in urban infrastructure as compared to the planned investment given in the CDPs. The main reason for the better performance of Kochi is because of its ability to attract private investments as it is the center of commercial activities in the state, standing much ahead of Thiruvanathapuram.

- The performance of the cities in Kerala under UIG is appalling in comparison to many other Mission cities. The share of the invested funds in urban infrastructure as compared to the planned investment is roughly 0.6 percent in both the cities. Because of the various capacity constraints both the cities could utilize only 5 percent of the total released funds under the urban infrastructure Sub-Mission. At the present level of progress, it cannot be expected that the cities will be able to overcome the present challenges in urban infrastructure delivery through JNNURM.

- In both the cities, solid waste management sector has performed far ahead of the other sectors. Though not significant, the other sector where investment could be made under JNNURM in the cities is water supply. The investments in other infrastructural sectors which were mainly dependent on private sector investment were negligible or absent.

- Irrespective of the economic conditions, a good number of the slum households are covered under the solid waste management service in both the cities. They are willing to pay for the service as they believe there are no other options to better their living conditions than to get the paid service. It was also noticed that irrespective of the level of income, the families residing in slums located near vacant public land, do not avail the paid service as they have the option to dump the waste in the open space.

- The main reason for the success of solid waste management sector in the state is the active participation of the common people in various activities involving service delivery. Besides creating numerous low skilled jobs these activities have also empowered the women economically and socially. Door to door waste collection by these women has made the service delivery efficient.

- Severe shortage in the number of technically qualified staff in the JNNURM wing of the ULBs is another problem the Mission cities in Kerala are facing at present. This further delays the project implementation making it more difficult to get the bids successfully from the private investors for various projects.

Progress of Basic Services for the Urban Poor (BSUP) in Kerala

- The nature of the slums in the two Mission cities of the state varies widely from one another in terms of size, settlement pattern, economic condition of the residents and availability of the infrastructural facilities. On one hand, there are slums with hardly 100 people living in them and on the other, there are slums with population well above 2000. Similarly, there are slums with well developed infrastructural facilities and those with very poor infrastructural facilities.

- The lack of reliable data and records on the slums and urban poor in the cities is another problem in the implementation of the poverty alleviation schemes in

Kerala. The responsibility to list the slums and the slum families in these cities is vested on the ward members. This gives enormous scope for manipulation of the reality by the elected members to suit their political needs.

- The lack of reliable data on slums in both the cities has led to wrong selection of the slums under various schemes while the more needy ones were left behind. There are a large number of slums which lack infrastructural facilities much acutely than the slums covered under the Mission. Thus, the argument that the slums under BSUP are selected on the basis of the intensity of shortage in the basic amenities cannot be accepted. The field observation has revealed the fact that the majority of the slums covered under the Mission are either located in the central parts of the city, or near to the strategic locations.

- *Kudumbasree* plays an important role in the implementation of programs under BSUP especially in beneficiary selection. The study has proved that the beneficiary selection for the various housing programs under BSUP is highly biased. It was clear from the field that many needy families were not covered under the housing scheme, while many better-off households with political connections were covered. The political intervention by various parties in the beneficiary selection as well as in the overall functioning of *Kudumbasree* is one major threat to BSUP in the state. The drop out in *Kudumbasree* membership has to be taken seriously as the increasing drop outs will nullify the objectives of the Mission in course of time.

- It was noticed that though 'giving tenure at affordable cost' is one option in slum housing under BSUP, the ULBs are least interested in implementing this option. It is only in case of a large slum namely 'Kissan colony' that the ULB agreed to give land tenure to the households. The official formalities involved under this took such a long time that only six families were given "*patta*" of legal ownership of land in the first four years of the Mission.

- The implementation of "housing in flats" is against the interest of the slum population. The implementation of 'flat model' housing in the slums like 24 Mury Colony with well developed infrastructural facilities and fully furnished houses will only deteriorate their living conditions.

- A large chunk of the urban poor will not benefit from the Mission firstly because a small number of slums are covered under BSUP and secondly, because of the disqualification of a good portion of urban poor from applying for the housing scheme. This is true in the case of slums where fishermen live in majority. A good share of these households does not have the legal ownership of land which is necessary to apply for housing scheme under BSUP.

- The beneficiary selection under the previous slums housing schemes in the cities was also highly biased because of the political interventions. The flats distributed to the beneficiaries did not improve their standard of living remarkably as these flats were not provided with basic amenities like electricity and water supply in the premises. A group housing of this sort in fact made their life more difficult than earlier.

- The individual housing scheme has gone way ahead of the group housing scheme because of comparatively simpler official formalities and the enthusiasm of the applicants because it enabled them to own their premises. Opposition from the slum population against the implementation of 'flat model' houses, lack of private contractors coming forward to participate in construction etc, have hindered the smooth progress of the group housing projects in the state.

- The city level comparison of the projects under BSUP clearly points out that Thiruvananthapuram is far ahead of Kochi in progress of projects under BSUP. This is clear from the fact that when Kochi could invest only 3.5 percent of the planned investments under BSUP, the corresponding share of Thiruvananthapuram is 14.4 percent. However, the state as a whole failed to get the funds under BSUP in proportion to the population of the urban poor.

Policy suggestions from the study

For the purpose of policy making, the present study brings out the following suggestions :

Suggestions for JNNURM (All India Level)

- In order to ensure the access of the urban poor to the basic amenities as well as the sustainability in the provision of urban services in the long run, the GoI can prepare a database to locate the areas of concentration of urban poor within every ULB. This data base can be used to frame cost recovery mechanism for various services in such a way that it will not marginalize the urban poor from accessing them. The cost recovery can be done at a minimal rate in the economically weaker localities while the rest of the service cost, will have to be paid by the Local body as subsidy taking financial assistance from the Central and State governments.

- GoI should reshape JNNURM in a fashion which will promote the active local participation and mobilization of the local resources rather than merely focus on the market oriented reforms. The success of the solid waste management service in Kerala through the active participation of *Kudumbasree* members is a good example.

- In order to tackle the long delay in the implementation of the Mission projects, adequate technically qualified staff should be recruited at all levels of Mission management.

- In order to ensure the integrated and sustainable development of our urban centers in the long run, the Mission should include the presently neglected aspects of socio-economic development under JNNURM. It has to be remembered that a good urban development plan is the one which is comprehensive in covering the entire urban community, or entire area, addresses all aspects of government activity, and has a long term involvement.[1]

- While distributing the flats to the urban households, the ULB should ensure the provision of the basic amenities in the flats. If the ULB fail to provide these essential amenities, the group housing projects under BSUP will fail to accomplish its objective of improving the life of the slum families.

Suggestions Specific to Kerala

- The successful involvement of *Kudumbasree* in the solid waste management sector should be replicated in other sectors of urban infrastructure like sewerage and water supply. This will lead to efficient service delivery, women empowerment and the creation of numerous employment opportunities for the economically weaker sections.

- The state as well as the ULBs should have a detailed data base of the slums and urban poor at the household level. The list of beneficiaries prepared by the elected members can be cross checked with this data base to eliminate biasness in beneficiary selection.

- The choice for "flat model' group housing should be based on the losses and gains to the slum families once the program is implemented. The implementation of the 'flat model' in the slums with well developed infrastructural facilities and fully furnished houses will only deteriorate their living conditions.

- Necessary steps have to be taken by the state so that the poverty alleviation Mission "*Kudumbasree*" is not diffused by political interventions. Necessary steps also should be taken to ensure more transparency in beneficiary selection.

- Some modifications in the procedures to apply for the Housing scheme under BSUP have to be initiated by the State Government. Unless this step is taken, a good number of households in fisherman colonies which make up a large share of the urban poor population in both the cities will not be covered under BSUP. The fisherman community can be considered as a 'special category' under BSUP.

It is expected that the Mission will give a 'big push' not only to economic growth of the country but also to provisioning of physical infrastructure.[2] The very slow pace of the progress of the Mission projects in the country have, however, cast doubts on the success that JNNURM could bring in the transformation of urban areas in the country. This was found true in the case of the two Mission cities of Kerala too. Various reforms included under the Mission have negative implications for decentralization of urban governance and the access of the urban poor to basic amenities. The market oriented funding strategy encouraged through the Mission could not enable all the cities and states to receive the funds under JNNURM in proportion to their population size. Under JNNURM, the failure to create an investment friendly atmosphere was found to be very costly for many states including Kerala. The stride to achieve high economic growth centered on the urban areas should not compromise with the quality of urban life and with the need to ensure equity in urban areas. The attempt to completely replicate the successful sagas of commercialized basic amenities in the developed world may prove to be wrong in a developing country like India. The encouragement of the participation of common people in various activities involving service delivery, rather than focusing solely on the private sector will give better results under JNNURM.

References

1. Hopkins., L.D. (2001), "Urban development; The logic of making plans", Published by Island Press, New York, p. 3.
2. JNNURM Official Website, Ministry of Housing and Urban Poverty Alleviation, https://jnnurmmis.nic.in/jnnurm_hupa/jnnurm/Fre%20asked%20questions1.pdf .

Bibliography

- A. Bhatt, C. Chawla, (2004), "Urban governance for sustainable development" , Working paper, pp. 1-14.
- A. F. Ades, E. L. Glaeser, (1995), 'Trade and circuses; Explaining the urban giants', *The Quarterly Journal of Economics*, Vol. 110, No. 1, pp. 195-227.
- A. Fung., E.O. Wright, (Jan. 2000), "Deepening democracy; Innovations in empowered participatory governance", Paper presented the seminar on 'Real Utopians versus experiments in empowered deliberative democracy conference', Wisconsin, pp. 1-37.
- A. Holm., (2006), "Urban Renewal and the end of Social Housing; The role of Neo-liberalism in East Berlin's Prenz Cauer Berg", *Social Justice; A journal of Crime, Conflict and World Order*, Vol. 33/3, pp. 1-20.
- A. K. Dutt, C.B. Monroe, R. Vakamudi, (Apr 1986), "Rural-Urban Correlates for Indian Urbanization", *Geographical Review*, Vol. 76, No. 2, pp. 173-183.
- A. Kumar., (Feb 1990), "Industrialization in Kerala", *Economic and Political Weekly*, Vol. 25, no. 7/8, pp. 379-380.
- A. Kundu., (July 1983), "Theories of City Size Distribution and Indian Urban Structure; A Reappraisal", *Economic and Political Weekly*, Vol. 18, No. 31, pp.1361-1368.
- ———., (June 1993), "Urbanisation and Alternate Policy Perspectives", *Economic and Political Weekly*, Vol. 28, No. 26, pp. 1351-1352.

- ———., S. Gupta, (1996), "Migration, Urbanization and Regional Inequality", *Economic and Political Weekly*, Vol. 31, No. 52, pp. 3391-3398.
- ———., (June 1997), "Trends and Structure of Employment in the 1990s: Implications for Urban Growth", *Economic and Political Weekly*, Vol. 32, No. 24, PP.1399-1405.
- ———., S. Bagchi, D. Kundu, (June 1999), "Regional Distribution of Infrastructure and Basic Amenities in Urban India: Issues concerning Empowerment of Local Bodies", *Economic and Political Weekly*, Vol. 34, No.28, pp. 1893-1906.
- ———., (2000), "Globalizing Gujarat: Urbanization, employment and poverty", *Economic and Political Weekly*, Vol. 35, No. 5/36, p. 3172- 3182.
- ———., (2000), "Infrastructure financing and emerging pattern of urbanization; A perspective", Working paper, pp. 1-28.
- ———., N. Lalitha, S. Arora, (2001), "Growth Dynamics of Informal Manufacturing Sector in Urban India: An Analysis of Interdependencies", (withn N, Lalitha., S, Arora.,) in A, Kundu, A, N, Sharma (eds.), *Informal Sector in India*, Institute of Human Development, New Delhi. pp. 93-123.
- ———., B. K. Pradhan, A. Subramanian, (Dec 2002), "Dichotomy or Continuum: Analysis of Impact of Urban Centers on Their Periphery", *Economic and Political Weekly,* Vol. 37, No. 50, pp. 5039-5046.
- ———., (July 2003), "Urbanization and Urban Governance: Search for a Perspective beyond Neo-Liberalism", *Economic and Political Weekly*, Vol. 38, No. 29, pp. 3079-3087.
- ———., (2008), "Trend and patterns of urbanization and their economic implications", India infrastructure report 2008, Published by Government of India, pp. 27-42.
- A. Pethe, M. Ghodke, (June 2002), "Funding Urban Infrastructure: From Government to Markets" , *Economic and Political Weekly*, Vol. 37, No. 25, pp. 2467-2470.

- A. Philip,(2001), "Rethinking U,K aid in urban India; reflections on an impact assessment of slum improvement projects", *Environment and Urbanization*,Vol.13, No.1, pp,101-113.
- A. Rastogi, (2008), "The infrastructure sector in India, 2007'India", *India infrastructure Report 2008*, Published by Government of India, pp. 1-36.
- A. Sen (1989), "Development as Capability Expansion", *Journal of Development Planning*, Vol. 17, pp. 42-58.
- A. Shariff, P. Ghosh, S.K. Mandal, (Mar.2002), "Adjusted public expenditure on social sector and poverty alleviation programs", *Economic and Political Weekly*, Vol. 37, No.8, pp.767-787.
- A. Smart. J. Smart, (2003), "Urbanization and the Global Perspective", *Annual Review of Anthropology*, Vol. 32, pp. 263-285.
- A. Von, Hoffman, (2000), "A study in contradictions; The origin and legacy of the housing act of 1949", *Housing Policy Debate*, Vol. 11, Issue.2, pp. 299-326.
- A. Cocharane, (1996), "Just another failed urban experiment? The legacy of the Urban Development Corporations?", Ed by R Imrie, H Thomas, Sage Publications, London, pp. 254.
- Asian Development Bank, (2004), "India; Promoting Urban Social Development Through Self Help Groups in Karnataka", pp. 1-43.
- ———, (Nov 2006), "Technical assistance promoting best practices in private sector participation in urban infrastructure in South Asia", Technical Assistance report, pp.1-10.
- ———,(2006), "Special evaluation study on urban sector strategy and operations", pp. 1-140.
- ———, (2008) "Country Assistance Evaluation Project for India", Operations evaluation department, pp. 1-172.
- ———, (2008), "Urban Innovations; Development of Poor Urban Communities", www.adb.org/urbandev, pp.1-2.
- ———, (2009), "ADB assistance on Public Private Partnership in infrastructure development- Potential for more success", pp. 1-78.

- B. Chattopådhayay (2008), "Sustainable Urban development in India; Some issues", NIUA, pp. 1-18.
- ———, (2008), "Public policy and sustainable development of small towns in India; A review", NIUA, Working Paper, pp. 1-16.
- B.H. Nordtveit, (2005), "Use of Public Private Partnership to deliver Social Services; Advantages and drawbacks", EFA report, Washington, pp. 1-24.
- B. Jessop, (2002), "Liberalism, neoliberalism and urban governance; A state theoretical perspective", Antipode, pp. 1-22.
- B. K. Pradhan, P. K. Roy, M. R. Saluja, S.Venkatram, (July 2000), "Rural-Urban Disparities: Income Distribution, Expenditure Pattern and Social Sector", *Economic and Political Weekly*, Vol. 35, No. 28/29, pp. 2527-2539.
- B. Kuruvilla, (Dec 2006), "ADB Kerala urban loan conditionalities; Facts or fiction?", *Focus on the global South- India*, pp. 1-5.
- B. M. Robert, M. Singh, J. Kalarickal, (2005), "Strategizing slum improvement in India; A method to monitor and refocus slum development programs", Global Urban Development Magazine, Vol. 3, No.1, pp. 1-24.
- C. Gulfer, K. Basu, (April 2008) "Two Years of Jawaharlal Nehru National Urban Renewal Mission (JNNURM)", p. 32.
- C. Harris, S.K. Tadiwalls, (December 2008), "Financing the boom in pubic private partnerships in Indian infrastructure", *Gridlines*, pp. 1-4.
- C. Kauffmann, (Nov. 2007), "Private sector participation in water and sanitation infrastructure", Background paper for regional roundtable on strengthening climate assessment and reform in NEPAD countries, Zambia, pp. 1-46.
- C. S. Lee, (Feb, 2005), "Income inequality, democracy, and public sector size", *American Sociological Review,* Vol. 7, No. 1, pp. 158-181.
- C. Schremmer, D. Stead, (June 2009), "Restructuring cities for sustainability ; A metabolism approach", Paper

presented at the Fifth Urban Research Symposium, World Bank, pp. 1-19.

- C. Vaidya, (2009), "Urban issues, reforms and way forward in India", NIUA, Working paper No.4/2009-DEA, pp. 1-40.
- ————., H. Vaidya, (2008), "Innovative Municipal resource mobilization in India", Paper presented at workshop on resource mo. 1-7.
- Charvak, (July 2000), "From decentralization of planning to people's planning; Experiences of the Indian states of West Bengal and Kerala", CDS, Discussion paper No. 21, pp. 1-80.
- CDS, (2006), "State human development report- 2005", Prepared by CDS for Government of Kerala, pp. 1-228.
- D. Bandyopadhyay, (Sep. 27 - Oct. 3, 1997), "People's Participation in Planning: Kerala Experiment", *Economic and Political Weekly*, Vol. 32, No. 39, pp. 2450-2454.
- D. Ghosh, S.Ghosh, L. Bounsley, (2006), "Water and the Urban Poor", NIUA, Working Paper, 06-11, pp.1-27.
- D. Harvey, (1989), " The condition of post- modernity", *Geographiska Annaler*, Vol. 71, No. 1, pp. 1-16.
- ————., (1989), "From managerialism to entrepreneurialism: The transformation in urban governance in late capitalism", *Geografiska Annaler*, Vol. 71, No. 1, pp. 1-16.
- ————, (1989), "The condition of post modernity: an enquiry into the origins of cultural change", Catalogingin-Publication, p. 326.
- ————, (2001), "The art of rent; globalization, monopoly and the commodification of culture", *Socialist Register*, http://www.generation-online.org/c/fc_rent1.htm, pp.1-14.
- D. Milton, J. Thompson, (1995), "Participatory approaches in urban areas; strengthening civil society or reinforcing the status quo?", *Environment and Urbanization*, Vol.7, No. 1, pp- 231- 251.
- D. Savage., S. Dasgupta, (2008), "Governance framework for delivery of urban services", *India Infrastructure Report 2008,* Published by Government of India, pp. 42-60.

- D. Thorner, (Mar, 1950), "Problems of Economic Development in India", *Annals of the American Academy of Political and Social Science*, Vol. 268, pp. 96-103.
- E. Idelovitch, K. Ringskog, (1997), "Private sector participation in water supply and sanitation in Latin America", Published by World Bank, Washington, p. 1-49.
- E. Lobina, D. Hall, (2000), "Public sector alternatives to water supply and sewerage privatization: Case studies", *International Journal of Water Resource Development*, Vol. 16, Issue. 1, pp. 35.
- E. Swyngedouw, F. Moulaert, A. Rodriguez, (2002), "Neoliberal Urbanization in Europe: Large–Scale Urban Development Projects and the New Urban Policy", *Antipode*, Vol. 34 , Issue 3 , pp. 542 - 577.
- E. Swyngedouw, F. Moulaert, A. Rodriguez, (2002), "Neoliberal urbanization in Europe: large-scale urban development projects and the new urban policy", *Antipode,* 2002, Vol. 34, Issue 3, pp. 542-577.
- E.T. Mathew, (Feb. 11, 1995), "Educated Unemployment in Kerala: Some Socio-Economic Aspects", *Economic and Political Weekly*, Vol. 30, No. 6, pp. 325-335.
- ———., (Sep. 25 - Oct. 1, 1999), "Growth of Literacy in Kerala: State Intervention, Missionary Initiatives and Social Movements", *Economic and Political Weekly*, Vol. 34, No. 39, pp. 2811-2820.
- F. Bianchini, M. Parkinson, (1994), "Cultural policy and urban regeneration; The West European experience", Published by Manchester University Press, p. 218.
- F. Miraftab, (2004), "Public Private Partnerships; The Trojan horse of Neoliberal Development", *Journal of Planning Education and Research*, Vol. 24, No. 1, pp. 89-101.
- ———, (2004), "Neoliberalism and casualization of public sector services: the case of waste collection services in Cape Town, South Africa", *International Journal of Urban and Regional Research*, Vol. 28, Issue 4, pp. 874-892.
- G. Breese, (Sep 1963), "Urban Development Problems in India", *Annals of the Association of American Geographers*, Vol. 53, No. 3, pp. 253-265.

- G. Cheema, G. Shabbir, D. Rondinelli, (ed), (1983), "Decentralization and development : Policy implementation in developing countries", Sage Publications, Beverly Hills, p. 319.
- G.E. Peterson, (2008), "Unlocking land values to finance urban infrastructure", World Bank, Trends and policy options No. 7, pp. 1-150.
- G.G.G. Clarke, K. Kosec, S. Wallasten (2008), "Has private participation in water and sewerage improved the coverage? Empirical evidence from Latin America", *Journal of International Development*, Vol. 21, No. 3, pp. 327-361.
- G. K. Lieten, (Apr. 20-26, 2002), "Human Development in Kerala: Structure and Agency in History", *Economic and Political Weekly*, Vol. 37, No. 16, pp. 1539-15.
- Government of India, (2006), "Jawaharlal Nehru National Urban Renewal Mission; Issues and Opportunities", Recommendations and proceedings of the mission workshop, pp. 1-15.
- Government of Kerala, (2002), "Social service", Tenth five year plan of Kerala, State Planning Commission, pp. 361-582.
- ———, (2002), "Urban Policy", http://www.kerala.gov.in/annualprofile/urban.htm
- ———, (2006), "Economic Review of Kerala", (2006), Kerala State Planning Board, pp. 1-552.
- ———, (2008), "Annual plan 2007-2008", Kerala State Planning Board, pp. 1-494.
- ———, (2009), '*Kerala Economic Review* 2008', pp. 1-542.
- ———, "*Kudumbasree*; State poverty eradication mission; Concepts, organization and activities", Department of local self governance, p. 27.
- ———, (2009), "Infrastructure", '*Economic Review 2008*', pp. 273-308.
- ———, (2009), "Housing", Economic Review 2008', pp. 313-323.
- H. Benjamin, (1983), "Growth poles to systems of interactions in space", *Growth and Change*, Vol. 14, Issue 4, pp. 3-13.

- H. P. M. Wichester, P.E. White, (1988), "The location of marginalized groups in the city", *Society and Space*, Vol. 6, No. 1, pp. 37-54.
- H. W. Richardson, (1978), "Growth centers, Rural Development and National Urban Policy; A defense", *International Regional Science Review*, Vol. 3, No. 2, pp. 133-152.
- ————, (1981), "National Urban Development Strategies in Developing Countries", *Urban Studies*, Vol. 18, No. 3, pp. 267- 283.
- H. Polly, (1986), "Kerala Is Different", *Modern Asian Studies*, Vol. 20, No. 4 (1986), pp. 779-792.
- http://jnnurm.nic.in
- http://www.corporationofcochin.net
- http://www.corporationoftrivandrum.in
- http://www.townplanning.kerala.gov.in
- http://www.urbanindia.nic.in
- http://www.urbanindia.nic.in/theministry/subordinateoff/tcpo/tcpo.htm
- I.S.A. Baud, J. De. Wit, (2002), "New forms of Urban Governance in India", Sage Publications, p. 420.
- I. Turak, (1992), "Property led urban regeneration; Panacea or Placebo?", Environment and Planning, Volume 24(3), pp. 361-379.
- I. Gupta, A. Misra, (2002), "Rural migrants and labor segmentation; Micro level evidence from Delhi slums", *Economic and Political Weekly*, Vol. 37, No. 2, pp. 163-168.
- "India Infrastructural Report", (2003), Published by Oxford University Press, pp. 1-350.
- J. Isham, (1995), "Does participation improve performance? Establishing causality and with subjective data", The World Bank and Economic Review, Vol. 9, No. 2, pp. 175-200.
- J. J. Thomas, (2003), "Labor and industrialization in Kerala", *Indian Journal of Labor Economics*, Vol. 46, No. 4, pp. 575-92.
- ————, (2005), "Kerala's industrial backwardness; a case of path dependence in industrialization?", *World Development*, Vol. 33, No. 5.

- J. John, (2009), "*Kudumbasree* Project: A Poverty Eradication Program in Kerala: Performance, Impacts and Lessons for the other states", Planning Commission Report, p.118.
- J.Kurien, (Jan 1995), "The Kerala Model: Its Central Tendency and the Outlier", *Social Scientist*, Vol. 23, No. 1/3, pp. 70-90.
- J. L. Baker, K. McClain, (July 2009), "Private sector initiatives in slum upgrading", World Bank Report, pp. 1-42.
- J. R. Logan, H. L. Molotch, (2007), *Urban Fortunes; The Political Aconomy of Place*, Published by California University Press, p. 378.
- J. Wood, (Nov. 1958), "Development of urban and regional planning in India", *Land Economics*, Vol. 34, No. 4, pp. 310-315.
- John B. Parr, "Growth poles studies in regional economic planning, A Retrospective View; Part1, Origins and advocacy", *Urban Studies*, Vol. 36, No. 7, 1195-1215 (1999).
- K. Choe, A. Laquian, H Kim, (August 2008), "Urban development experiences and visions; India and People's Republic of China", Asian Development Bank, pp. 1-71.
- K. K. George, (Sep. 15, 1990) "Kerala's Fiscal Crisis: A Diagnosis", *Economic and Political Weekly*, Vol. 25, No. 37, pp. 2097-2105.
- K. K. Subrahmaniam, M. P. Pillai, (1986): "Kerala's Industrial Backwardness: Exploration of Alternative Hypotheses", *Economic and Political Weekly*, Vol. 21, No 14, April 5, pp. 577-92.
- ———,(1990): "Development Paradox in Kerala. Analysis of Industrial Stagnation". *Economic and Political Weekly*, Vol. 25, No. 37, pp. 2053-2058.
- K.N. Harilal, Joseph, K.J., (2000), "Stagnation of Kerala Economy – An Open Economy Perspective", CDS, Thiruvananthapuram.
- K. P. Kannan, (May 1999), "Poverty alleviation as advancing basic human capabilities; Kerala's achievements compared", CDS,Working paper 294, pp. 1-45.

- ————, (Apr 2002), "The welfare funds model of social security for informal sector workers", CDS, Working paper 332, pp. 1-65.
- K. Pushpangadan, G. Murugan, (1998), "Pricing with changing welfare criterion; An application of Ramsey-Wilson model to urban water supply", CDS, Working paper 287, pp. 1-28.
- K. R. Conner, (1991), "A Historical Comparison of Resource-Based Theory and Five Schools of Thought Within Industrial Organization Economics: Do We Have a New Theory of the Firm?", *Journal of Management*, Vol. 17, pp. 121 -154.
- K. R. Nayar, (Feb. 12-18, 2000), "Decline of Co-operative Medical Services in Kerala", *Economic and Political Weekly,* Vol. 35, No. 7, pp. 519-521.
- K. P. Kannan, (Sep. 1-8, 1990), "Kerala Economy at the Crossroads?", ,*Economic and Political Weekly*, Vol. 25, No. 35/36, pp. 1951-56.
- K. T. Rammohan , (Apr 2000), "Assessing Reassessment of Kerala Model", Economic *and Political Weekly,* Vol. 35, No. 15, pp. 1234-1236.
- L. D. Hopkins, (2001), Urban development; The logic of making plans, Published by Island Press, New York, p. 294.
- Loyolla College of Social Sciences, (Dec 2004),"A comparative study of Self Help Groups organized and promoted by Non-Governmental Organization and *Kudumbasree*- A Government organized Non Governmental organization in Kerala, towards empowerment of poor women", Report submitted to Ministry of Human Resource Development, pp. 1-135.
- M. Li, (2005), "The rise of China and the demise of the capitalistic world economy; Exploring historical possibilities in the 21st Century", *Science & Society*, Vol. 69, Issue 3, pp. 420-448.
- M. A. Oommen (2008), "Micro finance and poverty alleviation; The case of Kerala's *Kudumbasree*", Center for Socio- economic and Environmental Studies, Working Paper No. 17, pp. 1-17.

- M. Barnhardt, S. Supriti, R. Ramanathan, (2002) "Urban Poverty Reduction Initiatives in India; A General Assessment and a Particular Perspective", Published by Ramanathan Foundation, p. 380.
- M. Eapen, (May 21, 1994), "Rural Non-Agricultural Employment in Kerala: Some Emerging Tendencies", *Economic and Political Weekly*, Vol. 29, No. 21, pp. 1285-1296.
- ————, (Mar. 25, 1995), "Rural Non-Agricultural Employment in Kerala: Inter-District Variations", *Economic and Political Weekly*, Vol. 30, No. 12, pp. 634-638.
- ————, (Apr 1999), "Economic diversification in Kerala; A spatial analysis", Paper presented at the Memorial seminar on development experience of South Indian states in a comparative setting, CDS, Thiruvananthapuram, pp.1-44.
- ————,(2001), "Rural non-farm employment: Agricultural versus urban linkages – some evidence from Kerala State, India", *Journal of Peasant Studies*, Vol. 28, No.3, pp. 67-89.
- M, Freire, J. Peterson, M. Heurtas, M. Valadaz, (ed) (2004), "Sustainable capital markets in developing countries; From theory to practice", Co-published by World Bank and Oxford University Press, pp. 1-697.
- M. Mehta, D. Mehta, (Apr, 1991), "Housing Finance System and Urban Poor", *Economic and Political Weekly*, Vol. 26, No. 17, pp. 1107-1114.
- M. P. Mathur, (April 2007), 'Impact of the Constitution 74th Amendment Act on the Urban Local Bodies; A review", NIUA working paper 07-02, pp. 1-21.
- ————, (Mar. 25, 1995), "Rural Non-Agricultural Employment in Kerala: Inter-District Variations", *Economic and Political Weekly*, Vol. 30, No. 12, pp. 634-638.
- M. Pillai, (Feb. 1990), "Whither state sector enterprises in Kerala?", *Economic and Political Weekly*, Vol. 25, No. 7/8, pp. M9-M16.

- M. R. Narayana, (Jan 2008), "Performance of urban India during globalization period; An economic analysis", Paper discussed at CIRJE, http://www.e.utokyo.ac.jp/cirje/research/03research02dp.html, pp. 1-41.
- M. S. John, J. Chathukulam, (May 18-24, 2002), "Building Social Capital through State Initiative: Participatory Planning in Kerala", *Economic and Political Weekly*, Vol. 37, No. 20, pp. 1939-1948.
- M.S. Pillai, (Aug. 3, 1996) "Social Security for Workers in Unorganized Sector: Experience of Kerala", *Economic and Political Weekly*, Vol. 31, No. 31, pp. 2098-2107.
- Ministry of urban development, (Jan 2007), "Peer Experience And Reflective Learning Initiative (PEARL)", pp. 1-94.
- "Mckinsey Report on Urban India 2030 ; Projections and Statistics", (2010), Mckinsey Global Institute, p. 234.
- N. Brenner, N. Theodore, (2002), "Preface; From the 'new localism' to the spaces of neoliberalism", Published by Blackwell Publishers Limited, UK, p. 280.
- ————, (2004), "New state spaces; Urban governance and the scaling of statehood", Published by Oxford University Press Inc, New York, p. 345.
- N. Cook, T. Dyson, (Mar. 1982), "Urbanization in India; Results from the 1981 Census", *Population and Development Review*, Vol. 8, No. 1, pp. 145-155.
- N. Johnson, L. Wood, R. Hearne, (September 1999), "The regulation of private sector participation in urban water supply and sanitation; Realising social and environmental objectives in developing countries", International Institute for Environmental Sciences, Discussion paper. 99-01, pp. 1-55.
- N. Kumar, S. C. Aggarwal, (2003), "Patterns of consumption and poverty in Delhi slums", *Economic and Political Weekly*, Vol. , No., pp. 5296-5300.
- N. Tiwari, (Nov 2009), "Recent trends in gender mainstreaming and poverty alleviation; The *Kudumbasree* initiative", *Common wealth Journal of Local Governance*, Issue 4, pp. 121-129.

- N. Padmanabhan, (1990), "Poor Performance of Private Corporate Sector in Kerala", *Economic and Political Weekly*, Vol. 25, No. 37, pp. 2071-2075.
- N. Nilekani, (2009), "An exploration of sustainability in the provision of basic urban services in Indian cities", Published by TERI Press, pp. 412.
- NIUA, (1993), "Evaluation of the Slum Upgradation Programs in Kerala; Case Studies of Kochi, Thiruvananthapuram and Calicut", pp. 1-157.
- ————, (2005), "Impact of the Constitution of 74th Amendment Act on the Working of Urban Local Bodies", pp. 1-124.
- P. C. Annez, (Nov.2006), "Urban infrastructure finance from private operators; What have we learned from recent experience?", World Bank policy research working paper, pp. 1-30.
- P. C. Bhattacharya, (2002), "Urbanization in developing countries", *Economic and Political Weekly*, Vol. 37, No. 41, pp. 4219- 4228.
- P. D. Jeromi, (Apr. 19-25, 2003), "What Ails Kerala's Economy: A Sectoral Exploration", *Economic and Political Weekly*, Vol. 38, No. 16, pp. 1584-1600.
- P.D. Dey, S. Dev, (Dec 2006), "Rent control laws in India; A critical analysis", NIUA Working Paper 06-04, pp. 1-57.
- ————, T. Ramanathan, (December 2006), "Urban poverty reduction strategies; Past, Present and future", NIUA Working Paper 06-06, pp.1-32.
- ————, S. Gupta (December 2009), "Community oriented City Development Plans", NIUA Working Paper 06-02, pp.1-23.
- P.E. Peterson, (1981), "City limits", Published by the University of Chicago press, p. 265.
- P. K. Mohanty, B.M. Misra, R. Goyal, P.D. Jeromi, (Dec 2007), "Municipal finance in India; An assessment", Reserve Bank of India, Dept. of Economic Analysis and Policy, p. 214.
- R. B. Solanki, R. N. Dubey, (March 2007), "Urban planning in India; Challenges and Sustainable

Development", Paper presented at the national seminar organized by University of Delhi, pp.1-15.

- R. Casinader, (Dec 1995), "Making Kerala Model More Intelligible: Comparisons with Sri Lankan Experience", *Economic and Political Weekly*, Vol. 30, No. 48, pp. 3085-3092.
- R. Chandra, S. Singh, B. Chattopadhyay, (April 2007),"Norms and standards of Municipal basic services in India", NIUA Working Paper 07-01, pp. 1-41.
- R. Imrie, H. Thomas, (1999), "British Urban Policy; An evaluation of the Urban Development Corporations", Sage Publications, London, p. 275.
- R. J. Gittell, A. Vidal, (1998), "Community organizing; Building social capital as a Development Strategy", *Canadian Journal of Urban Research*, Sage Publication, p. 196.
- R. Khosla, (2009), "Addressing gender concerns in India's Urban Renewal Mission", Report Submitted to UNDP, pp.1-62.
- R. Martin, P. Sunley, (1997), Lee R. Wills J. (eds.), "The Post –Keynesian state and the space economy", *Geographies of Economies*, London: Arnold, pp. 278–289.
- R. Mohan, (Dec 1985), "Urbanization in India's future", *Population and Development Review*, Vol. 11, No. 4, pp. 619-645.
- ————, (Sep 1992), "Housing and Urban Development: Policy Issues for 1990s", *Economic and Political Weekly*, Vol. 27, No. 36, pp. 1913-1920.
- R. Nallathinga, (2005), "Institutional innovations of Urban Governance; Some examples of Indian cities", *Urban India*, Vol. xxv, No. 2, pp. 1-28.
- R. Radhakrishna, K. H. Rao, (2006), "Poverty, Unemployment and Public Intervention", India Social Development Report, Council for Social Development, p. 1-560.
- R. Ramachandran,(1990), *Urbanization and Urban Systems in India*, Published by Oxford University Press, p. 380.

- R. Sharma, (Sep. 6-12, 2003), "Kerala's Decentralization: Idea in Practice", *Economic and Political Weekly*, Vol. 38, No. 36, pp. 3832-3850.
- R. Weber, (2002), "Extracting Value from the City; Neoliberalism and Urban Development", *Antipode*, Vol. 34, Issue. 3, pp. 519-540.
- R. Raman,(2004), "The Asian Development Bank loan for Kerala (India); The adverse implications and search for the alternatives", Working Paper 357, CDS, Trivandrum, p. 78.
- R. Reddy, (July, 2001), "Declining social consumption in India", *Economic and Political Weekly,* Vol. 36, No. 29, pp. 2750- 2751.
- S. Bagchi, (Sep 1999), "Myth of Empowering Urban Local Bodies" , *Economic and Political Weekly*, Vol. 34, No. 37, p. 2637.
- ————-, (Feb 2001), "Financing Capital Investments in Urban Infrastructure: Constraints in Accessing Capital Market by Urban Local Bodies", *Economic and Political Weekly*, Vol. 36, No. 4, pp. 385-398.
- ————-, (2002), "Decentralized Urban Governance in India; Implications for financing urban infrastructure", Working paper, pp. 1.28.
- S, Banerjee- Guha., K. Sita., V.S. Phadke., (1988), *The declining city-core of an Indian metropolis: A case study of Bombay*, Published by Concept Publishing Company, New Delhi, pp. 384.
- S. Gupta, S. Kumar, G. K. Saranagi, (December 2006), "Measuring the performance of water service providers in urban India; Implications for managing water utilities", NIUA Working Paper 06-08, pp. 1-21.
- S. Kamat, (2005), The privatization of public interest; Theorizing NGO discourse in a neoliberal era, *Review of international political economy*, Vol. 11, Issue 1, pp. (155-176).
- S. M. Vijayanad, (April 2009), "Kerala- A case study of classical democratic decentralization", Kerala Institute for Local Administration, For submission of 12th finance commission, pp. 1-84.

- S.Mitra, D. Mahadevia (ed), (2008), "Financing urban development in Delhi: Towards inclusive Globalisation?", *Inside the Transforming Urban India: Processes, Policies and Public Actions*, Published by Concept Publishing Company, New Delhi, p. 619.
- S. Mukherji, (1995), "Poverty Induced Migration and Urban Involution in ESCAP Countries", Paper presented at UN-ESCAP, Bangkok, pp. 1-45.
- S. Narayanan,(2000), "External sources os finincing for urban development in India", p. 13.
- S. Parnell, J. Robinson, (2006), "Development and Urban Policy; Johannesburg City Development Strategy", *Urban Studies*, Vol. 43, No. 2, p. 337-358.
- S. Thakur, (December 2006), "Evaluating the financial health of Indian cities; A diagnostic report", NIUA Working Paper 06-05, pp. 1-31.
- S. Wilks- Heeg, (1996), "Urban experiments limited revisited; urban policy comes full circle?", *Urban Studies*, Vol. 33, No.8, pp. 1263-1279.
- S.M. Vijayanand, (2007) "Planning for BSUP; Lessons from *Kudumbasree* experience", Department of local self governance, Government of Kerala, p. 20.
- S. Paul, (1994), "Public Services for the Urban Poor; Report Card on the three Indian Cities", *Economic and Political Weekly*, Vol. 29, No. 50, pp. 3131-3134.
- T.T. Minassian, (March, 2004), "Public Private Partnerships", International Monetary Fund, Fiscal affairs department, pp. 1-47.
- T.T. Sreekumar, (Sep. 1-8, 1990), "Neither Rural nor Urban: Spatial Formation and Development Process", *Economic and Political Weekly*, Vol. 25, No. 35/36, pp. 1981-1990.
- ————, (Feb 2001), "Financing Capital Investments in Urban Infrastructure: Constraints in Accessing Capital Market by Urban Local Bodies", *Economic and Political Weekly*, Vol. 36, No. 4, pp. 385-398.
- ————, (1993), "Urban Process in Kerala", Centre for Development Studies, Thiruvananthapuram, p. 1-320.
- T.M. Thomas,Isaac, Tharakan, P. Michael, (Aug. 5-12, 1995), "Kerala: Towards a New Agenda", *Economic and Political Weekly*, Vol. 30, No. 31/32, pp. 1993-2004.

- United Nations, (2003), "World Population to 2300", New York.
- ————-, (2008), "World urbanization prospects; The 2007 revision, highlights", Department of Economic and social affairs, New York, pp. 244.
- V. Baindur, L. Kamath, (August 2009), "Reengineering Urban Infrastructure; How the World Bank and Asian Development Bank shape urban infrastructure finance and governance in India", Asian Development Bank, pp. 1-52.
- V. Nath, (1986), "Urbanization in India; Review and Prospects", *Economic and Political Weekly*, Vol. 21, No. 8, pp. 339-352.
- V.A. Janaki, (1954), "Functional Classification of Urban Settlements in Kerala", *Journal of M S University of Baroda*, Vol. 3, pp. 79-104.
- U.P. Raghupathi, S. Thakur, S. Gupta, (November 2006), "Jawaharlal Nehru National Urban Renewal Mission; Looking back to look ahead background paper on CDP appraisals", NIUA Working Paper 06-01, pp.1-34.
- www.worldbank.org
- "World Population to 2300", (2002), Published by the United Nations, pp. 1-224.
- "World Bank, (2008), "World Development indicators; Poverty data supplementary to World development indicators, 2008", pp. 1-32.
- World Bank, (2009), "The World Bank urban and local development strategy; Concepts and Issus notes", pp. 1-22.
- World Bank, (2009), "Improving Municipal management for cities to succeed; An Independent Educational Group special study", http://www.worldbank.org/ieg, pp.1-126.

Appendix I -The share of BSUP investment in CDP in comparison to the share of urban poor population

CDP Plan Investment Under BSUP	*Share of Urban Poor in CDP Population of Cities*					*Total*
	10 and below	*10 - 20*	*20 - 30*	*30 - 40*	*40 and above*	
5 and below	14.3	14.3	42.9	14.3	14.3	100.0
5 - 10	25.0	35.0	15.0	15.0	10.0	100.0
10 - 15	33.3	16.7	33.3	16.7	0.0	100.0
15 - 20	33.3	22.2	22.2	22.2	0.0	100.0
20 and above	0.0	27.3	36.4	27.3	9.1	100.0
Total	22.0	25.4	27.1	18.6	6.8	100.0

Source- Official Website of JNNURM, http://jnnurm.nic.in/, CDPs of Mission cities.

Appendix II - The share of the urban poor population in comparison to the share of BSUP investment in CDP

CDP Plan Investment Under BSUP	*Share of Urban Poor in CDP Population of Cities*					*Total*
	10 and below	*10 - 20*	*20 - 30*	*30 - 40*	*40 and above*	
5 and below	7.7	6.7	18.8	9.1	25.0	11.9
5 - 10	38.5	46.7	18.8	27.3	50.0	33.9
10 - 15	30.8	13.3	25.0	18.2	0.0	20.3
15 - 20	23.1	13.3	12.5	18.2	0.0	15.3
20 and above	0.0	20.0	25.0	27.3	25.0	18.6
Total	100.0	100.0	100.0	100.0	100.0	100.0

Source- Official Website of JNNURM, http://jnnurm.nic.in/, CDPs of Mission cities.

Appendix III - Population distribution and funds released across the cities under JNNURM

Name of the City	*Population (in Lakhs)*	*Urban Poor Population (in Lakhs)*	*Funds Released (in Rs. Lakhs)*		
			JNNURM	*UIG*	*BSUP*
Srinagar	9.88	4.41	9007.66	6681.66	2326
Jammu	6.12	0.21	4265.75	3230.75	1035
Shimla	1.45	0.25	2116.65	1660.65	456
Amritsar	10.03	0.95	17531.2	17459.2	72
Ludhiana	13.98	1.4	3878.37	3046.37	832
Chandigarh	8.08	0.96	13049.01	3146.01	9903
Dehradun	5.3	1.21	3543.63	3101.63	442
Nainital	2.2	0.1	322.75	136.75	186
Hardwar	2.21	0.86	2086.83	2014.83	72
Faridabad	10.56	1.32	22206.61	19868.61	2338
Ajmer- Pushkar	5.04	1.25	29410.26	27296.26	2114
Jaipur	23.27	1.49	27623.71	25507.71	2116
Meerut	11.61	4.71	12760.52	7785.52	4975
Mathura	3.23	1.44	6032.65	1991.65	4041

(Contd.)

(Contd. Appendix - III)

Name of the City	*Population (in Lakhs)*	*Urban Poor Population (in Lakhs)*	*Funds Released (in Rs. Lakhs)*		
			JNNURM	*UIG*	*BSUP*
Agra M Corp.	13.31	0.37	9445.62	2067.62	7378
Lucknow	22.46	1.79	7081.2	478.2	6603
Kanpur	27.15	4.2	28674.29	23386.29	5288
Varanasi	12.04	0.96	22094.19	19247.19	2847
Allahabad	10.42	3.3	14539.03	13747.03	792
Patna	16.98	2.86	7497.7	646.7	6851
Bodh Gaya	3.94	0.5	968	0	968
Gangtok	0.29	0.08	1318.02	592.02	726
Itanagar	0.35	0.58	5189.18	4006.18	1183
Kohima	0.77	0.19	6010.76	730.76	5280
Liong Imphal	2.5	0.65	1802	704	1098
Aizwal	2.28	0.54	2549.41	546.41	2003
Agartala	1.9	0.91	2458.85	1760.85	698
Shillong	2.68	0.78	2197.3	594.3	1603

(Contd.)

(Contd. Appendix - III)

Name of the City	Population (in Lakhs)	Urban Poor Population (in Lakhs)	Funds Released (in Rs. Lakhs) JNNURM	UIG	BSUP
Guwahati	8.19	2.52	11486.28	7832.28	3654
Asansol	10.67	1.22	19887.54	9607.54	10280
Kolkata	132.06	24	117775.4	80726.4	37049
Dhanbad	10.65	0.72	5309.63	4214.63	1095
Ranchi	8.63	2.37	11932.61	8737.61	3195
Jamshedpur	11.04	1.34	0	0	0
Bhubaneswar	6.58	0.71	12379.55	11225.55	1154
Puri	1.57	0.48	1800	1600	200
Raipur	7	2.14	16646.53	8841.53	7805
Ujjain	4.31	1.89	2003.51	1671.51	332
Indore	16.4	2.6	26183.03	24152.03	2031
Bhopal	14.58	1.26	43410.56	35136.56	8274
Jabalpur	10.98	4.29	4812.5	3719.5	1093
Ahmedabad	45.25	8.84	127330.7	113422.7	13908
Rajkot	10.03	2	20974.52	17381.52	3593

(Contd.)

(Contd. Appendix - III)

Name of the City	Population (in Lakhs)	Urban Poor Population (in Lakhs)	Funds Released (in Rs. Lakhs)		
			JNNURM	UIG	BSUP
Vadodara	14.91	2.8	49111.24	44555.24	4556
Surat	28.11	4.91	97149.89	79004.89	18145
Nagpur	21.29	7.4	36946.56	26760.56	10186
Nanded	4.31	1.56	57466.58	45052.58	12414
Nashik	11.52	1.38	33308.74	28124.74	5184
Navi Mumbai	164.34	59.3	203894.3	164539.3	39355
Pune	37.6	12	143946	118284	25662
Hyderabad	57.42	5.4	140874.6	103515.6	37359
Visakhapatnam	13.45	3.43	45866.18	29888.18	15978
Vijayawada	10.39	2.95	36076.6	22021.6	14055
Bangalore	57.01	14.9	82451.63	76536.63	5915
Mysore	7.99	1.55	24576.94	20292.94	4284
Panaji	0.99	0.01	115	0	115
Kochin	13.55	4.25	9805.83	7777.83	2028
Trivandrum	8.9	1.21	10672.67	5682.67	4990
Chennai	65.6	3.93	61927.48	44408.48	17519
Coimbatore	14.61	2.91	22565.62	15018.62	7547
Madurai	12.03	3.03	28996.09	22492.09	6504
Pondicherry	5.05	0.95	7165	5085	2080

Source- Official Website of JNNURM, http://jnnurm.nic.in/

Appendix IV - Funds Released under JNNURM and in Sub Missions UIG and BSUP- State wise

Name of the State	Funds Released Under the Mission						Share of State in Population under Mission	Fund Released Pop Share Ratio
	JNNURM	Share	UIG	Share	BSUP	Share		
Andhra Pradesh	222817	12.2	155425	10.89	67392	16.1	7.54	1.62
Arunachal Pradesh	5189	0.3	4006	0.28	1183	0.3	0.03	8.93
Assam	11486	0.6	7832	0.55	3654	0.9	0.76	0.79
Bihar	8466	0.5	647	0.05	7819	1.9	1.94	0.26
Chandigarh	13049	0.7	3146	0.22	9903	2.4	0.75	0.93
Chhatisgarh	16647	0.9	8842	0.62	7805	1.9	0.65	1.38
Goa	115	0.0	0	0.00	115	0.0	0.09	0.00
Gujarat	294566	16.1	254364	17.82	40202	9.6	9.13	1.76
Haryana	22207	1.2	19869	1.39	2338	0.6	0.98	1.22
Himachal Pradesh	2117	0.1	1661	0.12	456	0.1	0.13	0.74
Jharkhand	17244	0.9	12954	0.91	4290	1.0	2.82	0.32
JK	13273	0.7	9912	0.69	3361	0.8	1.49	0.47
Karnataka	107028	5.9	96829	6.79	10199	2.4	6.04	0.98

(Contd.)

(Contd. Appendix - IV)

Name of the State	*Funds Released Under the Mission* JNNURM	*Share*	*UIG*	*Share*	*BSUP*	*Share*	*Share of State in Population under Mission*	*Fund Released Pop Share Ratio*
Kerala	20479	1.1	13461	0.94	7018	1.7	2.08	0.53
M.P	76409	4.2	64680	4.53	11729	2.8	4.30	0.98
Maharashtra	476562	26.1	383761	26.89	92801	22.1	22.20	1.18
Manipur	1802	0.1	704	0.05	1098	0.3	0.23	0.43
Meghalaya	2197	0.1	594	0.04	1603	0.4	0.25	0.40
Mizoram	2549	0.1	546	0.04	2003	0.5	0.21	0.47
Nagaland	6011	0.3	731	0.05	5280	1.3	0.07	4.20
Orissa	14181	0.8	12826	0.90	1355	0.3	0.76	1.06
Pondicherry	7165	0.4	5085	0.36	2080	0.5	0.47	0.85
Punjab	21410	1.2	20506	1.44	904	0.2	2.23	0.54
Rajasthan	57034	3.1	52804	3.70	4230	1.0	2.63	1.18
Sikkim	1318	0.1	592	0.04	726	0.2	0.03	3.71
Tamilnadu	113489	6.2	81919	5.74	31570	7.5	8.56	0.72
Tripura	2459	0.1	1761	0.12	698	0.2	0.18	0.57
U.P	147969	8.1	116046	8.13	31923	7.6	9.31	0.87
Uttarakhand	5953	0.3	5253	0.37	700	0.2	0.90	0.33
West Bengal	137663	7.5	90334	6.33	47329	11.3	13.25	0.57

Source- Official Website of JNNURM, http://jnnurm.nic.in/

Appendix V - The number of projects approved under JNNURM- State-wise

Name of the State	*Total*	*UIG*	*BSUP*
Andhra Pradesh	84	48	36
Arunachal Pradesh	5	3	2
Assam	4	2	2
Bihar	26	8	18
Chandigarh	4	2	2
Chhatisgarh	7	2	5
Goa	1	0	1
Gujrat	83	67	16
Haryana	6	4	2
Himachal Pradesh	5	3	2
Jharkhand	15	4	11
JK	9	4	5
Karnataka	65	47	18
Kerala	17	10	7
M.P	42	20	22
Maharashtra	132	77	55
Manipur	3	2	1
Meghalaya	5	2	3
Mizoram	5	1	4
Nagaland	2	1	1
Orissa	11	5	6
Pondicherry	5	2	3
Punjab	7	5	2
Rajasthan	16	14	2
Sikkim	4	1	3
Tamil Nadu	102	51	51
Tripura	2	1	1
U.P	98	31	67
Uttarakhand	17	9	8
West Bengal	130	39	91

Source- Official Website of JNNURM, http://jnnurm.nic.in/

Appendix VI - Funds Released under JNNURM and in sub missions UIG and BSUP- City wise

Sr. No.	Name of the Mission City	Percentage of Share of the Funds Released			Share of City in Population Under Mission	Fund Released Pop Share Ratio
		JNNUR	UIG	BSUP		
1.	Srinagar	0.50	0.48	0.58	0.58	0.55
2.	Jammu	0.24	0.23	0.26	0.26	0.42
3.	Shimla	0.12	0.12	0.11	0.11	0.88
4.	Amritsar	0.98	1.27	0.02	0.02	1.05
5.	Ludhiana	0.22	0.22	0.21	0.21	0.17
6.	Chndigarh	0.73	0.23	2.46	2.46	0.97
7.	Dehradun	0.20	0.22	0.11	0.11	0.40
8.	Nainital	0.02	0.01	0.05	0.05	0.09
9.	Hardwar	0.12	0.15	0.02	0.02	0.57
10.	Faridabad	1.24	1.44	0.58	0.58	1.27
11.	Ajmer- Pushkar	1.64	1.98	0.53	0.53	3.52
12.	Jaipur	1.54	1.85	0.53	0.53	0.72
13.	Meerut	0.71	0.56	1.24	1.24	0.66
14.	Mathura	0.34	0.14	1.01	1.01	1.13
15.	Agra M Corp.	0.53	0.15	1.84	1.84	0.43

(Contd.)

(Contd. Appendix - VI)

Sr. No.	*Name of the Mission City*	*Percentage of Share of the Funds Released*			*Share of City in Population Under Mission*	*Fund Released Pop Share Ratio*
		JNNUR	*UIG*	*BSUP*		
16.	Lucknow	0.40	0.03	1.64	1.64	0.19
17.	Kanpur	1.60	1.70	1.32	1.32	0.64
18.	Varanasi	1.24	1.40	0.71	0.71	1.11
19.	Allahabad	0.81	1.00	0.20	0.20	0.84
20.	Patna	0.42	0.05	1.71	1.71	0.27
21.	Bodh Gaya	0.05	0.00	0.24	0.24	0.15
22.	Gangtok	0.07	0.04	0.18	0.18	2.74
23.	Itanagar	0.29	0.29	0.29	0.29	8.93
24.	Kohima	0.34	0.05	1.31	1.31	4.70
25.	Liong Imphal	0.10	0.05	0.27	0.27	0.43
26.	Aizwal	0.14	0.04	0.50	0.50	0.67
27.	Agartala	0.14	0.13	0.17	0.17	0.78
28.	Shillong	0.12	0.04	0.40	0.40	0.49
29.	Guwahati	0.64	0.57	0.91	0.91	0.84
30.	Asansol	1.11	0.70	2.56	2.56	1.12
31.	Kolkata	6.59	5.86	9.22	9.22	0.54
32.	Dhanbad	0.30	0.31	0.27	0.27	0.30
33.	Ranchi	0.67	0.63	0.80	0.80	0.83

(Contd.)

(Contd. Appendix - VI)

Sr. No.	Name of the Mission City	Percentage of Share of the Funds Released			Share of City in Population Under Mission	Fund Released Pop Share Ratio
		JNNUR	UIG	BSUP		
34.	Jamshedpur	0.00	0.00	0.00	1.03	0.00
35.	Bhubaneswar	0.69	0.81	0.29	0.61	1.13
36.	Puri	0.10	0.12	0.05	0.15	0.69
37.	Raipur	0.93	0.64	1.94	0.65	1.43
38.	Ujjain	0.11	0.12	0.08	0.40	0.28
39.	Indore	1.46	1.75	0.51	1.52	0.96
40.	Bhopal	2.43	2.55	2.06	1.35	1.79
41.	Jabalpur	0.27	0.27	0.27	1.02	0.26
42.	Ahmedabad	7.12	8.23	3.46	4.20	1.70
43.	Rajkot	1.17	1.26	0.89	0.93	1.26
44.	Vadodara	2.75	3.23	1.13	1.38	1.98
45.	Surat	5.43	5.73	4.52	2.61	2.08
46.	Nagpur	2.07	1.94	2.54	1.98	1.05

(Contd.)

(Contd. Appendix - VI)

Sr. No.	Name of the Mission City	Percentage of Share of the Funds Released			Share of City in Population Under Mission	Fund Released Pop Share Ratio
		JNNUR	UIG	BSUP		
47.	Nanded	3.21	3.27	3.09	0.40	8.03
48.	Nashik	1.86	2.04	1.29	1.07	1.74
49.	Navi Mumbai	11.40	11.93	9.80	15.26	0.75
50.	Pune	8.05	8.58	6.39	3.49	2.31
51.	Hyderabad	7.88	7.51	9.30	5.33	1.48
52.	Visakhapatnam	2.57	2.17	3.98	1.25	2.05
53.	Vijayawada	2.02	1.60	3.50	0.96	2.09
54.	Bangalore	4.61	5.55	1.47	5.29	0.87
55.	Mysore	1.37	1.47	1.07	0.74	1.85
56.	Panaji	0.01	0.00	0.03	0.09	0.07
57.	Kochin	0.55	0.56	0.50	1.26	0.44
58.	Trivandrum	0.60	0.41	1.24	0.83	0.72
59.	Chennai	3.46	3.22	4.36	6.09	0.57
60.	Coimbatore	1.26	1.09	1.88	1.36	0.93
61.	Madurai	1.62	1.63	1.62	1.12	1.45
62.	Pondicherry	0.40	0.37	0.52	0.47	0.85

Source- Official Website of JNNURM, http://jnnurm.nic.in/

Appendix VII - Status of implementation of important state level reforms under JNNURM – November 2009

Name of the State	*Repeal of Urban Land Ceiling Regulation Act (ULCRA)*	*Transfer of 12th Schedule Functions*	*Enactment of Community Participation Law*	*Enactment of Public Disclosure Law*	*74th CA (Constituti MPC)*
Andhra Pradesh	Achieved	Achieved	Achieved	Achieved	Achieve
Arunachal Pradesh	Achieved	(N A)	(N A)	(N A)	(N A)
Assam	Achieved	(N A)	Achieved	Achieved	(N A)
Bihar	Achieved	Achieved	(N A)	(N A)	(N A)
Chandigarh	Achieved	(N A)	(N A)	(N A)	(N A)
Chhattisgarh	Achieved	Achieved	(N A)	(N A)	(N A)
Goa	Achieved	(N A)	(N A)	(N A)	(N A)
Gujarat	Achieved	Achieved	Achieved	Achieved	Achieve
Haryana	Achieved	(N A)	(N A)	(N A)	(N A)
Himachal Pradesh	Achieved	(N A)	(N A)	(N A)	(N A)
J&K	Achieved	(N A)	(N A)	(N A)	(N A)
Jharkhand	(N A)	(N A)	(N A)	(N A)	(N A)
Karnataka	Achieved	(N A)	(N A)	(N A)	(N A)
Kerala	Achieved	Achieved	(N A)	(N A)	(N A)
Madhya Pradesh	Achieved	Achieved	(N A)	(N A)	(N A)

(Contd.)

(Contd. Appendix - VII)

Name of the State	*Repeal of Urban Land Ceiling Regulation Act (ULCRA)*	*Transfer of 12th Schedule Functions*	*Enactment of Community Participation Law*	*Enactment of Public Disclosure Law*	*74th CA (Constitut MPC)*
Maharashtra	Achieved	Achieved	(N A)	Achieved	(N A)
Manipur	Achieved	(N A)	(N A)	(N A)	(N A)
Meghalaya	Achieved	(N A)	(N A)	(N A)	(N A)
Mizoram	Achieved	(N A)	(N A)	(N A)	(N A)
Nagaland	Achieved	(N A)	(N A)	(N A)	(N A)
Orissa	Achieved	(N A)	(N A)	(N A)	(N A)
Punjab	Achieved	(N A)	(N A)	(N A)	(N A)
Puducherry	Achieved	(N A)	(N A)	(N A)	(N A)
Rajasthan	Achieved	(N A)	(N A)	(N A)	(N A)
Sikkim	Achieved	(N A)	(N A)	(N A)	(N A)
Tamilnadu	Achieved	Achieved	(N A)	(N A)	(N A)
Tripura	Achieved	Achieved	(N A)	Achieved	(N A)
U P	Achieved	(N A)	(N A)	Achieved	(N A)
Uttarakhand	Achieved	(N A)	(N A)	(N A)	(N A)
West Bengal	(N A)	Achieved	(N A)	(N A)	Achieve

Source- Official Website of JNNURM, http://jnnurm.nic.in/

Appendix VIII - Status of implementation of important ULB reforms under JNNURM

Name of the City	*Important ULB levels Reforms (Given as Code)*								*Total Points (equal weights for the Reforms taken)*
	R-1	*R-2*	*R-3*	*R-4*	*R-5*	*R-6*	*R-7*	*R-8*	*Total*
Srinagar	0	0	0	0	0	0	0	0	0
Jammu	0	0	0	0	0	0	0	0	0
Shimla	1	0	0	0	0	0	1	0	2
Amritsar	0	0	0	1	1	0	0	1	3
Ludhiana	0	0	0	0	1	0	0	0	1
Chndigarh	0	0	0	0	0	0	0	0	0
Dehradun	0	0	0	1	0	0	0	0	1
Nainital	0	0	0	0	0	0	0	0	0
Hardwar	0	0	0	0	0	0	0	0	0
Faridabad	0	0	0	0	0	0	0	0	0
Ajmer- Pushkar	0	0	0	1	1	1	0	1	4
Jaipur	1	0	0	1	1	1	1	1	6
Meerut	1	0	0	1	0	0	0	1	3
Mathura	0	0	0	1	0	0	0	1	2
Agra M Corp.	0	1	0	1	0	0	0	1	3
Lucknow	0	0	0	1	0	0	0	1	2

(Contd.)

(*Contd. Appendix - VIII*)

Name of the City	*Important ULB levels Reforms (Given as Code)*								*Total Points (equal weights for the Reforms taken)*
	R-1	*R-2*	*R-3*	*R-4*	*R-5*	*R-6*	*R-7*	*R-8*	*Total*
Kanpur	0	0	0	1	0	0	0	1	2
Varanasi	0	0	0	1	0	0	0	1	2
Allahabad	1	1	0	1	0	0	0	1	4
Patna	0	0	0	0	0	0	0	0	0
Bodh Gaya	0	0	0	0	0	0	0	0	0
Gangtok	0	0	0	0	0	0	0	0	0
Itanagar	0	0	0	0	0	0	0	0	0
Kohima	0	0	0	1	0	0	0	1	2
Liong Imphal	0	0	0	0	0	0	0	0	0
Aizwal	0	0	0	0	0	0	0	0	0

(*Contd.*)

(Contd. Appendix - VIII)

Name of the City	Important ULB levels Reforms (Given as Code)								Total Points (equal weights for the Reforms taken)
	R-1	R-2	R-3	R-4	R-5	R-6	R-7	R-8	Total
Dhanbad	0	0	0	0	0	0	0	0	0
Ranchi	0	0	0	0	0	0	0	0	0
Jamshedpur	0	0	0	0	0	0	0	0	0
Bhubaneswar	0	0	0	1	0	0	0	1	2
Puri	0	0	0	1	0	0	0	1	2
Raipur	0	0	0	1	0	0	0	0	1
Ujjain	1	0	0	1	0	1	0	1	4
Indore	1	0	0	1	1	1	0	1	5
Bhopal	1	0	0	1	1	1	0	1	5
Jabalpur	0	0	0	1	0	1	0	1	3
Ahmedabad	1	0	0	1	1	1	1	1	6
Rajkot	1	1	0	1	1	1	1	1	7
Vadodara	1	1	0	1	1	1	1	1	7
Surat	1	0	0	1	1	1	1	1	6
Nagpur	1	0	0	1	1	0	1	1	5

(Contd.)

(Contd. Appendix - VIII)

Name of the City	*Important ULB levels Reforms (Given as Code)*								*Total Points (equal weights for the Reforms taken)*
	R-1	*R-2*	*R-3*	*R-4*	*R-5*	*R-6*	*R-7*	*R-8*	*Total*
Bhopal	1	0	0	1	1	1	0	1	5
Jabalpur	0	0	0	1	0	1	0	1	3
Ahmedabad	1	0	0	1	1	1	1	1	6
Rajkot	1	1	0	1	1	1	1	1	7
Vadodara	1	1	0	1	1	1	1	1	7
Surat	1	0	0	1	1	1	1	1	6
Nagpur	1	0	0	1	1	0	1	1	5

Source- Official Website of JNNURM, http://jnnurm.nic.in/

Reform implementation status codes; 1- Achieved, 0- Not achieved

R-1. Double entry accounting

R-2. Property tax coverage above 85

R-3. Full cost recovery for services

R-4. Internal earmarking of funds for urban poor

R-5. Revision of building laws,

R-6. Simplification of legal procedure for conversion of agricultural land for nonagricultural uses

R-7. Computerized registration of land and property

R-8. Encouraging Public Private Partnership (PPP)

Appendix IX - Class wise distribution of urban population in Kerala

Class	*Number of Towns / Cities-Kerala- 2001*	*Percentage of Total Towns-Kerala-200*	*Percentage of the Urban Population Kerala-2001*	*Percentage of the Urban Population-India-2001*
I	10	6.3	44.66	61.86
II	24	15.1	19.21	12.11
III	72	45.3	27.78	14.77
IV	37	23.3	6.85	8.21
V	15	9.4	1.44	2.77
VI	1	.6	.06	.27
Total	159	100.0	100.0	100.0

Source- Census of India, 2001.

Appendix X - Size classification of the family

Name of the Mission City	*Family Size Categories*		
	5 and below	*5 – 8 Members*	*8 Members and above*
Thiruvananthapuram	45.9	49.4	4.7
Kochi	65.2	34.8	0.0
Total	57.0	41.0	2.0

Source- Field work in the slums of Kochi and Thiruvananthapuram.

Appendix XI - MPCI classification of the slum households

Name of the Mission City	*Monthly per capita income of households (in Rupees)*				*Total*
	1500 and above	*1000-1500*	*500-1000*	*500 and below*	
Thiruvananthapuram	17.6	5.9	17.6	58.8	100.0
Kochi	21.7	15.7	33.0	29.6	100.0
Total	20.0	11.5	26.5	42.0	100.0

Source- Field work in the slums of Kochi and Thiruvananthapuram.

Appendix XII - Nature of interaction of the slum households with the ULB

Name of the Mission City	*Nature of Interaction*					
	Very good	*Good*	*Bad*	*Very bad*	*No opinion*	*Total*
Thiruvananthapuram	0.0	29.4	29.4	25.9	15.3	100.0
Kochi	8.7	49.6	27.0	5.2	9.6	100.0
Total	5.0	41.0	28.0	14.0	12.0	100.0

Source- Field work in the slums of Kochi and Thiruvananthapuram.

Appendix XIII - Cross-tabulation of MPCI and Perception of the household about the positive changes in the slum

Perception about changes in the slum	*Per capita income*				*Total*
	500 and below	*500-1000*	*1000-1500*	*1500 & above*	
Observed no betterment of slum facilities	17	14	4	10	45
Observed betterment of the slum facilities	67	39	19	30	155
Total	84	53	23	40	200

Source- Field work in the slums of Kochi and Thiruvananthapuram.

Appendix XIV - Cross-tabulation of MPCI and Level of satisfaction of the households with the available facilities in the slum

Level of satisfaction in available facilities in the slum	*Per capita income*				*Total*
	500 and below	*500-1000*	*1000-1500*	*1500 & above*	
Not satisfied with the present facilities	68	34	16	26	144
Satisfied with the present facilities	16	19	7	14	56
Total	84	53	23	40	200

Source- Field work in the slums of Kochi and Thiruvananthapuram.

Appendix XV - Cross-tabulation of MPCI and Preference of the household in case of slum housing schemes

Preference for the Housing Options	*Per capita income*				*Total*
	500 and below	*500-1000*	*1000-1500*	*1500 & above*	
Prefers house at the same place	76	44	21	33	174
Prefers flat	3	1	1	4	9
Anywhere	4	8	1	3	16
Total	83	53	23	40	199

Source- Field work in the slums of Kochi and Thiruvananthapuram.

Appendix XVI - Cross-tabulation of status of land ownership and payment of user charges

Status of Land Ownership by the Household	*User Charge*		*Total*
	Doesn't Pay User Charge	*Pays User Charge*	
Has no legal ownership of land	61	55	116
Has legal ownership of land	16	68	84
Total	77	123	200

Source- Field work in the slums of Kochi and Thiruvananthapuram.

Appendix XVII - Cross-tabulation of Kudumbasree membership and Coverage of the households under any developmental schemes in the past

Status of Membership in Kudumbasree	*Received Financial Aid from Govt;*		
	Hasn't Availed Financial Aid from the Govt.	*Has Availed Financial Aid from the govt.*	*Total*
Don't have membership in Kudumbasree	33	13	46
Has membership in Kudumbasree	87	67	154
Total	220	80	200

Source- Field work in the slums of Kochi and Thiruvananthapuram.

Questionnaire of Household Level Slum Survey in Kochi and Thiruvananthapuram Cities (Conducted in 2009 October)

1. Name of the respondent, M/F (1. male, 2. female) ☐

2. Name of the slum (mention if it is notified/ notified) (1. notified, 2. non-notified) ☐

3. Native place/ state/district (1. Kerala, 2. Tamil Nadu, 3. Karnataka, 4. Other states) ☐

4. Number of family members

Sl no.	*Name of the family members*	*Age*	*Educational Qualification*	*Main occupation*	*Monthly earning*

5. Do you have the legal ownership of the land and house? (Codes 1-yes, 2-No) ☐

6. Do you own land/house in your native place? (Codes 1-yes, 2-No) ☐

7. The length of stay in the slum (Codes, 1. less than 4 years, 2. 4-7 years), 3. 7-15 years, 4. above 15 years) ☐

8. Have you found any kind of betterment of the slum during the period of your stay? If yes, specify. (1-yes, 2- no), ☐
Improvement in the slum facilities

1	2	3	4	5	6	7	8	9

(1. sanitation, 2. water supply, 3. waste disposal, 4. drainage, 5. accessibility, 6. Education, 7. Health, 8. Entertainment, 9. other facilities)

9. Do you go for community development society meetings? If yes, how often?
(1. yes, 2. no) (frequency, 1. Always, 2. Not always, 3. Rarely) ☐

10. Is your family covered under the Kudumbasree scheme? Do you believe that it is useful for the common people?
(1. yes, 2. no) ☐

11. Civic amenities available at the household level

Sl no.	*Civic amenities available*	*Yes / no*	*Source*	*Is it enough Yes / no*	*Facilities in the slum Yes / no*	*Problems*
1. 2.	Access to the slum / house Drinking water supply					

(Contd.)

(Contd. Table)

Sl no.	*Civic amenities available*	*Yes / no*	*Source*	*Is it enough Yes / no*	*Facilities in the slum Yes / no*	*Problems*
3.	Water for other					
4.	uses					
5.	Garbage disposal					
6.	Sanitation facilities					
7.	Storm water					
8.	drainage					
9.	Educational					
10.	facilities, specify					
	Health facilities,					
	specify					
	Entertainment					
	sources					
	Electricity					

(Problem codes, 1.absent, 2. inadeqaute, 3. distance, 4. poor maintenance, 5. affordability)

12. Are you satisfied with the available facilities in the slum? If not, mention inadequate facilities.
(1- yes, 2- no) ☐

1	2	3	4	5	6	7	8	9

(infrastructural facilities, 1. road, 2. drinking water, 3. water for other uses, 4. garbage disposal, 5. sanitation, 6. drainage, 7. education, 8. health, 9. entertainment, 10. electricity)

13. Are you paying any kind of user charges for the services that you get?
(1- yes, 2- No) ☐

14. The nature of interaction with the corporation office
(1. Very good, 2. good, 3. bad, 4. very bad, 5. no opinion)

☐

15. Have you ever received any benefit from the various programs for the urban poor and slum population? If yes specify the source.
(1-yes, 2- no) ☐
(1. state, 2. center, 3. corporation, 4. NGOs, 5. don't know) ☐

16. If you are given the option of either constructing a new house in the same place or to live in a flat given by the corporation, which will you prefer? Specify the reason
(1. New house in the same place, 2. flat) ☐

(Reason code- 1. Ownership of land, 2. Attahment with the place, 3. wants separate house, 4. other reasons) ☐

Index

T

U

V